Social Class in the Writings of
Mary Hallock Foote

Western Literature Series

Christine Hill Smith

SOCIAL CLASS IN THE WRITINGS OF

Mary Hallock Foote

UNIVERSITY OF NEVADA PRESS

RENO & LAS VEGAS

Western Literature Series
University of Nevada Press, Reno, Nevada 89557 USA
Copyright © 2009 by University of Nevada Press
All rights reserved
Manufactured in the United States of America
Design by Omega Clay

Library of Congress Cataloging-in-Publication Data
Smith, Christine Hill.
  Social class in the writings of Mary Hallock Foote / Christine Hill Smith.
    p. cm. — (Western literature series)
  Includes bibliographical references and index.
  ISBN 978-0-87417-764-0 (alk. paper)
  1. Foote, Mary Hallock, 1847–1938—Criticism and interpretation. 2. Social
classes in literature. 3. Sex role in literature. 4. Women in literature. 5. West
(U.S.)—In literature. I. Title.
PS1688.S65 2009
  813'.4—dc22   2008043533

The paper used in this book is a recycled stock made from 30 percent
post–consumer waste materials, certified by FSC, and meets the requirements
of American National Standard for Information Sciences—Permanence of
Paper for Printed Library Materials, ANSI/NISO z39.48–1992 (R2002).
Binding materials were selected for strength and durability.
First Printing
18 17 16 15 14 13 12 11 10 09   5 4 3 2 1

To:

My grandmother Ruth Elizabeth Hillyar Hill
(1899–1987)
ABD Yale 1931, intellectual, lover of books

My mother, Katherine Hill Smith Udall
Indefatigable, strong, smart

My father, James Duane Smith
For the book he always wanted to write

and

Donald Revell,
Graduate school mentor, who said,
"You can be poor or even on the streets.
But they can't take the Ph.D.
away from you."

CONTENTS

Following page 72

Portrait of Mary Hallock ca. 1874

"At the foot of the pass," illustration of freight wagons in *The Led-Horse Claim*

"Between daylight and dark," illustration of the lovers in *The Led-Horse Claim*

"There were sounds which might have been miles away," illustration of Cecil Conrath in a mine in *The Led-Horse Claim*

"The engineer's mate," illustration of a Victorian lady with baggage at a western train station

"The cabin by the ditch," illustration of the Footes's cabin interior in Leadville, Colorado

"Dream horses," illustration of Polly on a pony in Idaho

"Afternoon at a ranch," illustration of Foote's daughter napping on the family's desert porch

Portrait of Helena de Kay Gilder, 1870s

"A pretty girl in the West," illustration of friends of the Footes at their Idaho canyon house

Mary Hallock Foote, ca. 1876

"Between the desert and the sown," illustration of a woman walking and a man on horseback by an irrigation ditch

"And the spreading waters below," illustration of an irrigation ditch

The Foote family in Boise, ca. 1894–1895

This work explores the complicated and sometimes contradictory manifestations of social class as they appear in the novels, short stories, autobiography, and letters of Mary Hallock Foote. I use Foote's texts to argue that her own class background and the changing nature of publishing, capitalism in general, transportation, and class formation in the late nineteenth century helped her play a significant role in both validating and questioning social hierarchies in the eastern and western United States.

This book begins with a discussion of the historical and literary contexts of the time in which Foote lived, and lays out the trajectory of her life and work for a close examination of how her experience of social class and sturdy belief in "character" both determined and limited her outlook in life. Chapter 2 demonstrates how Foote's first three novels, set in Leadville, Colorado, rely on traditional literary allusions and the conventions of the romance genre to establish a genteel tone. The Leadville novels are also the subject of chapter 3 and show how Foote tackles the subject of class issues for both men and women, which she felt strongly as a newcomer to the West. In spite of Foote's adherence to traditional feminine boundaries, in her own way she often promoted new, progressive, and sometimes liberating attitudes and behaviors for western women. In chapter 4, the concept of class is explored in Foote's modest output of children's stories vis-à-vis the larger background of the class-conscious children's books, stories, and periodical magazines of the day. Chapter 5 focuses on the concept of the New Woman, a feature of Foote's last novel, and contrasts the class position and attitudes of both fictional and nonfictional New Women around the turn of the twentieth century. Finally, chapter 6 provides an analysis of the formative personal attitudes toward class through an examination of some 250 letters between Foote and her best friend, Helena de Kay Gilder, during the first twenty years of their nearly fifty-year friendship.

The links between these varying topics become apparent when we view Foote as a turn-of-the-century woman dealing with the era's rapid social changes. She often tried to downplay these mutating relations in her fiction. Her "status anxiety," to use Alain de Botton's phrase, led her to present a world in which entrenched social class counted for something, both personally and professionally. But as Wallace Stegner notes insightfully in his anthology of American realism, she was "too honest" to be dismissed as merely dated (*Selected American Prose* xi). Although Foote craved class stability, and sometimes seemed to look only to the past for examples, in spite of herself she often wrote positively about the new social and technological forces catapulting the formal nineteenth century into the more fluid twentieth.

Social historians have taken a broad view of the technological and social changes of Foote's time, positing the appearance of a new class in the United States after the Civil War (see Blumin; Bledstein and Johnston). Elaine Showalter is correct that the "old Yankee aristocracy [was] no longer viable in the post-war environment" (*Sexual Anarchy* 28). What Richard Ohmann calls the professional-managerial class arose, made up of new professionals who were trained, urban, literate, and upwardly mobile (see also Brodhead). As they created a more rational and national bureaucracy to replace closely knit but inefficient small-town structures, they were ready to jettison some of the Victorian pieties and rigid standards that went along with them. They still valued some of these traditions, however, as long as they did not interfere with the new, more flexible way of life that the class itself was inventing and improving upon. Foote's husband, an engineer, was part of this new professional elite, a member of what was called "the lace-boot brigade"—the engineers who reshaped much of the world in the late nineteenth century (see Spence). Mary Hallock Foote herself straddled two worlds: she came from the old land-based, family-based elite (as did her husband) but also enjoyed the cachet of this new class, as well as the technological advances empowering it.

The transcontinental railway was finished when Foote was twenty-two, in 1869. This milestone changed much of the face of the West and allowed professionals to relocate with their families without having to cross the continent in covered wagons. Foote identified with the new professionals' relentless backward-and-forward tug in time and space. In her novels this is most obviously reflected in educated eastern types living professional lives in the West. Foote and her characters were well situated as part of the rising educated middle class that took advantage of these improvements in transportation and, in her case, publishing technology that increased readership in the genteel magazines in which she published (see Casper et al.). She was in fact part of an emerging group of "outsourced" freelance professionals who earned a livelihood from distant clients.

This study will add needed depth to the textual criticism of western American writings. Using terminology and concepts of class defined by historians, sociologists, political scientists, and literary critics, I analyze Foote's fiction and nonfiction, addressing how she came to think and write as she did. I compare Foote with other writers of her age, delve into her upbringing and literary tastes, and scrutinize how being a woman affected her attitudes toward class. Given our own (post)modern, individualistic ideas about gender roles, it somehow disappoints us that Foote did not grow and change in the West as much as we might have wanted. But presenting the literary and historical contexts for Foote's real and fictional worlds in both the East and the West will unearth the social density beneath her apparently simple plots and stock characters. Foote rode the cusp of a wave of popular fiction that was part of the rise and education of the new professional middle class.

. . .

Class is no longer a particularly popular topic in the United States. We do not talk about it; we pretend that social class depends merely on how much money one has amassed. The very idea of class is often "stigmatized . . . as premodern," according to German sociologist Klaus Eder, and, in fact, a good case can be made that academic discussions of class perpetuate ideas of class (91, 63). However, a glance through *Renewing Class Analysis* (2000) explodes this myth of a classless twenty-first century (Devine et al.). Class still exists, albeit in transformed ways.[1] As recent dynastic presidencies prove, the elite class has a way of perpetuating itself, with or without talent.

Today, as the gap between rich and poor widens and a new Gilded Age emerges—with its own robber barons and immigrant underclass—a new kind of "class struggle without classes" is forming (Edwards 141). To understand this transformed legacy of class in American society, we must explore its history. Through an examination of Mary Hallock Foote's keen review of class structures in her own era, we see how power relations continue to influence American society. Indeed, her nineteenth-century attitudes illuminate the intricacy of class issues that are presently underacknowledged in studies of western American literature.

. . .

Please note I use the following abbreviations throughout the book:

MHF   Mary Hallock Foote
HKG   Helena de Kay Gilder
RWG   Richard Watson Gilder

ACKNOWLEDGMENTS

To begin with, I want to thank Daniel Sarewitz for being the catalyst to my finishing my dissertation, out of which came this book. Also thanks to Kristen Iversen, Tom Noel, Peter Fields, and Sands Hall for being supportive all the way through this long process.

At The Huntington Library, Peter J. Blodgett, Lita Garcia, and Jill Cogan helped me navigate the complexities of the collections there. At Stanford University, John E. Mustain, Special Collections librarian, was helpful for citations of Foote's letters, as was Anthony Tedeschi from the Lilly Library at Indiana University for Helena de Kay Gilder's letters. Janice E. Ruth, manuscript specialist at the Library of Congress, went out of her way to help me with online and in-person searches.

Leslie A. Morris aided my searches for *Century* correspondence at the Houghton Library at Harvard, as did the wonderful librarians at the Harry Ransom Research Center at the University of Texas at Austin and Coi Gehrig at the Denver Public Library Western History Room. Many thanks also to the Cambridge Public Library and the Widener Library at Harvard University for aiding me in last-minute fact-checking.

Ann Gardiner and her mother, brother, and sister, Evy and Bob Gardiner and Katharine Gardiner Hale, generously shared their time, photos, and family lore with me. Bob and I even roamed through the cemetery in Grass Valley together, eventually finding, typically on its margin, his great-grandmother's grave.

Professor Mary Ellen Williams Walsh was kind enough to share her copies of half of her transcripts of the Foote-Gilder correspondence.

When I revised the manuscript in Europe and did not have books or articles with me, Linda Karell, Melody Graulich, Judy Austin, and especially Darlis Miller were my long-distance support for fact-checking via e-mail.

Thanks also to the University of Nevada Press for being patient with my revised timetable since I was always teaching an overload, though technically I was for many years a "part-time" college instructor—that is to say, adjunct contract slave-labor, so-called affiliate faculty at various Denver-area colleges and universities.

Thanks goes to the *Dictionary of Literary Biography* and the Boise State University Western Writers Series, as I used and revised some of my own descriptions of Foote's novels first written for them, from my Foote profile in the dictionary and my article *Reading "A Victorian Gentlewoman in the Far West: The Reminiscences of Mary Hallock Foote"* in the series.

I also thank Alex Drummond for supporting me materially, for talking out some of the chapter logic during the revisions in Europe, and for reading a final draft with a helpful pen in hand. In addition, my dearest and oldest friend, Steve Liss, came through with a "laptop grant" that enabled me to revise the manuscript while traveling for a year with only a backpack. I couldn't have done it without you. And finally, as I finish the publication process, I am thankful for the faith of Steve Lacy and the inspiration of Levi, Caleb, and John Lacy.

Social Class in the Writings of
Mary Hallock Foote

Introduction

To undertake a discussion of class in America is to
venture into an area fraught with perils.

—Willard B. Gatewood, *Aristocrats of Color:
The Black Elite, 1880–1920*

Mary Hallock Foote (1847–1938) was born at the right time and in the right place to take advantage of the cultural capital of her birth class and turn it into a moneymaking career. Talented and educated, she moved in the 1870s from New York State to the West and became an early and prominent western illustrator and writer. She was able to parlay a genteel middle-class background and her own illustrating and writing skills into a career in magazines and books at a time when American publishing was burgeoning and wanted to hear voices like hers from the American West.

Several factors contributed to her success. To begin with, she was raised in an Old World Quaker family on a longtime family property in the Hudson River Valley. This background put her in the orbit of the reigning values of the eastern establishment. As a young woman, she acquired marketable artistic skills as one of the first generation of educated middle-class women in the United States. She then married and went west with her mining engineer husband, a move that gave her an advantaged, technological perspective on the settling of the West. Furthermore, she began her career just when new publishing and transportation technologies made it possible for someone in rural California, Colorado, or Idaho to make a living from eastern publishers.

As a result of this fortuitous set of circumstances, Foote became a success. She was renowned for her elegant drawings of life in the East and West and for her stories and novels, many of which depict easterners and their families coming to terms with both the cultural isolation and the vicissitudes of professional opportunities in the West.

. . .

Mary Hallock Foote's Quaker family had farmed for five generations near the Hudson River in Milton, New York, about seventy-five miles north of New York City. If it takes three generations to make a gentleman (or a gentlewoman), her family qualified. Although they were not well off, they had history and traditions that gave them a sense of pride, status, and rootedness.

Mary's literary influences as a girl were transatlantic. She read most of the classic nineteenth-century texts, including the novels of Sir Walter Scott, William Makepeace Thackeray, and George Eliot and the poetry of the British Romantics and later the Victorians, especially Robert Browning. In her letters she also mentioned continental authors, such as Turgenev and Tolstoy. Of Americans, she was fond of citing James Fenimore Cooper, Oliver Wendell Holmes, and James Russell Lowell and frequently quoted Ralph Waldo Emerson in her books and letters. Foote kept up over the years with the serious writing of her day, often through serializations of novels in the *Atlantic Monthly, Harper's,* and *Century,* "those exclusive portals," as California writer Gertrude Atherton termed them (*Adventures* 145).

As a young woman in the 1860s, Foote attended the nearby Poughkeepsie Female Collegiate Seminary and later the Cooper Union in New York City, one of the few places at the time that a young woman could obtain art training. It was there that she met Helena de Kay (Gilder), whose background included old family and the old money to go with it; the two would become lifelong friends. At art school, Foote found that she excelled in the then popular genre of woodcut illustration and began working for *Century* and other magazines as well as adorning gift books by Henry Wadsworth Longfellow and Bret Harte.[1]

Mary Hallock's professional career as an artist was on the ascendancy when at an 1873 New Year's Day party in New York she met Arthur De Wint Foote. Arthur, whose Connecticut family was more socially prominent than Mary's, trained briefly at the Sheffield Scientific School at Yale University to be an engineer. Due to poor eyesight, however, he quit his academic studies and subsequently learned mostly on the job in western mining and irrigation projects. By the time of her 1876 marriage to Foote, Mary Hallock had been illustrating for magazines and books for five years. Marriage did not end her professional career, however, as it did for so many women of the period. Armed with book commissions, wooden engraving blocks, and pen and ink, she moved to the West with her husband and lived there for most of the next fifty years.[2]

At first Foote continued illustrating, but around 1878 friends Helena and her new husband, Richard Watson Gilder, encouraged Foote to write travel sketches to accompany her drawings. They had enjoyed her glowing letters describing California and knew of her financial troubles, as Arthur struggled to find steady work. Conveniently, Richard Gilder was the editor of *Century,* which developed into the leading mass-circulation magazine in the 1880s and was, again according to Gertrude Atherton, "as exclusive as Mrs. Astor" about whom it published (*Adventures* 145).[3] It is an important fact of Foote's personal and professional life that Helena, her good friend and confidante in letters for almost fifty years, lived a high-society life in New York City and Washington, D.C., with trips to Newport and Europe. The two women bridged the geographical, financial, and class differences between them but at what personal and artistic cost to Foote we shall never know.

In the beginning of her career, Foote's short pieces were published in *Century*, *Scribner's*, *Atlantic*, and the children's magazine *St. Nicholas*, periodicals marketed predominantly to upper-middle-class eastern audiences. Due to improved printing quality, marketing, and distribution, readership was greatly increased in Foote's era, and she caught the wave of the new technologies changing American magazine form and content. Once her travelogues and short stories were well received, she tried her hand at novel writing, with the chapters first serialized in the magazines. Foote does not seem to have felt that her gentility or femininity was compromised by writing, though, as some women did.[4] As Louisa May Alcott noted in the 1870s, "Story-writing was a genteel accomplishment and reflected credit upon the [family] name" ("How I Went" n.p.). Like Alcott's, Foote's endeavors augmented the family's always precarious income in essential ways, since Arthur Foote, though a brilliant mining and irrigation engineer, was not always practical and often lacked funding for his projects. As Wallace Stegner observes, Mary and Arthur Foote were "the upper crust of pioneers—in this case, the upper crust in brains and talents rather than in money" (Stegner and Etulain 91). Arthur did not succeed in landing a steady, well-paying job until twenty years after their marriage. By that time, the family, having lived in several towns in three western states, had grown to five, with the addition of a boy and two girl children.

. . .

It seems that Foote acquired her sense of social class mostly from her family, and to some degree from her formal schooling. Unlike most Americans, however, when she moved west, Foote did not join community or national organizations that perpetuated class divisions, such as garden or women's clubs, churches, or the Daughters of the American Revolution. In Boise Foote helped found the Columbia Club at the public library but joined little else. In Grass Valley, California, she contributed money to the local Episcopal church but did not attend regularly (E. Gardiner personal interview). It may seem unusual that Foote was not eager at least to improve her adopted home in the West. Given her personal shyness and dire need for time to write, however, her self-imposed isolation seems more understandable. Her birth family had been an island of culture unto itself amid the many villages along the Hudson, and it is clear where Foote learned self-sufficiency.

Like any immigrant, Foote missed the familiar, especially at first. She regularly compared her new region and social setting to her former cultured life at home with her parents and in New York City. Carol B. Pearson, editor Rodman Paul's researcher for the 1972 edition of Foote's *Reminiscences,* observes that Foote was "never able to put this Easternness, this Quaker gentility behind her" (1). James Maguire and Richard Etulain concur, noting that she filled her novels with "genteel reticence" and a "style and outlook . . . strongly tied to Victorian sensibilities" (Maguire 44; Etulain, "Mary Hallock Foote" 145). Foote felt comfortable only in familiar situations, reflecting her insular Quaker upbringing. An exchange in her early novel *The Last Assembly Ball* (1889) succinctly reflects this narrow-mindedness. In a discussion about servants, an exasperated young man demands of his snobbish landlady, "'Them'—'they'! Who are 'they,' Mrs. Dansken?" She instantly responds, "Anybody who is n't [sic] us" (80). Even though Foote seems to have written this exchange to be facetious, her own views were not much different from the landlady's. Of course, we do not know the extent to which Foote's insistence on this gentility was due to her own impulses or the polite expectations of the editors of her elite eastern magazines. She was, after all, willing to change the ending of her first novel to please *Scribner's*—as she admitted years later—adding an unlikely reunion and subsequent marriage for the protagonists (Davidson 123). But in a letter explaining this literary faux pas, she does not express artistic frustration or regret. She had come to accept that her art might be compromised by the need for money for her struggling family.

The Footes' constant financial insecurity contributed to Mary Hallock Foote's strong sense of class consciousness. In many ways, she used it to ground herself and bolster her self-confidence. She took her white privilege for granted, grateful to enjoy the unearned assets that her birth afforded her, especially when economic times were bad (see MacIntosh). And she proved by her actions that one could draw on class background and succeed without having much cash flow. To use French sociologist Pierre Bourdieu's terms, the Footes' "strong cultural capital" helped lessen the impact of their "weak economic capital" (*Distinction* 57). In fact, Mary Hallock Foote's writing maintained the family's social class, as was true for several nineteenth-century women writers, including Alcott and Harriet Beecher Stowe. Foote's income from eastern sources also allowed her to stay detached from the provincial societies where she was based without important economic or personal repercussions. As Janet Floyd notes, it was common for autobiographers in the mining camps to "assume a disengaged distance from their subject by reason of their class" ("Mining the West" 151). Foote usually socialized only with those of her own background, even while living in small mining and ranching towns in California, Colorado, and Idaho. She created for herself and her family oases of books, conversation, and cultural traditions with a few like-minded relatives and friends.

Foote continued writing novels for forty years, at first out of financial necessity and later for more personal and creative reasons. Her husband finally established a stable career in Grass Valley, in 1895, where the Footes lived for thirty years. Foote's last novel, *The Ground-Swell,* was published in 1919; she wrote an autobiography in the 1920s that was not published until 1972, *A Victorian Gentlewoman in the Far West: The Reminiscences of Mary Hallock Foote.*

In old age the Footes moved in with one of their children in Massachusetts. But when Mary Hallock Foote died in 1938, according to her wishes she was buried in Grass Valley. Her tombstone in Grass Valley is appropriately at the edge of the graveyard, several yards away from the hundreds of other graves of the townsfolk, in a separate Foote family plot near an irrigation ditch.

. . .

In death and in life, then, Foote set herself apart from her neighbors. She was raised to this and came by her desire for seclusion naturally. Her family had split from the New York Quakers in the 1800s over the issue of slavery, and they lived and worshiped in large part separately from the local community in the Hudson Valley. Foote describes a family like hers in *Edith Bonham* (1917): "The family, bred in an exclusiveness peculiar to our old eastern farming aristocracy, cultivated very little social intercourse with their neighbors" (13–14). Foote maintained an isolation like this in the West.

Although one might think Mary Hallock Foote ostensibly chose the West when she married Arthur, it is clear from her letters that she never conceived she might live her whole life there. When she was first married and visited San

Francisco, she was horrified and mystified by what she described as the well-bred wives of engineers and other professionals who cheerfully exchanged horror stories about the challenges of living in remote areas.

Foote's generation has been characterized as "indulged children of the post–Civil War era," with the education and confidence to explore new terrain both physically and metaphorically (Mapel-Bloomberg n.p.). And Foote was at first intrigued by the idea of seeing the West when it became clear that her husband needed to work there. She wanted to experience more of the world and was thrilled, for example, when he accepted a trip for the two of them to the interior of Mexico to assay a silver mine. But Foote did not want to end up isolated and stranded away from the East, as eventually happened in Idaho when her husband's irrigation projects failed and she was left trying to educate her children to elite eastern standards in a dusty canyon home and keep up her subscription to the *Atlantic,* too. For years Foote clung to the idea that somehow Arthur's work in the West would lead to a good job in the East and the family could settle down near friends, family, and culture (MHF to HKG and RWG, September 29, 1877).[5] It did not happen, of course, and though Foote's disappointment eventually mellowed during the years in Grass Valley, it is not surprising that some bitterness crept into her writings. At first my study was to be about Mary Hallock Foote and *exile,* but I have come to see that for her class was the larger topic. Foote's exile from the centers of culture drove class consciousness deep into her psyche; this ossification informed her images, themes, and characters.

But to say that Foote's approach to class was simplistic or monolithic would be inaccurate. Her insights into her own and others' pretensions and limitations in fact deepened her writings. The honesty that Stegner saw saved her from being a mere mouthpiece for the values of nineteenth-century American snobbery, and her own candid self-assessments help to reveal the complexity beneath her apparent narrowness. Describing a character who is clearly a stand-in for herself in the late novel *Edith Bonham,* Foote writes that Anne Aylesford had "her little rigid way of seeing [things]" and "an inflexibility that showed the stock she came from" (7, 23). These comments exhibit both pride at the legacy of entrenched traditions and at the same time awareness that this legacy is restrictive. Thus, if Foote made statements in her writings that sometimes seem patrician, she often undercut them too. Many times, in letters to Helena in particular, Foote both complained about her surroundings' lack of taste and culture but also begged her friend's pardon for taking so narrow a view. As a character in *The Chosen Valley* (1892), a young man stranded in his irrigation engineer father's remote house, comments wryly: "Proud, poky families like ours; we ought to mix up more, and be more like other people" (206). Such self-depreciation, especially in her letters, makes Foote an often charming as well as adept chronicler of class position in both the East and the West.

. . .

Neither Foote nor her husband did well financially in the West, at first at any rate. They had to struggle for material and economic security in order to sustain their class position. They had been raised, however, with "expectations, resources, and connections"—in other words, "assets, not just income" (Dalton Conley quoted in D. W. Miller A15). Peter Calvert sums up this ambiguous social situation by explaining that class is "a self-assigned, constant picture of one's place in the world, defined not only, and possibly not even dominantly, in terms of one's economic position but also in terms of other variables, now commonly labeled status and power" (94). These "other variables" are Bourdieu's "cultural capital," a concept with much relevance to this study. It is by means of her modest writing skills in conjunction with significant cultural capital that Mary Hallock Foote made her family's living for many years. Her artistic talents were evidenced early in her life, and are beyond dispute, but writing was more of a learned trade for her; she was not a natural novelist and often talked in her letters about how difficult it was for her to think creatively and find the time to write well. She considered what she did to be journeyman "potboiling," writing books that would sell and bring needed checks from the East to the family in the West (*A Victorian Gentlewoman* 359). As she somewhat ruefully and somewhat proudly notes in her autobiography, Foote used every scrap of eastern background and western travail, relentlessly mining her life for material. That the combination of what she was born to and where she ended up living was what editors and the public wanted at the time was her luck, as well as a boon to later analysts of late-nineteenth-century sociology.

In Foote's sentimental tales and family sagas, the conventional plots and characters belie the thorny social expectations and connections depicted. In *West of Everything: The Inner Life of Westerns*, critic Jane Tompkins makes a case that despite English teachers' scorn and because of its popularity, formulaic writing reflects and in turn affects readers and society significantly.[6] And although one cannot call Foote truly formulaic, she is not fundamentally realistic either, nor is she experimental. Her training in two-dimensional art transferred to her writing, as her often rich and detailed settings served as the backdrop for frequently predictable plots and mere character "types." More probing and risk-taking authors presented more nuanced views of class and effectively sidelined Foote, even during her lifetime, including Samuel Clemens, William Dean Howells, and Henry James.

In addition to the mainstream white mostly male writers of realism and naturalism, newly acknowledged nineteenth-century women from the margins and ethnic subcultures of the United States now capture critical attention for both their skill and their depiction of social context. The likes of Eva Emery Dye, Alice Dunbar-Nelson, Winnifred Eaton (Onoto Watanna), and her sister Sui Sin Far tackled class in both subtle and overt ways. Their usually less privileged position made them perhaps more able to expose patriarchy and racism than Foote. Yet Foote's combination of unique artistic talent and geographical peregrinations makes her worthy of study. Her lucid portrayal of social class as it went west exposes a moment of change and retrenchment in the public and private worlds of late-nineteenth-century America (see Roberts).

Western American Stratification

Authors from the northeastern United States, and particularly those from the South, have not infrequently chosen to focus on class issues, but the topic is less popular with authors as well as critics and historians of western American literature. Foote was one of the first western writers to foreground class—her subjects are predominantly upper-middle-class women and men on the frontier. Other western writers addressed class, from Samuel Clemens's pastiches of the gold and silver rush settlements to Agnes Smedley's views on worldwide and western American privilege, Willa Cather's aristocratic clergy, and Wallace Stegner's working-class heroes and ranchers. Foote chose a different path from male western writers such as Clemens and Bret Harte, who had already carved out their niche with the rougher elements of western society; she wrote of a more sheltered world suited to her experience. She also often explicitly situated her characters as professionals working within a national economic context of absentee capitalist owners, a setting that helped her succeed in the kind of middle-class magazines in which she published.

Western American literature and diaries of the era were not usually concerned with class and refinement; usually, the more dramatic struggle with the land and native populations took center stage. That marvelous snob Gertrude Atherton, however, focused on the doomed culture of the old Spanish gentry in California, as well as the sometimes humorous efforts of California's nouveau Anglo elite to best each other. Likewise, Willa Cather's writing is steeped in class issues, particularly "Old Mrs. Harris," *A Lost Lady,* and her later works such as *Death Comes for the Archbishop* and *Shadows on the Rock.* Foote's romances and family sagas, letters and autobiography, show a West in which status looms as large as the struggle to subdue terrain or found towns. As one essay notes, "Foote tries to present a West which can be tied to a traditional past" (Cragg, Walsh, and Walsh xiv). It was her way of justifying her background in a new context that did not always value it.

This book is in many ways a "defensive rereading" of Foote—to use Annette Kolodny's term—in order to reintegrate her into an appropriate historical and literary location in American letters (148). My analysis of Foote's fascination with class uses historical, sociological, and literary lenses.[7] This polyvalent approach is especially useful, as a biographical and cultural approach makes more sense than a purely literary one when discussing Foote's fiction. Barbara Cragg, Dennis M. Walsh, and Mary Ellen Walsh disparage some of Foote's critics for being too biographical and not literary enough in their discussions of her. They prefer James Maguire's literary analysis to Mary Lou Benn's or Lee Ann Johnson's biographical discussions, pleased that Maguire "tends to evaluate [Foote's] novels and stories on their own merits," as they term it, comparing her to George Eliot, Edward Fitzgerald, Bret Harte, and Frank Norris (vi). Whereas Maguire's analysis has utility as it attempts to integrate Foote's oeuvre into the existing literary tradition, other more wide-ranging Foote critics do important historical and critical work as well. Darlis Miller, Foote's recent biographer, gives us the worried, busy, talented woman, noting that because Foote was "conservative and traditional in outlook, she championed existing social arrangements in both fiction and private life" (270). Janet Floyd notes in her discussion of Foote's mining fiction that Foote kept aloof even literarily and was not "much given to positioning herself in relation to other writers of the West" ("Mining the West" 203). Benay Blend shows just how ambiguous Foote's relationship with the West was, given "her relationship to power" (93). Appropriately, then, most recent Foote critics engage less in literary criticism and more in social history when discussing Foote's writing. They recognize that Foote's strengths as a writer lie in her western settings and cultural juxtapositions, not in her literary style or character types. Her work often has more to say to us now when placed in its economic and historical context than when compared to the literary genres and trends of Foote's own time.

Foote's personal odyssey also fitted in with what *Century* editors and readers wanted in a family magazine for the upwardly mobile professional class. And so it came to be that along with Samuel Clemens, Bret Harte, Joaquin Miller, Josiah Royce, Charles Warren Stoddard, Helen Hunt Jackson, Frank Stockton, and Gertrude Atherton, Foote's genteel version of the West helped to shape American readers' attitudes about the region and about nationhood in general. Most articles in the elite magazines of the day, which were published in New York or Boston, centered on events and people on the eastern seaboard or in Europe. Stories covering other parts of the United States were less frequent, focusing on "the scenic and untamed West" of gold rush camps, the Indian wars, or the fashionable neighborhoods of San Francisco or the upper Midwest (Ohmann 231). Eastern and even western readers' notions of class formation in the West were thus influenced by the fiction and nonfiction of these carefully edited magazines.

It is difficult to pin down exactly how class was enacted in the nineteenth-century western United States, since the settlements and towns, cities and mining areas, varied so much and often saw rapid changes in population. In one short story, "The Harshaw Bride," a Foote narrator dryly notes that "westward lies the way of escape from social complications," but certainly sophisticated San Francisco was very different from the raw, makeshift worlds of New Almaden, California, or Leadville, Colorado, when Foote was there (*A Touch of Sun* 259; see also S. Johnson; Roberts). Ohmann asserts that the "nation was not really one" at this time, citing Robert Wiebe's phrase "island communities" to describe the self-contained towns that stretched from coast to coast (57).[8]

The expectations about women regarding social conventions in these western locales ranged anywhere from strict to lax. Still, although class boundaries might have seemed unstable in the West, we know a good deal about Foote's sheltered circles in Colorado, Idaho, and California from her letters and fiction, as well as from period and more recent historical research. Foote carried her class assumptions with her and lived them out with remarkable fidelity, given her modest means.

· · ·

In both her public and private writings, Foote frequently touched on social distinctions, but usually to validate, not criticize, them. She does not seem to have minded that there were people perpetually at the bottom of the social and economic ladder, even if she herself was not at the top. Social inequality and eastern white privilege are complacently accepted in her writings, the classes "engaged in a contractual relationship," in nineteenth-century German sociologist Ferdinand Toennies's phrase (quoted in Calvert 92). In *The Desert and the Sown* (1902), Colonel Middleton expresses surprise that his idealistic future son-in-law believes that having servants is wrong. "Has the boy read history?" he cries. "It's a relation that began when the world was made, and will last while men are in it" (5). This passage represents what I believe to be Foote's attitude, although she exhibited tolerance by presenting more egalitarian views in the avowals of a likable young man.

In Foote's world the reader may sustain the fiction that the classes lived harmoniously together and did not fret at their narrow, prescribed, and inherently unequal roles. Conveniently, this was exactly the world that *Century* and many other late-nineteenth-century magazines wanted to present to their readers. Whereas working-class newspapers and elite intellectual magazines such as the *Atlantic Monthly, Arena, Forum, North American Review,* and the *Nation* dealt with the serious issues of the time—immigration, labor unrest, racism, women's rights, radical political ideas, urban degradation—family and literary magazines did their best to sustain "a space unvexed by conflict," as Ohmann terms it (255). The class focus in these magazines was either upwardly mobile or peer centered. The new professional middle class who paid for magazine subscriptions wanted to learn about those like themselves or above them, but they were less interested in those below.

Within this fictional space, Foote was able to sidestep the antagonistic aspects of class that so disturbed Karl Marx and generations of later idealists. Her philosophy of class might be summed up in the words of Mrs. Dansken in *The Last Assembly Ball,* who, when a gentleman boarder expresses sympathy for the subservient position of the pretty but working-class housemaid, declares confidently, "We can't change places in this world, my dear boy. We have our little fitnesses and unfitnesses, and we'll find ourselves in the long run pretty much where we belong" (74). Foote perceived class less in exploitative and more in gradational terms. She saw social differences not as pitched Marxist battles between the haves and have-nots but, like Max Weber, as relations more defined by issues of status, power, education, and skills. Except in the 1894 *Coeur d'Alene,* which, tellingly, depicts Idaho mine owners as reasonable gentlemen, whereas the striking miners are either dim rustics or outside agitators, Foote rarely portrayed classes in conflict at all and instead constructed what can be termed "an illusory coherence" in her tales (McNall, Levine, and Fantasia 262).

This false harmony served her well in her career in mainstream publishing, of course, since to maximize sales magazines adhered to a worldview that tended to validate existing power relations by treating them as normal, natural, and right. It was an unspoken rule that one did not present social conflict in magazines such as *Century;* what was wanted was "a sunny and conflict-free representation of the social world" (Ohmann 252).

Foote's sense of God-given class and privilege may have had its origins in the self-serving tradition of "natural" superiority, such as the Manifest Destiny justification of the settling of the American West or Rudyard Kipling's imperialist injunctions in "The White Man's Burden." In any event, Foote identified with the elite of her era, which, unconsciously or not, worked like any elite "to legitimize its rule, making its interests seem natural, inevitable, and universal" (Ohmann 43). She did not question the status quo even as much as William Dean Howells, for example, who makes a wry comment in *The Rise of Silas Lapham* about the cost of maintaining social distinctions: "It is certain that our manners and customs go for more in life than our qualities. The price that we pay for civilisation is the fine yet impassable differentiation of these. Perhaps we pay too much; but it will not be possible to persuade those who have the difference in their favour that this is so" (n.p.). In a modest way, Mary Hallock Foote's acceptance of the social hierarchy thus served the interests of the old guard—"those who have the difference in their favour"—but also the new professionals, too. She modeled the standards of the old elite for the new upper middle class, usually in new western settings.

Realism and Naturalism in Foote

Mention of the "space unvexed by conflict" in family magazines and Foote's fiction brings us up against the two major literary trends in her lifetime: realism and naturalism. While Foote was skimming above class conflict and the brutal side of human nature, other writers were choosing to focus on such topics, endeavoring to present modern American life more frankly, with its regional sterility, class disparities, institutional indifference, and racial and gender inequalities. Generally, realism centered on the rapid changes available to the middle class, whereas naturalism, coming later, toward the turn of the twentieth century, focused more on the struggles of the lower classes. It can be argued that realistic novels were merely catching up with what had been a reevaluation in personal relations in Europe and the United States. At first the sentimental ruled in the States.[9] With industrialization, the formal, role-bound expectations of American small towns and extended families in the eighteenth century gave way to more intimate, "intense sentimental relations" in middle-class nuclear families in the urbanizing mid-nineteenth century (Pfister 3). Hawthorne's "scribbling women" novelists and their peers dwelled in this fertile zone. Sentiment, in turn, became less in demand when in the post–Civil War world it became apparent to philosophers, journalists, and writers, as well as the reading public, that all the sentiment and heroic personal efforts in the world might not help one in a society more often controlled by impersonal economic and historical forces than by one's own will or character. Readers who had gobbled up E.D.E.N. Southworth and Harriet Beecher Stowe now found resonance with the more rational and less cloying ethos of realism and naturalism, which portrayed the individual as part of a complicated and not infrequently heartless social system.

Realism wars with romance in Foote's early novels, set in Leadville, Colorado, and romance wins out in the end. Nonetheless, her clingy heroines and their vaguely heroic paramours enact their formal courtships against realistic, practical, and economic backdrops that bring a reader out of the drawing room and onto the crude capitalist streets of a western boomtown. But Foote's high-toned fiction has an edge to it that occasionally jars the reader with scenes of grim western realism. The moonlit, melodramatic descriptions of the final seconds of Babe's life in *John Bodewin's Testimony* (1886), for example, are in stark contrast to the pitiful, naturalist-like description of her body laid out for the public to see the next day. Likewise, the genteel parlor games at Mrs. Dansken's boardinghouse in *The Last Assembly Ball* are interrupted by her impassioned and somewhat progressive speech about the unjust treatment of Chinese immigrants in Leadville.

Foote's brand of realism was to present detailed descriptions of actual places in the West or East and people them with stock upper-middle-class Anglo characters and their faithful family retainers. Foote's narrators might make occasional mention of contemporary ideas or deplorable social conditions—usually far from the novel's setting—but the focus of the plot nonetheless remains the socially circumscribed world of the well-bred protagonists in love. In a review of *The Cup of Trembling, and Other Stories* (1895), the *Nation* extolled writers like Foote who renounced the growing tide of American realism, and noted with approval that such "story-tellers cultivate a gracious intention to entertain, and an amiable desire to give pleasure rather than pain" (February

27, 1896, 181). Foote's is thus a "selective, a respectable, an official realism," as Carl Van Doren called that of William Dean Howells, who himself published Foote's first short story in the *Atlantic* (n.p.). In her fiction Foote does allude to "the clang of the larger America [and] the sense of the manipulation of vast forces" that were remaking the country, but she forbears to linger on the crushing or pathetic effect those forces have on individuals who cannot maneuver them successfully (Van Doren n.p.).

As we have seen, this selectivity dovetailed with the kind of fiction many readers wanted. The burgeoning middle class chose to read magazines such as *Century, Harper's, Scribner's,* and the *Atlantic* in part to educate itself about the new world of opportunity; naturally, it was not appealing to read about those who failed in it. Tales such as *Silas Lapham* could appear in *Century* because Lapham's failures serve to improve his character and spiritual depth, thus demonstrating a useful lesson suitable for family fare. In addition, *Century* readers could take wicked pleasure in Howells's condescension to the nouveau riche as the novel opens. If readers were of a class higher than the Laphams, they could laugh and wince at their faux pas; if they were of the Laphams' rising class, they could take notes. A story like Howells's had some educational value for an upwardly mobile professional class, whereas many of naturalism's dark tales merely reinforced for anyone who had risen in the world the obvious truth that the lower reaches were indeed better off abandoned.

The insistence on gentility in Foote's realism prefigured some of the writers of color a generation later. The mannered tales of Sui Sin Far, her sister Onoto Watanna, and Jessie Fauset often exhibit a deferential, almost defensive, tone about class.[10] Respectability and decorum are treated seriously in stories that also deal with the grimmer issues of both institutional and personal racism.[11] Working with less oppressed types, Foote established a presumed gentility in her characters, who even if they wear flannel shirts or lack fashionable bonnets are above all ladies and gentlemen. Foote stayed in this polite world for some of the same reasons that the segregated Asian and black writers did. She too was depicting people with a precarious social status—in this case, deracinated Anglos in remote western places that eastern readers might have dismissed out of hand as being outside the bounds of polite society. For Foote's stories to sit well with her educated, urban readers, they needed to be peopled with westerners impeccable in behavior and thus beyond reproach. She skirted the edges of realism and presented only a few downright grim moments.

Even with lifelike backdrops and occasionally gritty situations in her writing, she nonetheless disliked the uncouth reality that was making its way into the realism and particularly the naturalism of her day. She referred to Bret Harte's and George Miller's descriptions of California as "coarse" (MHF to RWG, December 14, 1877). After reading Edgar Watson Howe's *Story of a Country Town* (1883), she decried its realism in a letter to Helena. Citing one of the scenes of squalid family life, she vociferously asserted that the book was "revolting" and had actually made her ill (January 5, 1885). Foote found fault with it for the very reasons the *Atlantic Monthly* did in its review of January 1885. The people of this country town, the *Atlantic* lamented, "are engaged in a sordid struggle for existence; they have lost their ideals, and the world seems to mock at them. A more dreary waste than the country town which Mr. Howe describes could not well be imagined. It appears to have no traditions even of beauty, and certainly no anticipations of hope. It is degraded spiritually and mentally, and nature itself seems to take on the prevailing gray hue, and to shut in upon the narrowing circle of life" (125). In a later letter Foote commented on the novel again and its relation to the themes of the West: "The movement in its largeness [is] not individual tragedies or even race tragedies—for in the main, the movement of life in the West is hopeful and strong. That is why I cannot feel that books like the Country Town are *true*. There are stagnant spots, halts, and deserters in every march, but the march moves on" (MHF to HKG, January 8, 1888).

Thus, Foote generally chose a more positive tone than the hard-core realists, despite her personal misgivings about the West. She wrote to Richard Gilder about her unwillingness to take on unpleasant, unladylike subjects: "I know a beautiful scheme for a short story, strong and new, and tragic, and very western: but someone else ought to write it: [Wolcott] Balestier or Rebecca Harding Davis. It is too strong for me. I shouldn't succeed, and if I did all my lady friends would wish I hadn't. Can't I write it anonymously?" (c. 1894). If Foote had ever read the salty "Dame Shirley" (Louise Amelia Smith Clapp) letters about the California gold rush camps, she would have been particularly appalled that a woman could write such honest and brutal descriptions of local western color.

At the end of her *Reminiscences,* Foote admitted that reality was sometimes too unpleasant and that she could not help being an "old romancer," even about her own life (*A Victorian Gentlewoman* 400). In her fiction, she often portrayed the sometimes heartless power relations underpinning western mining or irrigation concerns, but she kept the tone light and used metaphor and allusion to soften the realism. In her first novel, *The Led-Horse Claim* (1882), for example, instead of presenting the dark side of boomtown life in Leadville, Colorado, she playfully described the mines' financial dependence on eastern syndicates as "the ark of the mining industry . . . awaiting the olive-leaf of Eastern capital" with its "uncertain doves of promise" (9). The headlong forces of emerging capitalism were not absent in this new region, but they were transformed into the literary and allegorical. In *Angle of Repose*, Wallace Stegner asserts that the frontier West where his fictional couple, much like the Footes, lives was less mythological (and less unruly) than its reputation, asserting that "in fact large parts of it were owned by Eastern and foreign capital and run by iron-fisted bosses" (117). The history and economics of the West bear this out.

An additional facet to the tempered realism of Foote's writing set in Leadville is that most of her characters have options and agency in their lives; they are not trapped in one place or in a specific job. This reflects the situation of Foote's husband and herself, too, who had more mobility than many westerners, in spite of severe financial setbacks. In a poignant short piece about loneliness in the West, Foote talks compassionately about disheartened people who "get left" there, as she colloquially terms it (Cragg, Walsh, and Walsh 301). Her fictional protagonists do not have complete autonomy, however; they must go where they are sent like the modern professionals they are. But they are not tied down to a farm or town forever. Often, they leave their situations and start again with new hope, like the couple in Foote's early novel *John Bodewin's Testimony* or the ne'er-do-well pilot husband in her last work, *The Ground-Swell*. In addition, Foote's usually rural *isolatoes* generally lack the narrow, bleak outlook of the characters in realist Hamlin Garland's *Main-Travelled Roads* or Cather's darker Nebraska stories such as "The Sculptor's Funeral." Likewise, Foote's characters rarely approach the sordidness or starkness in Elizabeth Stuart Phelps's *Silent Partner* or the works of Stephen Crane or Theodore Dreiser.

Foote had a distaste for blank verisimilitude, one shared by the editor of *Ladies' Home Journal* at the time, Edward Bok, who "primly opposed what he took to be the impropriety of realism and naturalism and fussed with writers over unsuitable subjects like the stage, suicide, and the consumption of alcohol" (Ohmann 291). Foote steered clear of these topics, too, except to touch on them obliquely. In a California story, "A Touch of Sun" (1903), a middle-aged matron who seems to speak for Foote on several subjects disapproves of activities for women that bring any publicity on themselves, including going onstage. Foote avoided suicide in her fiction, too, aside from a few pat tragic endings for some Idaho short stories. Alcoholism, which touched Foote's life closely due to her husband's failings, has some presence in her work, usually in connection with down-and-out western types. Rarely does a protagonist have a real drinking problem, however. In a classic redemption trajectory, *The Prodigal* (1900) alludes lightly to the patrician hero's weakness for the bottle, first letting the reader revel in the more picturesque sides of his lowlife rambles through old San Francisco and then having the young man overcome addiction by means of his own aristocratic "character" and the love of a good woman.

We know from her letters that Foote was explicitly critical of realism and naturalism, but as we have seen, aspects of both crept into her novels and stories. As Carl Van Doren describes the world of William Dean Howells, Foote started out in a literary era "when taste ran rather to discipline than to variety or vividness, rather to decorum than to candor, rather to learning than to experience, rather to charm than to passion" (n.p.). But Foote kept abreast of contemporary social and literary ideas and drew on them freely, though inconsistently, in her writing. Influenced by transnational currents, as well as Victorian respectability and the sentimental tradition, she first used the idealized romance formula for her novels, with clear-cut moral and immoral character types to match. Despite her initial gestures to the certitude of tradition, however, she increasingly began to explore the equivocal and mutable social relations of the times. Her backdrops had always been realistic, even in the first novels, but now, inching toward naturalism, she allowed the control her characters have over their fates to grow less and less as the century waned. As a putative realist, then, Foote straddled the fence, frequently trying to impute success or failure to class status and inbred character, but in the end depicting a bleaker landscape with less personal agency than a sentimentalist would.

Female and Male Roles

Foote's female protagonists in the early Leadville novels languidly drift into their traditional marriage plots and never lose contact with the eastern structures that bred them. Later Idaho characters, on the other hand, such as Rose Gilroy in "Maverick" or Dolly Dunsmuir in *The Chosen Valley*, are western-born women living in regions whose geography essentially holds them prisoner. Desperate, stage-stop waitress Rose lights out across treacherous lava fields to certain death in order to avoid marriage to a scarred roughneck. In *Chosen Valley*, Dolly, the daughter of a gentleman, is saved from a wasted, isolated life in a dry canyon only because she is beautiful and somehow well bred enough to attract a professional man for a husband. Foote's female characters generally have less autonomy than the male, especially in the Idaho novels, and for that Laura Katherine Gruber rightly argues that Foote's situations can be viewed as naturalistic. But even though they sometimes encounter dire, deterministic situations, Foote's Idaho heroines never sink to the level of Maggie of the streets, Sister Carrie, or their ilk. Sometimes they die somewhat sentimentally and sensationally, like the hapless Rose in "Maverick" or Ruth Mary in "A Storm on the Mountain." Foote was unwilling to portray what might really have happened to nonelite women when life dealt them a rough blow, so she killed them off. In any event, most of Foote's western female characters are sheltered, middle-class women with limited life choices. They remain chaste and marry well, a far cry from naturalism's unfortunate and often desperate drabs.

In her male characters, too, Foote evolved. Her knight errant hero waiting alone for his adversary with pistol in hand inside a Leadville mine in *The Led-Horse Claim* gave way to engineers struggling to find eastern funding for an Idaho-based irrigation project in *The Chosen Valley*. This latter work is a good case study for Foote's realist tendencies, for though it is ostensibly about the personal tension between two irrigation engineers—one scrupulous, one not—a more compelling focus is the broader economic and indeed ecological forces affecting these men's moral behavior and success. Class comes into it also, since the more moral engineer has better training and comes from a more solidly upper-middle-class background. But what remains for the reader at the end is a Frank Norris–like sense of helplessness and isolation in the remote dry canyons of Idaho, and not the principled or unprincipled actions of either the men or the predictable romantic subplot involving their children. Foote might have preferred to demonstrate that success lies with the individual, but she ended up showing that success depends in large part on the vicissitudes of history, region, and birth class. Amy Kaplan notes that literary realism at the turn of the twentieth century helped create a "strategy for imagining and managing the threats of social change" as characters work through some of the uncharted social possibilities and pitfalls the new age had wrought (9). In this light we can see that in spite of herself, Foote had moved beyond the sentimentality of Stowe and Alcott's era to explore the daunting idea that even with a sturdy character and great personal effort, an individual and his or her life chances could be greatly influenced by extrapersonal realities.

...

Although much of Foote's work deals with class differences in a provincial western setting, she should not be considered a true regionalist. Like many other western writers, Foote wrote about the West from an eastern perspective, usually portraying not natives of the region at all but instead easterners and their efforts to establish lives and standards in the new locale. Regionalists, by contrast, are emotionally rooted in locale and as such "present regional experience from within"; they empathize with their local characters (Fetterley and Pryse xii, xv). Even though Foote could occasionally be sympathetic to local and non-well-connected characters, she did not get inside their skin; only rarely does one forget that an outsider is telling the story. When Foote did depict westerners exclusively, such as in the short stories "Maverick" or "How the Pump Stopped at Morning Watch," she was superficial, rendering the quaint customs of the natives from a detached and often superior perspective. She had the "ethnographic distancing" that Sandra Gilbert asserts some local colorists chose to adopt, which resulted in a sometimes insulting portrayal of anyone different from herself (quoted in Showalter, "American Gynocriticism" 120). By contrast, in "At the 'Cadian Ball," Kate Chopin can refer to the former slave George as a "darkey" and not be dismissive because her narrator clearly respects him as an individual; she is merely using the terminology of the day (65–74). Foote avoided racial epithets when describing nonelite characters, but not infrequently she exuded a polite condescension.

. . .

Book groups, common readers, and even western historians and literary scholars often know of Mary Hallock Foote only through the somewhat distorted lens of Wallace Stegner's 1971 Pulitzer Prize–winning novel, *Angle of Repose*. Although he changed the names, Stegner meticulously re-created the facts of the Footes' biography and borrowed many phrases and sentences from her letters and autobiography, including the geologic title phrase "angle of repose" itself. The original scholar who "outed" Stegner on this, Mary Ellen Williams (Walsh) of Idaho State University, detailed the similar and indeed identical nature of parallel passages in Foote's writing and Stegner's throughout *Angle of Repose*. Linda K. Karell of Montana State University has recently written about what she terms the "collaborative" nature of this new creation, although not without some condemnation for Stegner's cavalier disregard for Foote's sovereignty (*Writing Together;* see also "The Postmodern Author"). Most Foote scholars and all of her descendants are less forgiving; even Jackson J. Benson, Stegner's biographer and staunch defender, estimates that 10 percent of Stegner's novel is from Foote's letters (354). California playwright Sands Hall adds that if Foote's autobiography is taken into account, it is probably a higher percentage. A recent play by Hall titled *Fair Use* dramatizes the effect of Stegner's considerable "borrowings" by having not only Stegner and Foote onstage together but also their "creations"—Susan Burling Ward and young Mary Hallock Foote—and the modern-day playwright herself.

Nonetheless, Stegner generally remained true to what I believe is the spirit of Foote's outer and inner life—that is, until the last quarter of the novel. At that point, Stegner exaggerated the tensions between Susan Burling Ward—his Foote-like character—and her best friend over Susan's husband's lack of success in Idaho and later the tensions between her and her husband and son. Most egregiously, however, when Stegner depicted the distance that grew between Susan and her husband during the Idaho canyon years, he had her turn for comfort to one of her husband's associates and inadvertently cause the accidental death by drowning of her five-year-old daughter during an emotional meeting with her would-be lover. The associate then commits suicide. Nothing of the sort happened in real life: Foote's youngest daughter, Agnes, died of appendicitis in her teens, not because of parental neglect but due to remoteness from a hospital, and none of Arthur De Wint Foote's Idaho associates committed suicide, though one had a nervous breakdown and came to the Footes' home to recuperate; an old Leadville friend did commit suicide in Montana around this time when a mining scheme failed (D. Miller 145, 151).

Despite Stegner's offenses against family history and particularly against character—since I do not believe that Mary Hallock Foote was the sort of woman who would have committed adultery—he portrays Foote's class attitudes accurately, especially in her first years in the West. Listing the remote places where his protagonist has lived, he notes that Susan Burling Ward "stayed a cultural snob through it all" and that she "made not the slightest concession to the places where she lived" (19, 85). This might be a bit overstated, as some recent critics have pointed out, including both Linda Karrell and Janet Floyd, who assert that Foote was more in tune with the West than previously thought (Karell, *Writing Together;* Floyd, "Mining the West" and *Writing*). Nonetheless, Foote continued to live away from others, even during her thirty years in Grass Valley, choosing to interact only with those who were like her. At the end of her autobiography, written in her seventies, she is still fighting a western identity, wistfully noting that as important as an eastern background has been to her, her thoroughly western grandchildren have little connection to their ancestral roots in her beloved Hudson Valley.

· · ·

Due to a constellation of historical forces and personal attributes, then, Mary Hallock Foote enjoyed a long and successful career in late-nineteenth-century and early-twentieth-century illustration and magazine and book publishing. No matter what she wrote—fiction, travel essays, letters, or an autobiography—she saw the world as minutely stratified. Social class in the West and East emerged as one of her underlying concerns. Her connections to the upper middle class of New York State served her well, as did her insistence on maintaining the social gulf between the genteel and the ungenteel in her writings. In her life she might have been happier had she jettisoned her rigid way of keeping the uncouth West at bay. But her loss of assimilation is our gain, since along with other nineteenth-century novelists she detailed for us the rich and sometimes seemingly byzantine texture of social-class distinctions in her time. Still, as Loretta Wasserman observes about Cather's embarrassing and disappointing anti-Semitism, "attitudes toward race, class, and gender are not dismissed as awkward blemishes but are perceived as deeply significant clues both to dominating cultural thought patterns and to individual habits of mind" (n.p.).

Foote, too, gives one pause with her conservative and sometimes ungenerous insistence on the maintenance of class boundaries. This no doubt contributes to the reason she is not more popular in the early twenty-first century: her views are at odds with an era that gives at least lip service to social, cultural, and ethnic inclusivity. Nonetheless, living as she was "at the moving edge of the present" in a time of great social change, Foote usefully charted where the old elites of the Northeast had been and where the new professional middle and upper middle class was headed (Ohmann 233). Until we can critique power relations and better understand how historical social forces—and their embodiment in hierarchies, ideologies, and claims for morality—shape and create public perceptions and norms, we will not fully understand how we navigate our own "moving edge of the present."

Foote's Cultural Moment

"They Had Stayed in One Place and Cultivated Character"

Class structure in nineteenth-century America was certainly more stratified than in the twentieth, when world wars, mass-produced consumer goods, and global communications and transportation changed the face of privilege, white and otherwise. Yet nineteenth-century industrialization, immigration, urbanization, and increasingly impersonal bureaucracy had already begun to loosen barriers to social mobility. Mary Hallock Foote found this trend disturbing, and in most instances continued to present her own established eastern background as the bedrock of taste and discrimination. Any elite westerners in her tales, male and female, are types comfortable in at least middle-class eastern settings, if not higher. Foote obscured this classism, however, by making privilege the result of upright moral character, not necessarily advantaged background. She usually held that one's good character grows out of one's (upper) social class.

This idea relates to upward mobility. This mythic feature of American life is a rarity in Foote's novels, stories, and letters, despite the fact that the magazines she wrote for were vehicles for class assimilation. In her work, Foote intimated that attempted class mobility in the West usually failed, even though some of the real western lives around her might have led her to question this convenient assumption. In Foote, those in the lower class and less geographically "placed" sometimes exhibited the vaunted "character" and thus qualified for upward mobility. But Foote used this reward sparingly, and usually nonelite characters are mere sketches with little individuality. Either Anglo or of color, they exist often merely as background for her protagonists. Only a few deserving types are able to maneuver their way up the fraught class ladder successfully.

For many reasons, Foote did not jettison her narrow class vision even after decades of living in the shifting democracies of the West. If not by Foote, however, the changes nonetheless possible in nineteenth-century class position were played out by many other writers. Most famously, in *The Rise of Silas Lapham* (1885), William Dean Howells depicted the hapless, if decidedly rich,

Laphams at a loss about how to break into Boston society. In the early twentieth century, Edith Wharton also focused on this theme in her work, and in fact on Foote's own turf in *Hudson River Bracketed* (1929), where the old aristocratic estates along the Hudson River are being bought up by the newly rich who want the comfort and prestige of a summer home.

Any idea of a monolithic elite is inaccurate, however, even if Foote seems to have believed it existed. Historians suggest that "a self-conscious and united ruling class was an impossibility" at this time, since the "island communities" of the United States had not yet been united by easy transportation and national media (Ohmann 57). In the 1880s Gertrude Atherton found this to be the case, noting how different upper-class New York society was from her own San Francisco: "It took me little time to discover that belonging to the best society in San Francisco cut no ice in New York. Our first families had never been heard of. . . . New York brooked no rival" (*Adventures* 142).

In the Northeast, the prestige of the first colonial families was being co-opted by and combined with that of the new mercantile and professional elite, who in turn devised mechanisms and institutions to differentiate themselves from those less successful. Privilege was fiercely guarded, as the now extraordinary creation by Mrs. Astor in 1892 of her "Newport 400" guest list attests. This concern about class and its boundaries was due to industrialization and its effects, which slowly or rapidly dismantled the old rank structures and brought into being modern and more impersonal social strata. Many wanted clear demarcations retained between classes; the social register and cotillion both had their origins at this time. As the narrator wryly notes in *Silas Lapham,* the nouveau riche Lapham daughters "had learned to dance at Papanti's; but they had not belonged to the private classes. They did not even know of them, and a great gulf divided them from those who did" (n.p.). Atherton makes wicked fun of the exclusivity of San Francisco's society in *The Californians* (1898), where idle Paris-dressed wives from "old" California money—made in the 1849 gold rush—snub those with "new" money who are trying to buy their way into the right neighborhoods.

That status was difficult to attain if you weren't born to it was a sustaining theme of American fiction up through *The Great Gatsby.* Etiquette books and magazines such as Foote's *Century,* however, aided the upwardly mobile, teaching them the tastes and behaviors of the upper classes, following norms that were "modeled on the usages of the Old World" (Schlesinger 5). *Century*'s readers might have been raised with dime-novel sensibilities, but they aspired to

those of James and Wharton. Foote was accessible middle ground. Her rootedness in and internalization of elite traditions focused—and narrowed—her as an
artist and writer but made her outlook and sensibilities perfect for *Century.*

...

Foote's approach to class, literature, and history assumed the cultural primacy
of the eastern Anglo United States and Europe. Her 1903 story "Pilgrims to
Mecca" blatantly calls the West "the wrong side of the continent for art and
culture" (*A Touch of Sun* 145). In her day, the northeastern American cities and
those of northern Europe were indeed the centers of industry and culture,
although as the century waned some Americans wanted to celebrate a more
homegrown sensibility. With varying degrees of self-consciousness, they endeavored to throw off the yoke of the genteel tradition emanating from European and eastern metropolises (see Alexander; Wertheim). In the mid-twentieth century, Raymond Williams and others analyzed and politicized these
efforts, advocating that instead of accepting the "metropolitan interpretation
. . . as universal," scholars should instead validate the talent and new ideas in the
"hinterlands," "where different forces are moving" (quoted in Ardis and Lewis,
The Politics 47, 5). This trend later exploded into various subaltern, regional,
ethnic, feminist, and queer interpretive camps.

As tempting as it might be to analyze Foote's work from one or more of these
margins, however, it proves difficult, since she did her best to ignore the local
talent and culture in the West. She was unabashedly metropolitan-centric—
New York being the touchstone of her worldview—and though she often depicted the regional customs of the West, she made it clear that such backwater
ways should not be used as models for her eastern protagonists. Writers such
as Willa Cather and Mary Austin made more of an effort to portray western
people and themes on their own terms, and thus they can be usefully studied
from a regionalist, or "hinterland," perspective. But revisionist critics, given
half a chance, are quick to pounce on Cather and even Austin for elitist, racist,
or Anglo-centric attitudes.[1] Such critics usually don't bother with Foote at all,
due to her consistently elitist views. It is clear, then, that Laura Katherine Gruber is accurate when she says that "Foote's nightmare . . . [was] the disappear-
ance of familiarity. . . . [A]ll the unsettling backgrounds of the frontier were
unfamiliar to her—and felt so for years. The East was Foote's original context."
I am less convinced, however, by Gruber's subsequent assertion that "the West
. . . forced her to reevaluate that old context as well as come to terms with a new

one for her characters" (355). I do not believe that Foote did reevaluate the old context. Benay Blend agrees: "It was Foote's rigid adherence to class and caste, even in the face of her husband's repeated business failures, that prevented her from valuing the wilderness as anything more than vacant land upon which to re-create hierarchical society as she had known it in the East. And there was no question in her own mind as to what class she should belong" (98). We don't have to go that far, since Foote did try in her own way to accept aspects of the West. But her embeddedness in eastern culture and class still degraded all she saw there. This is evident in her treatment of her characters, elite and humble. Gruber is correct that Foote's western situations could border on the naturalistic, depicting the dreariness and limited options for women and some men there, but Foote rarely allowed the situations to become truly scary for the truly genteel. Her eastern characters do not have to come to terms with the West. They succeed or fail there, but they rarely become one with it and prosper, like Cather's pioneers, for example. Foote created some westerners with dignity and worth, but in the words of a character in her last novel, ultimately they were not "our kind of folks" (*The Ground-Swell* 144).

Tragedies in Foote's fiction, and there are some, generally happen to expendable western "types" and often seem more melodramatic than naturalistic. Old, befuddled Adam Bogardus in *The Chosen Valley* (1892), who has become a western mountain man, gets himself stuck inside an empty house in the East and implausibly starves to death. Frantic, rustic Rose in "Maverick" runs off to die in lava fields, fleeing an oafish suitor, and impoverished Babe in *John Bodewin's Testimony* (1886) and river child Ruth Mary in "A Cloud on the Mountain" perish in misguided romantic attempts to save the lives of eastern professional men they know are out of their ken socially. This last example is less like western naturalism and more like the old English ballad "Lass from the Low Country" updated to the American West: a "common" Idaho female is summarily ignored by one above her and dies forgotten. "Cloud" in particular is filled with charming but incongruous "ye olde Englishe" allusions to Tennyson's "Lady of Shallot." Characters with solid ties to eastern or European gentility do not die or come to bad ends unless they have been very immoral, like Conrath in *The Led-Horse Claim* (1882); very foolish, like Frank in *The Last Assembly Ball* (1889); or too idealistic for this world, like Dunsmuir in *The Chosen Valley* or Katherine in *The Ground-Swell* (1919).

Determined to preserve eastern standards of propriety, Foote's idea of fictional tragedy is a threatened scandal or a mixed-class marriage—not one of naturalism's more sordid scenarios. Better death than lowering one's standards of association. Death is in fact a clean and respectable end for several of Foote's compromised upper-middle-class lovers, from callow, impulsive Frank in *The Last Assembly Ball* to the fragile, adulterous Esmee in "The Cup of Trembling." When Richard Gilder's sister is reported to have made an ill-advised engagement, Foote expresses horror in a letter to Helena, saying, "I could wish poor Tina were dead for her sake" (Spring 1882).

Since Foote herself was tormented by her exiled love of eastern places and ways, she was able to illustrate convincingly the tensions between her old and new contexts. In one of her best short stories, "Pilgrims to Mecca," she presents the dilemma confronting westerners who want to amount to something in the larger world. A snobbish, eastern-looking mama muses to her carefully reared western daughter, "Sometimes I wonder why we do cling to that old fetish of the East. Why can't we accept the fact that we are Western people? The question is, Shall we be the self-satisfied kind or the unsatisfied kind? Shall we be contented and limited, or discontented and grow?" (*A Touch of Sun* 148). The mother finally decides after much soul-searching to let her high school–age daughter remain in San Francisco instead of shipping her off to Boston to be "finished." Nonetheless, Foote had only occasional interest in those who are contented and, to her, limited by the West, such as the forthright young western couple in "The Watchman." She tended to create protagonists who, if not exactly unhappy, yearn for more ambitious and often eastern horizons.

Foote's longing gaze to the East resulted in the ossification of her view of its culture and standards, due to infrequent trips back as well as her less than swift adoption of new literary trends owing to a lack of contact with peers. Richard Ohmann talks about the "greatly extended axis of respectability" that the new professional middle class developed in their suburbs and city neighborhoods, clubs and watering holes, as "closely monitored circles of local acquaintance had given way to metropolitan and national affinities" (159). But Foote did not experience that newfound respect; she and her husband were too isolated from such society. They remained far-flung members of this new socioeconomic stratum. All Foote knew was the model of a tightly knit, exclusive, rural New York family like her own, and she reproduced that ideal as best she could in the West in fact and fiction. At the end of an 1896 review in the *Nation*, a discerning comment sums up most of Foote's characters: "At all events, [Foote's] people have always come from somewhere else, and one feels sure that, if they are permitted to live long enough, they will go home again" (February 27, 1896, 182).

As for Foote's literary approach, though it deepened psychologically as she grew older, the fact that she was writing in a vacuum is manifest in many ways. She read the better magazines such as the *Atlantic* and *Century*, and tried to keep abreast of the trends. But by inclination and location, she limited her exposure to the emerging unpleasantness of realism and naturalism and chose not to dwell on the underlying political and economic reasons for them. This kept her work tied not only to an old-fashioned literary style but also to a social code and class structure of an earlier age.

To understand what seems to be a surprising restrictiveness on Foote's part, it is necessary to understand the rigid class ideology she accepted. Her kind of point of view held sway in mid-to late-nineteenth-century eastern and often western America, despite the prevalence of upward (and downward) mobility. For Foote, social class should be a fixed mark of background and personality, based on birth and that quaint and often racist term *breeding*. And most people apparently felt as she did, that class was "written on minds and bodies," in Valerie Walkerdine's somewhat figurative phrase (n.p.).[2] We see this assumption in other writers' works, from the aristocratic confidence of Olive Chancellor in Henry James's *Bostonians* (1886) to Constance Fenimore Woolson's faded spinsters insisting on gentility even in poverty. You either had it or you didn't, and it was difficult and foolish to try to change your station.

In fairness, Foote's exclusiveness was not always mere snobbery. It was also due to personal shyness, and longtime habits of solitude, which Robert Coles notes are often ingrained in elite children. As part of the development of an individual self, children of privilege often "do not like large groups of people in public places," having been "taught the value not only of privacy but of the quiet that goes with being relatively alone" (57).[3] Foote was used to time to herself for art and reflection. She had grown up where others managed the housekeeping responsibilities; she commented to Helena that she felt it a burden even to have to make her bed in the morning (December 13, 1885). Foote's tendency to avoid both quotidian tasks and local people in the West may therefore have stemmed as much from a wish to avoid distractions as a wish to avoid local western "yahoos," as she once termed them (May 19, 1884; September 15, 1889). Moreover, she did need to concentrate and keep the *Century* checks coming for the family. Accordingly, before, during, and even after the especially lean Idaho years, she retreated daily from local society to write and draw.

The kind of stratified world Foote grew up in and found reassuring is echoed in an obscure autobiographical piece by Willa Cather. Cather describes her birthplace, a region in old Virginia from which she came to Nebraska. It sounds very much like the New York State of Foote's youth. Cather describes it as "an old conservative society; from the Valley of Virginia, where the original land grants made in the reigns of George II and George III had been going down from father to son ever since, where life was ordered and settled, where the people in good families were born good, and poor mountain people were not expected to amount to much. The movement of life was slow there, but the quality of it was rich and kindly. . . . Foreigners were looked down upon, unless they were English or persons of title" (quoted in Porter 53). Cather goes on to say that as a young girl she found the immigrants and struggles in Nebraska of greater interest than the "definitely arranged" structure of her old region. Yet her positive regard for that settled and secure way of life is palpable here—as it is in "Old Mrs. Harris"—despite the glowing depiction of the exciting Nebraska frontier that follows this Virginia passage.

Imagine Foote, then, from a similar stronghold of landed gentry in upstate New York, a place that had been an old royalist territory like Virginia. Since Foote did not go West until she was well into her twenties, she had had time to become fond of what Cather calls "comfort and picturesqueness" (53). The upshot was, as Foote critics have politely noted, that Foote was "handicapped by certain attitudes and conventions and her own sense of fitness," caught in a "genteel trap" (Benn 2; James, James, and Boyer 644). In a letter to Helena during her first year or two in California, Foote wondered if she would be able to change her frame of reference and doubted it: "Will we be Western and 'brag' about this glorious country—and the general superiority of half civilized over civilized societies? That sounds bitter. There are such good people here but I cannot care for them! I am too old to be transplanted. The part of me which friendship and society claim must wait or perish in the waiting" (January 1878). She was thirty-one when she wrote this. Once in the West, Foote clearly missed her friends and the old land-identified, family-bound way of life, even as she and Arthur modeled what was possible for members of the new, mobile, professional middle class.

In her writings Foote assumed that not only New York City but also her own little part of the Hudson Valley had important cultural and social characteristics. She continued to enact the "genteel performance," to use historian Willard B. Gatewood's clever term (182). In this she was different from Caroline Kirkland, Mary Austin, Mari Sandoz, or Cather in the Nebraska novels, who viewed the West as a place where Old World and eastern American models of living could be simplified and improved upon.

Upon first reading Foote's letters and published works, it might seem that her frequent regional allusions to the East were merely her personal frame of reference. They were, of course, but in her case they also served as class markers. Like many nineteenth-century American male writers, as well as Louisa May Alcott and Ellen Glasgow, Foote happened to be from an old, established family in an old, established region that dictated the national cultural standards. She knew and cherished the old dispensations and felt at home in that world. It was her luck that, as wrenching as it was, leaving that milieu and going west with an engineer for a husband enhanced her economic life chances, since she could not only draw and write about western settlement firsthand but do so from a privileged perspective, not a more marginal, pioneering one. She was able "to benefit from the experience of her own alienation," as Michael Nowlin notes about Edith Wharton's ambivalence toward the United States (101).

· · ·

We see class lines clearly drawn and Foote's attitude toward upward mobility further revealed when she recounts in her *Reminiscences* the way in which her parents' farm came to be sold. Times were precarious for small farmers in the Hudson Valley, especially for those who did not have enough family members to help them, or who did not choose crops or investments wisely. Foote's parents had fallen deeper and deeper in debt, and when her father died in 1889 the family sold the farm. At this time, Foote had lived in the West for about thirteen years and was in her early forties. Her description of this event points up her discomfort—like Henry James's—with a new and changing world where gentility must cede to crass bottom-line realities: "The man who outbid [us] was one of that class of farmers who are not affected by the rise in wages. They work on the land, as our forefathers did; but they were not unlettered hinds, those old Quaker Hallocks and Townsends" (314). Foote felt the loss of the farm very keenly because it represented a cherished, genteel way of life lost. Some years later, Edith Wharton took a more detached view of this region, which she dissects in *Hudson River Bracketed*. Noting that an estate there had been in the Lorburn family for more than two hundred years, the narrator muses: "It was too long, perhaps, for Americans to live in any one place; and . . . it had become a sort of tribal obligation to go on doing so" (77). From her insecure perch in a dusty canyon in remote Idaho, however, Foote would have liked to be *more* connected to tribal obligation and its accompanying stability and status.

Foote relates that the buyer of the Hallock Farm had started out years earlier as a lowly farmhand there, and had struck the family as unmannerly and uncouth for his refusal to accept the exclusivity and privacy of his employers. She recalls that he had looked into rooms where he was not allowed and was remembered as having sometimes stared through the parlor window into the house. Foote says that her mother had not liked his ways: "Mistresses were mistresses in those days, and she had the ideas of her time as to behavior proper to his class." Foote does give the upstart grudging compliments: "He married and raised a family of sons who were rough young fellows, but he taught them to work, and he knew how to save. While the old farm went on lending money without interest and piling up debts, he was piling up a bank account" (314). She does not like the man but has to admit she respects him on one level. Foote cannot but assert, though, that "it was not a house suited to him or his family" and lament that her father "belonged to the last of his breed of thinking and reading American farmers, working their own lands which they inherited from their fathers" (314, 316). This may sound like nostalgia or self-aggrandizement, but there apparently was indeed a class of such farmers in the northeastern states. Author Mary Ellen Chase, for example, describes her father and mother living similarly literate lives on their farm in rural Maine (in MacLeod 115). Although the buyer of the Foote farm seems to have been merely hardworking and thrifty, Foote treats him as if he were the opportunistic Ivy Peters in Willa Cather's *Lost Lady,* sullying and destroying beautiful but economically unviable land and lifestyles with philistine ways. In this vein, she decries a new mechanized turbine wheel that replaced the charming old mill waterwheel at the farm; to her it was one of the "wonders of efficiency replacing the joys of the beautiful past" (92).

This incident in Foote's family history reveals her views about those who work to improve their material conditions, let alone try to move up in the social hierarchy. It also exposes worries about her family's ability to remain within their birth class. Clearly, Foote was offended, and a bit defensive, that a poorly educated and "common" brood should take over her family's patrimony. The social changes possible in her era caused her anxiety, even as they propelled her elite magazines to bigger circulations and hence indirectly paid her bills. Yet she could mount no substantial case against the classic American upward mobility of the family farm's new owner except to feel, as Neil does in *A Lost Lady,* that a lovely, leisurely, civilized way of life is passing. Foote might have agreed with Eileen Slocum that "there is definitely such a thing as an aristocracy in America. It is based on breeding and behavior—*superior* behavior—and a willingness to work and to do what needs to be done. The word 'lady' and the word 'gentleman' meant a great deal to Mummy and Daddy. We were gentlefolk, and people who weren't were—well, we could tell who they were" (quoted in Birmingham 292; emphasis in the original). Foote did not usually make such direct pronouncements in her fiction, but her omniscient narrators generally share these attitudes.

Perhaps because she took the status quo for granted, Foote's use of class markers in her fiction is understated. She had a reticent, perhaps even Quaker, ethic of not broadcasting one's heritage, wealth, or status. Her attitudes are echoed in those of an upper-class woman in a 1950s study of social class in New Haven, Connecticut, who explained, "One does not speak of classes; they are felt" (quoted in Blumberg 162). With Atherton, Foote might have said about those who possess class, somewhat vaguely but with equal certitude, that "what they did or had or were was of an indisputable rightness" (*Adventures* 60). Like those with more secure "class confidence," Foote assumed gentility on the part of her protagonists and left it at that (Ohmann 289).

In most of her novels, after the initial setting is presented—usually western—Foote describes the characters with deft touches that "place them," using social markers to distinguish the upper middle from the working class, after which she puts the plots in motion. In her first novel, *The Led-Horse Claim,* the genteel hero, Hilgard, is "from one of the little [Long Island] Sound cities" in Connecticut—like Foote's husband; middle-class Mrs. Denny looks coarse and prematurely aged from the altitude in Leadville, Colorado; Molly the maid is Irish—there is no need to say more about her. These examples also illustrate that although Foote was always clear about relative status, she usually did not delve into the finer points. She was not a western Edith Wharton or Henry James; she steered clear of the deep psychological probing and subtle jockeying that make their novels acute anthropological studies of status and affiliation.

. . .

Foote was part of her cultural moment in that she shared a belief in the popular concept of "character," the meaning of which she explores throughout her work, often equating good character with upper-class status. Peter Dobkin Hall defines the mid-nineteenth-century twist on the term as "internalized authority," noting that "an individual possessed character to the extent to which he could be counted on to act correctly and responsibly of his own accord in situations in which he would have been free to act otherwise" (182). Foote's stories abound with upright and proper male and female protagonists, who, usually being in the isolated "Wild West," are indeed free to act any way they like, but who invariably do act correctly and with restraint. Sometimes, in fact, they seem overly punctilious in observing moral distinctions. In turn, this upright behavior validates the right to privilege. Rashna B. Singh makes a good case that the "inculcation of productive, responsible, and accountable character traits" has justified white privilege and imperialism throughout the world (32). In Foote, not only does her characters' moral rectitude justify their privilege, but it also keeps them within genteel bounds and conveys to the *Century* reader that drawing-room manners and forms are being observed in the soon-to-be-no-longer-wild West.

Frances Ellen Watkins Harper, a black antislavery activist, grandly evoked the term *character* in an 1893 address: "Men may boast of the aristocracy of blood, may glory in the aristocracy of talent, and be proud of the aristocracy of wealth, but there is one aristocracy which must ever outrank them all, and that is the aristocracy of character" (quoted in Guy-Sheftall 41). That this progressive woman would cite so many kinds of aristocracies gives us a window on the epoch's obsession with hierarchies of all kinds, and her elevation of character is an interesting addition to them. Ohmann discusses the practical utility of character at the time, explaining that exhibiting so-called character set one apart from the uncouth classes as well as the burgeoning immigrant population. Impersonal capitalism relied less on nepotism and privilege than earlier economic systems, he notes. More than before, though not on anything like an equal playing field, an individual's skill set and personal capabilities made him (or her) successful. Thus, the cultural capital implicit in manifestations of character gave one an advantage over those who merely had job skills and ambition. Managed correctly, this cultural capital "amounted to a plan for the economic reproduction of family and class over time," and Foote worked hard to ensure that her children carried on the family's cultural capital (Ohmann 161). She notes in her autobiography how gratified she and her husband were when they sent their son to boarding school in the East and received a letter from the distinguished headmaster of St. Paul's praising the boy for what she refers to as his "good and gentlemanly" ways (317). All the years of moving around the remote West had not drawn down the boy's class position, for which his parents were thankful.

Concerns about character abound in Foote's novels, letters, and autobiography, with good character for her usually growing out of an upper-middle-class upbringing. In *Edith Bonham* (1917) the narrator says about Edith's rural New York family, one much like Foote's own, "They had stayed in one place and cultivated character, and with it some of the excrescences of character that go with old standard types like theirs" (11). Foote is vague about what exactly the "excrescences" might be, perhaps out of her considerable delicacy. As with her comments in the same novel on the inflexibility of old stock, Foote both boasts of and is also a bit chagrined about the effects of "background." She clearly endorses the concept yet sees that it can be carried to extremes. Interestingly, her use of the word *types* shows that although she not infrequently calls others "types" in her letters and fiction in ways that may sound condescending, she here acknowledges that she, too, is a "type." Some types have good character and some do not, and despite "excrescences," those from rural Quaker New York can be trusted, at least in Foote's eyes. In defense of the use of typing, other authors of the day used such shorthand, from the serious fiction of Henry James to the page-turners of Gertrude Atherton. "You belong to the wrong category," says Dr. Sloper to his feckless would-be son-in-law (James, *Washington Square* 90). Atherton, too, enjoyed setting types against each other and sitting back to watch the sparks fly.

This tendency to pigeonhole people by class or character or type works against psychological depth in Foote's fiction, although it need not necessarily do so. James playfully addresses the idea in "The Real Thing," where high and low types unknowingly vie with each other. In this story, having "the real thing"—being a person with elite background and superior breeding—turns out to be less useful than having the flexibility and canniness of a commoner. Foote biographer Darlis Miller states in her summation of Foote that she "remained sensitive to class boundaries, even though on occasion . . . she explored the superficialities of class biases" (270). Foote faced this issue early on in the West, when her famous honesty forced her to admit in Leadville that a more adaptable sort of woman than her own kind would have better success there. Yet her female protagonists remain the "protected" sort, as she termed it, through her last novel, and the heartier women, the unclassified western "types," are relegated to supporting roles (quoted in Davidson 123).

Integrating Into the West

Class mobility and the economic frontiers in the West made new social fluidity possible, but how much flexibility in class relations existed is open to debate, particularly for women. Foote did not want to allow too much indeterminacy one way or another. Some scholars of western women's history, echoing the liberation ethos of the 1960s, find proof of "a spirit of adventure, nonconformity, and adaptation"; they assert that some women enjoyed "the rejection of constraint, the embrace of active work and open spaces, the escape from a stifling domesticity" (Moynihan, Armitage, and Dichamp xiii; Floyd, *Writing* 167). Less idealistic historians, studying similar texts and historical evidence, contend that, on the contrary, many women "brought eastern sex-role standards west with them and refused to modify their principles even when they proved a hindrance" (Moynihan, Armitage, and Dichamp xiii). They assert that a good number of female pioneers did not "take advantage of the relative flexibility of Western society" (Floyd, *Writing* 203). Foote was of this last group of pioneer women, which is not surprising, given that she had more ties to upper-class culture and education than most westering women. This helped her make a living in the West, but it also kept her from having to accept the West on its own terms, to her personal and even literary detriment, as Wallace Stegner and Rodman Paul both note. Laura Katherine Gruber tries to make a case that Foote chose both to "re-create and combat the restrictions of the nineteenth century woman's life in the American West," but again I take issue with her and hold that Foote's forays into new roles for women were limited and class bound (353). Not for her are girls or their mothers riding bareback through the canyons or making friends with the rustic locals. They keep close to home and sally forth only with brothers or husbands riding shotgun. Nineteenth-century women in particular, especially in the West, were symbols of civilization and class, and their correct behavior and dress could raise or lower both their own reputations as well as the stature of their families.

For Foote, how women integrate into their new life in the West can be studied by looking at her record for marriages between characters of different classes and backgrounds. For her, even western marriages of happenstance must be between social equals, except in rare circumstances, such as in *Coeur d'Alene*, where a wealthy young Englishman finds happiness with the daughter of a drunken, if somehow upper-crust, mine manager. Usually, Foote meted out destruction for those who would disturb the standing order, however. In *The*

Last Assembly Ball, when well-connected Frank Embury precipitously marries a housemaid in Leadville, he is quickly dispatched in a duel. Interestingly, the maidservant he marries is not punished, since she has been a reluctant pawn in the socially scandalous scheme. The reader will likely have compassion for an unfortunate girl who finds herself flattered by a sympathetic man from a higher social stratum, but Foote leaves no doubt that a marriage between them would never have worked out. Milly the maid is sufficiently humble and passive, however, to be allowed to live. By not actively or crassly seeking her betterment, she gets a second chance at life with a rich Montana rancher.

The Bogardus marriage in *The Desert and the Sown* (1902) is doomed and impossible, since it is between a ladylike if poor Hudson River landowner's daughter and her farmhand. Foote makes sure to separate the two soon after a second child is conceived, and disallows any later reconciliation. The very title may indicate Foote's belief that the class divide is insurmountable. The title also shows her concern about how the West destroys some people. I take "the desert" of the novel's title to be unlettered husband Adam and the West he retreats to after inadvertently committing a crime. Drifting around the mountains for twenty years as "Packer John," the barely verbal Adam is the seed that falls on bare ground and cannot germinate. His dignified wife, Emily, on the other hand, and her East are "the sown," since like Alexandra Bergson in Cather's *O Pioneers!* Emily becomes a good woman of business and greatly increases her modest New York holdings. She is the seed that falls on fallow ground and thrives.

In "The Harshaw Bride," Foote must make the highborn but degenerate Harshaw son a complete lout in order to deserve his simple common-law Idaho wife, like Arthur in Edith Wharton's *Sanctuary* (1903), who "at his lowest ebb . . . drifted into living with her as a man drifts into drink or opium" (334). An interracial (Anglo–Native American) union in "The Trumpeter" produces a beautiful if ill-fated offspring, Meta, who in turn marries a feckless Anglo army private husband. Both she and he are doomed to an early death; a child lives on, never knowing his father. In Foote's last novel, *The Ground-Swell*, we finally are presented with the possibility of a promising interclass marriage, but in the end Foote nixes it, having made her heroine a free-spirited New Woman who refuses to marry on principle. Here, as with the housemaid Milly in *The Led-Horse Claim*, Foote bestows upward mobility as a reward for humbleness. Rejected suitor Tony, a naive, self-taught California orphan, is grateful to be mentored concerning taste and lifestyle by the girl's upper-middle-class family. What he loses in love, Tony gains in class. Foote makes her western rough diamonds suffer to deserve their elegant settings.

. . .

The idea that the West changes some people and not for the better came to Foote early on. It did not take her long to see that the myth of the great West was indeed just a myth, and though many thrived there, many were not cut out for its liberties and physical and mental challenges. She vacillated between blaming the individual and blaming the region. When first in Colorado, she cautioned Helena against investing in mines because they were so unstable, noting, "One way in which I *do* respect [the mines] is as discipline to a man's conscience. I glory in the temptations which surround Arthur and which are not even temptations to him. In the general wreck of men's characters in places like this, it fills one with pride and joy to feel that *that* at least is a trouble which can never come into one's own life" (July 10, 1880). This passage is poignant, given that Foote's husband started having drinking problems soon after. But the phrase especially to be noted is "the general wreck of men's characters in places like this." Foote sounds disgusted with the West here, which belies her occasionally soaring prose in her fiction about the landscape and its freedoms. She trusted in strength of character and the class hierarchies and privilege that she believed create it, but she quickly became fatalistic that her adopted region would override even these advantages and worm its way into someone who initially seemed sturdy. She felt that the altitude of Leadville "did queer things to many persons—developed latent germs of trouble; the weakest spot (physically and morally) betrayed itself promptly. It was a climate that selected its victims and was merciless" (in Davidson 124–25).

Around this time Foote wrote Helena from Leadville about a mutual friend: "If you know his mother and sh'd [should] ever meet her I wish you w'd [would] tell her what a good boy 'Van' is in this wild place and how much respected here. No, you needn't either—for a mother needs no one else's assurance about her boy—He is twenty-three, handsome and high spirited, and it is no small credit to twenty-three to be irreproachable in a place like this" (June 13, [1880]). Foote often called the remote, two-mile-high boomtown of Leadville "a place like this" in her letters, demonstrating her view that the West was outside normal eastern parameters—full of unknowns and dangers.

Often the literature of the West is optimistic, for many reasons, but Foote usually has an undercurrent of fatalism in her fiction, even as she skirts the horrors of naturalism. Not many western writers until Frank Norris portrayed the West in a really grim light, except for a few depressed pioneer diarists, usually published later in the twentieth century. And actually, Norris seems to have felt that the whole human race was appalling, not particularly westerners. Jack London perceived the tendency of people to go to seed in the West and blamed the inhumanity of capitalism (Etulain, *Re-imagining* 18), but although Foote discerned that men like her husband were but pawns in rich men's investments, she did not question the system. Cather showed the loneliness, nay despair, that overtook some western immigrants, and she occasionally depicted truly evil men, such as Wick Cutter in *My Antonia* (1918) or Buck Scales in *Death Comes for the Archbishop* (1927). But she did not imply that the West itself ruined them. Nor did Mary Austin, who, in investigating how Anglos, Hispanics, and Indians adapted to lonely places, sought to learn what sort of interesting ideas isolation inspired in them. Foote had no such anthropological bent. When a friend of the Footes, "Pricey," a lively and educated Englishman, deteriorated mentally and physically in Leadville, Foote squarely attributed his decline and early death to what she termed the "altitude of heartbreak" (*A Victorian Gentlewoman* 205).

Shipwrecked is another term Foote frequently used to describe this phenomenon, meaning the alcoholism, moral decay, and physical wasting that she observed in some men in the West. It dismayed her, but she had to admit that despite class, some people will slip. This deterioration of otherwise well-bred men would continue to horrify and fascinate Foote all her life. Within five years of her Leadville sojourn, she had cause to worry about her own husband's character, as he turned to drink when his irrigation schemes in Idaho failed miserably. In *The Led-Horse Claim*, set in Leadville, Foote presents two people, the Doctor and the heroine's brother Conrath, whose good characters have eroded to varying degrees. She attributes this decline to their move west. About the Doctor, an older and slightly disreputable friend of the hero, Hilgard, the narrator notes that "the moth of long isolation from gentle communications had corrupted his good manners, and the thief of discouragement had stolen his pride" (73). In his case, lapsed manners do not mean lapsed morals, however, which is why Foote's upright hero can still be his friend. About the less than pleasant Conrath, Foote indicates that even though he is from a "good eastern family," he has gone to seed in the West and lost his moral compass—he drinks and is dishonest in his business dealings (191). He is similar to Frederick Bingham, the degenerate mine manager in *Coeur d'Alene* (1894), who comes from good eastern stock and has somehow lost his moral compass. So even at the be-

ginning of her long western life, Foote was trying to assess in what ways character and class, such as those of the Doctor, Conrath, Bingham, her own husband,
and her friend Pricey, were at risk. She would have liked to find firm ground
upon which to base her ideas of unchanging character and class, but instead
was faced with the mutability of personal morality and inner resources, as well
as the conundrum of addiction psychology. The one-bad-apple theory was appealing to her, but she saw too many instances of it to make it credible. The
West brought into question the role of innate personality versus life-changing
circumstances, of nature versus nurture.

Foote came to accept that even the strongest sorts of people, those with discipline and talent, could come to a bad end if they "get left" in dreary, hopeless
places with no peers, useful work, or intelligent stimulation. At least her own
sketching and writing could be done anywhere, and she could read magazines
and books to keep up with her profession. But for many it was different, as
she admitted. In a series of drawings and captions titled "Pictures of the Far
West," which ran in *Century* in 1888 and 1889, Foote soberly explains that (like
her husband) "the capable man with his hands tied, in a community where
life means nothing if not action, finds there is a bitter difference between the
'something' that takes the place of work . . . and the divine gift of a man's own
work" (Cragg, Walsh, and Walsh 301–2). This bitterness and underappreciation
is reflected in *The Chosen Valley,* where Dunsmuir, the ethical, well-trained, but
failed irrigation engineer, has become diminished in the West. We hear that
"the dry summers bred in him a low fever that wasted his flesh, and quick-
ened his pulse" (208). Stress from the intractable land is killing him. A similarly
paragon-like character, young Californian Helen Benedet in "A Touch of Sun,"
is described as being like the desert roses, none of which is perfect since they
bloom too early, get "a touch of sun," and become blighted. The wealthy, strict-
ly reared Helen breaks out during the relentlessly hot summer of her sixteenth
year, elopes with a cowboy, and escapes only at the last moment. Impossible
weather and western isolation almost ruin the reputation of a carefully reared,
wealthy young woman.

Western Elites

Foote's preferred kind of fictional creation was a lady or gentleman who has
character and never waivers from the correct path, despite what the West might
throw at him or her. In defiance of the new journalistic and literary voices in

Rebecca Harding Davis, William Dean Howells, Stephen Crane, and Theodore Dreiser, who dealt with the heartlessness, shame, and tragedies in both rural and urban American settings, Foote stuck to her genteel guns, determined to depict the West as a civilized place where background counted for something. If she referred to alcoholism or violence, for example, she did so obliquely and quickly moved the focus back to respectable activities. In a wildly improbable romance, "On a Side-Track," the story opens with a scene on a remote western train of a murderer being transported under armed guard. At first the reader presumes that the tale will reflect the gritty underbelly of lawless western life, but it is soon revealed that not only is the chaperoned ingenue in the same car from a good eastern family, but the handsome murderer himself is too! Even how the accused came to kill a man stays within honorable bounds: he relates to the young miss as he woos her that it was by accident and in self-defense, in the course of defending the reputation of a friend's wife. The reader is left at the end with the expectation of judicial lenience for the lad and a quiet Quaker wedding for the youthful pair. Foote recoiled from untimely death much like the sheltered Kate Orme in Edith Wharton's *Sanctuary:* "The blinds were drawn again on the ugly side of things, and life was resumed on the usual assumption that no such side existed" (325). Similarly, at the opening of Foote's 1900 novel, *The Prodigal,* Clunie Robert, a New Zealand magnate's well-bred but ne'er-do-well son, appears in San Francisco with a checkered past of dubious South Sea liaisons. When he makes a righteous vow to straighten out his life, however, his good character eventually prevails sufficiently to impress his new love interest, a respectable spinster, and his past shortcomings are forgiven. His degradation and failings are glossed over.

Foote could approach her paragons and strict standards humorously, however, even if at her own expense. In "Pilgrims to Mecca," she severely critiques westerners (like herself) who slavishly emulate elite eastern culture. When snobby Mrs. Valentin observes an elite and seemingly eastern woman on the train, we hear just what sorts of traits the elite should have. Mrs. Valentin's geographical assessment is incorrect—the elegant woman in question is in fact from Los Angeles—yet Foote's characterization of her describes a perfect upper-class "type": "She was of the benignant Roman-nosed Eastern type, daughter of generations of philanthropists and workers in the public eye for the public good; a deep, rich voice, an air of command, plain features, abundant gray hair, imported clothes, wonderful, keen, dark eyes overlapped by a fold of the crumpled eyelid—a personage, a character, a life, full of complex energies and domineering good sense" (*A Touch of Sun* 151). The narrator here associates positive attributes and admirable morality—intelligence, generosity, complexity—with the woman's tasteful, expensive clothing and regal air.

The punctilious dress and behavior evident in novels of manners pepper Foote's fiction, with the polite classes leading the way. They model their good character with scrupulous exactitude, justifying their class privilege and the deference owed them. In "The Harshaw Bride," a British father hurries out from England to marry a young woman stranded in the West after his wastrel son has reneged on a promise of marriage. Foote's narrator drives home the point about the older man's gentility: "He is a gallant widower of fair estate, one of those splendid old club-men of London; a very expensive article of old gentleman, with fine old-fashioned manners and morals" (*A Touch of Sun* 260–61). Foote did not participate in the popular nineteenth-century American hobby of demonizing decayed aristocracy. This degenerate Harshaw son is one of Foote's few instances of high birth degenerating into low morals.

In another story, "A Touch of Sun," heiress Helen Benedet journeys alone to her fiancé's parents' home to explain why a youthful indiscretion will not bring scandal to their respectable name. The boy's mother has been beside herself, at one point wishing that her son had gone to Cuba in the Spanish-American War rather than make an ill-advised, scarlet choice of wife. San Francisco society whispers that the teenage Helen had eloped with a cowboy desperado. When the poised, soft-spoken young woman bravely details the truth to her fiancé's parents, it turns out that her wayward youthful impulses were nipped in the bud, and the beautiful, well-educated Helen is revealed to be the most articulate and appealing of Foote's spotless virgins. After her confession, when the son arrives to find all reconciled, the exasperated lad says to his mother about her fussy suspicions, "Mother, do you think a man can't see what a girl is?" (78). Foote's modern readers in 1900 would have shared his frustration and dismissed the mother's overanxious propriety as outmoded.[4] They may have also assumed, as Foote no doubt did, that any jewel of a girl brought up so elitely would have had strong morals and a sterling character.

The correct behavior of Foote's privileged people might seem simply to reflect human efforts to do the right thing—a timeless theme in drama and fiction—but Foote made sure the reader knows these individuals would not have such strength of character if they had not been well bred. Compare this attitude to contemporaries James, Wharton, or Ellen Glasgow, where elevated status was no predictor of moral behavior. As they saw it, those higher on the social scale may have more manners and restraint than those below, but they are not necessarily more decent or honorable. Since Foote, on the other hand, either believed or would like to have believed that mere gentility generates moral rectitude, she set about enacting this in her fiction. She not infrequently conflated the distinction between polished upper-middle-class accoutrements and sturdy morality.

Nonetheless, mere wealth did not make the grade. Merle Rubin's insight into James holds true for Foote here, that "although James deplored the lack of manners, he also seems to have recognized the pointlessness of hastily acquired, inauthentic manners, which could not be a true reflection or distillation of moral and cultural tradition" (n.p.). Both James and Foote respected this cultural tradition, and neither liked pretenders. Fellow easterner Oliver Wendell Holmes, who Foote quoted in her letters, maintained in "The Autocrat of the Breakfast Table" (1858) that his favorite people were those who "[inherited] family traditions and the cumulative humanities of at least four or five generations" (quoted in P. Hall 199). From her isolated perches in rural Colorado, Idaho, and California, Foote missed such company and idealized it.

Foote may seem to have had the class confidence of James and Holmes, yet seeing how she was wedded to her stock characters—high, low, and in-between—one sometimes cannot help but wonder if some of her insistence stemmed from insecurity. If not, why did she stick to her class-bound cast of courtly young engineers and demure virgins, correct matrons and incorruptible professional men, faithful Irish servants and hapless western girls? Perhaps one answer is that if she explored more ambivalent and complicated characters, it might upset the applecart of class privilege in uncomfortable ways. The furthest Foote was willing to go was to admit that sometimes the upper class could produce a few seedy men—although never such women; her realist inclinations balked at that notion. She seemed a bit embarrassed about even those male lapses, however, such as when she explains the change in the bridegroom manqué in "The Harshaw Bride": "Possibly he was nicer four years ago. Men get terribly down at heel, mentally, morally, and mannerly, poking off by themselves in these out-of-the-way places" (*A Touch of Sun* 203). Note that morality and manners are lumped together here. Insisting on the infrequency of this kind of situation, Foote asserts that the "old club" father of the irresponsible son is "a very superior sort of father for such a son to have, but accidents will happen in the best-regulated families" (260). With this aside, she blithely attempts to uphold the high ground for the upper class.

When Foote first came west to California, she was confused and appalled by what the lack of social constraints did for some people, even some who had apparently been raised with as much tradition and discipline as she had. In a letter to Helena, Foote described a young man she and her husband had met on the train. He was "the son of a Louisiana Creole and one of those old Virginia Peytons—a rather handsome fast young fellow—very stuck up about his family and with an uneasy consciousness of being rather 'bad form' himself. We see so many of these half-ruined young lives and it is perfectly sickening!" (September 29, 1877). Foote's vehemence here is surprising. Was she worried that her own relatively young life—she was thirty at this point—might be ruined by life in the West? Even if she honestly did find it sickening that people with such promise had lost their way, why the irritation? Why not sorrow or compassion, too? Perhaps she feared seeing changes in the kinds of people she was familiar with; she could not let go of her own background, even for a moment. Whatever young footloose Peyton was learning in California, whatever new kind of Peyton he was becoming, it was not within structures that Foote recognized, and it scared her. This was early in her time in the West, but even in a novel fifteen years later, *The Chosen Valley,* when a young gentleman's son in Idaho gets involved with the locals for unsavory parties and gunplay, it is a temporary phase brought on by boredom. Like Shakespeare's Prince Hal, he soon forsakes his low life when family duty calls.

Upward Mobility and the Lower Classes

If the elite can come to grief in the wastes of the West, what happens to the less highbrow? What kind of character do they warrant? With Foote, lower-class characters do not fare any worse, and sometimes they actually outshine the diffident upper-class types, even though they are rarely the focus of the story. They may be more stolid, but they are predictable and often better survivors than the fastidious elite. When Foote writes about less privileged people in her novels and stories, it is often sympathetically, but condescension usually creeps in. Not infrequently, their lives and struggles seem to be solely as foils or regional wallpaper for her middle-class professionals. Literary historians argue that this sort of shallow portrayal of the lower classes by nineteenth-century middle-class writers, many of them women, "aimed at the subjugation of different classes and even races who were compelled to play not the leading roles but the human scenery before which the melodrama of middle-class redemption could be enacted" (Laura Wexler quoted in Pfister 7; see also Wexler). Although I would not assert that Foote's goal was the subjugation of anyone per se, I do think that the end result indicated to *Century* readers that the lives of the professional middle class were more important than others' lives. By contrast, Louisa May Alcott presents interesting and significant nonelite characters throughout *Work: A Story of Experience* (1873), including a fugitive slave and illiterate laundress mentor, who give wise advice to her middle-class female protagonist. Foote lacks such wide-ranging scope, although as Elaine Showalter cautions, "it is more productive to look at what a work contributes, and what it leaves open, than to pounce triumphantly on where it has 'failed'" ("American Gynocriticism" 126). Let us say, then, that Foote's limitations can be used to reveal the mentality of the old Anglo elite as it sensed that new money, immigrants, and technology would supplant its geographical and cultural hegemony. We can examine the way literature both reflected and shaped social norms and values.

It helps that the nonelite in Foote tend to be more reconciled to the land—they are not pining to be elsewhere like Foote herself or Ruth Mary's mother in "A Cloud on the Mountain." The dulcet if unexciting Ruth Mary herself is content by her lonely Idaho river, as is the couple in "The Watchman." They also earnestly try to do the right thing, she by her sour father, he by the impersonal ditch company employing him. This simple, romantic tale shows that Foote could have empathy for frontier people who are happy to live lives without the cultured trappings of the East. For their steadfastness, the couple in "The Watchman" is rewarded with employment and a decent place to live. The same is true for Irish factotum Molly and her Leadville timberman husband in *The Led-Horse Claim*, both of whom exhibit trustworthiness and compassion toward the decorous but dependent heroine. Molly protects Cecil when the girl becomes prostrate after the death of her swinish brother, again showing that less delicate women are more useful than the "protected" kind. The noble Babe in *John Bodewin's Testimony*, however, who behaves with courtesy and honor despite having been raised by ruffians in the hills, does not survive, due not to poor character, though, but to her inappropriate love of a man her social superior.

Like the Irish couple in *The Led-Horse Claim*, the often unpaid, loyal servants in *The Chosen Valley*, Margaret and Job, are more useful as well as perhaps better people in general than their employer, in this case the obsessed, meticulous engineer Dunsmuir. They are steadfast and practical, whereas Dunsmuir is just steadfast. His painstaking plans for a large-scale irrigation project are bankrupting them all and depriving his children of education and opportunities. Foote's narrator wryly notes that the well-educated Dunsmuir has "the inbred conviction that it must be a privilege for persons of Margaret's class to be connected with persons of his own, with or without remuneration. It is a sentiment that dies hard in the blood of those accustomed to be served, which many pleasing illusions and traditions help to keep alive, even in new countries, where it is imported under conditions often curiously the reverse of feudal" (207). Dunsmuir heartily respects Margaret and Job and all that they have given up for his family, but he still thinks of them as fixtures, tellingly referring to them as "honest, worthy folk" (209). They are valuable appendages to his long-stalled scheme. He is presented as a throwback in the novel due to his high ideals and gentlemanly nature, and when he dies in the end because of a rival engineer's faulty work, the question remains if even this sacrifice can justify his patrician faults.

The creation of admirable westerners such as Margaret and Job may seem to indicate that Foote was becoming more flexible as she lived in the West, but she still made them less interesting and complex than her elite protagonists. Dunsmuir's character is more multifaceted—the narrator somewhat condescendingly describes Margaret and Job as "two faithful friends; plain, poor people, staple products of the older countries, proved by every form of discipline known to the new" (207). Note again Foote's penchant for reverting to "types": individuals have become "staple products." Throughout the novel, Dunsmuir is presented with more sympathy and depth, as each character in turn mulls over his or her often difficult relationship with him. If someone were to do a study of "the tragedy of American patricians," as John Lukacs suggests, Dunsmuir could take his tortured place in line with the likes of Newland Archer and Ellen Olenska in Wharton's *Age of Innocence* (1920) (18).

Foote's most moral and complicated nonelite character may be soft-hearted Adam Bogardus in *The Desert and the Sown*, but his confusing conduct toward his estranged family is based on a childlike (in)comprehension of the world, not cogent consideration. In the end the reader all but dismisses him as a well-meaning but naive primitive. Tony Kayding in *The Ground-Swell* is a likable local California fellow, and worthy to rise from his lowly roots, but he fails at sufficiently attracting the accomplished, independent Katherine Cope—she knows he is not stimulating enough. Foote thus did make tentative stabs at presenting ordinary people who possess good character that was not instilled with a silver spoon and parlor manners. The issue fascinated her; note this exchange in *The Desert and the Sown,* which lays out both an exclusive and a more democratic case for the humanity of the lower classes. Stolid Colonel Middleton complains, "'These young philanthropists! They assume that the Hands and the Feet of the world, the class that serves in that capacity, have got the same nerves as the Brain.'" To which his guest mildly replies, "'There's a sort of connection. . . . Some of our Heads have come from the class that you call the Hands and Feet, haven't they?'" The narrator purrs in explanation, "The colonel admitted the fact, but the fact was the exception" (5–6). That is what upward mobility was for Foote: the exception. Isolated individuals may rise by means of hard work, intelligence, or lucky mentoring, but Foote did not delve into the coarse realities of getting there.

Journalist Rebecca Harding Davis and even optimistic Louisa May Alcott detailed how difficult it was for the underprivileged and uneducated to remain even clean and sober in the face of poverty, let alone focused on higher ideals of polite behavior or enriching culture. Foote's fiction usually skirts the realistic problems of keeping fed, warm, and safe, although in her letters to Helena she occasionally wrote of such practical concerns about her own life in remote western locations.

. . .

Not surprisingly, Foote's notions about innate class and predetermined character dictate that those lower on the social scale have inferior discernment and less exacting tastes and manners than their social superiors, even if they have hearts of gold. Foote, however, confused moral virtue with the culturally specific tastes of a particular class in a particular region, in this case the old Quaker gentry of the Hudson Valley. When talking about a woman like her mother in a children's story, "The Spare Bedroom at Grandfather's," the narrator asserts, "Ordinary self-respect would have prevented her wearing an edge of lace that was not 'real,' or a stuff that was not all wool, if wool it professed to be, or a print that would not 'wash'; and her contempt for linen that was part cotton, for silk that was part linen, or velvet with a 'cotton back,' was of a piece with her truthfulness and horror of pretense" (*The Little* 178). This is Foote at her most obscure, conflating personal honesty and authenticity with rigid preferences in fabrics and styles of clothing. Yet if we look at Pierre Bourdieu's analysis of how taste and what he calls "symbolic capital" are used to define class, Foote's sartorial rant makes sense. Bourdieu notes that we are not only what we choose to wear or listen to or eat but also most emphatically what we would *never* wear, listen to, or eat. "The most everyday choices of everyday life" elevate or lower us in the eyes of others and in our own eyes, he asserts (*Distinction* 5–6). As in James, Wharton, and later Cather and Fitzgerald, taste figured importantly for Foote. She lovingly details upper-middle-class lifestyles and fittings at every opportunity, and since most of her stories are set in the rustic West, the occasional luxuries stand out more than they might in New York City, Philadelphia, or Boston.[5]

In addition to having simpler tastes and ignorance of the larger world, Foote's fictional lower classes lack the moral complexity of the elite. They also have less of a sense of their moment in history. Usually dull and plodding, sweet but shallow, the less well heeled seem content to live out their lives doing their jobs faithfully, as devoted servants, deferential cowboys, or local laborers. If, however, they are not salt-of-the-earth types whom their employers take for granted, Foote is on shakier, though sometimes no deeper, ground. Her less appealing western characters often lack backbone and upright morals, and sometimes even rational thought. Foote seemed to feel that without in-bred class, some people will end up rudderless or crude or both. Milly the housemaid in *The Last Assembly Ball* is a wisp of a character: with barely a peep from her she is wooed and wed by an inappropriately aristocratic boy. No excuses are made for her drifting or her silence, whereas when upper-class characters slip Foote always makes excuses. Mrs. Norrisson in *The Chosen Valley*, the petted, spoiled wife of a wily engineer, escaped ranch life in California as a girl and now is a superficial creature with nouveaux riches and little loyalty to either family or region. Meta, the half Native American, half Scottish girl in "The Trumpeter," is witless, whereas Stella in the overland saga *A Picked Company* (1912), a rare loose woman in Foote's writing, becomes a pathetic prostitute and is saved from further degradation by being killed by her own husband.

The unsavory male lower-class types mirror their female counterparts. Sometimes the classic strong, silent, western male types, they are not so much immoral as premoral, brutish in their understanding. Both Adam Bogardus in *The Desert and the Sown* and Maverick in "Maverick," an uncouth sheriff, make Shakespeare's half-human Caliban look articulate. These western characters know the land, but their humanity and morals are of the most basic kind. In oafish ways, they try—unsuccessfully—to make their families and women happy. They discern little, whereas the upper-middle-class people whom their lives impact—Adam's wife and grown children and "Maverick"'s narrator—thought-fully deliberate and then act rationally. This is not to say that all of Foote's immoral or destructive characters hail from quotidian backgrounds, but since most do, we can tell where Foote stood on the subject. Despite good intentions, individuals who have not been carefully brought up with her kind of standards will more readily waver from the straight and narrow, or lack civilized subtle-ties. Foote insisted on "privileging" the "old verities," even as her life played out amid new professional and regional possibilities (Ohmann 221). But since she accurately depicted those civilized subtleties and old verities, an upwardly mo-bile *Century* reader paying attention to such things could absorb their lessons and learn the ropes.

. . .

Foote's writings usually hold a caution for those who would climb to do it prop-erly. She wrote to her editor about which name to use for a nouveau riche boy in "Pilgrims to Mecca," explaining why she was resisting naming him Billy. She in-stead suggested using "Reggy," because "his 'folks' were aspiring sort of people in the matter of names. They wouldn't have been content with anything 'plain'" (MHF to RWG, November 12, 1898). Foote had an eye for the subtle differences of dress, manner, and speech that separate upper from middle class, which the story both parodies and validates. The discerning matron traveling with her daughter to the East regales the poor girl with dos and don'ts concerning such weighty matters as custom-made belts for the new fashionable shirtwaists and how to walk like a lady and affect a dignified poise.

If someone has risen to a higher class in Foote's fiction, we do not see the struggle or occasional mistakes committed. Foote establishes whether charac-ters have background, and not much time is spent on complicating their sta-tus with upward or downward mobility. She disliked those actively seeking to climb, shamefacedly laughing to Helena at the friendly, vulgar women of Boise who dressed in bright colors and left tacky New Year's cards one year, thinking they were being so very genteel. Foote sent one to Helena to make her laugh—the elegant Helena, one of the founders of the Arts Students League of New York, friend of President and Mrs. Cleveland, Augustus Saint-Gaudens, and John La Farge. One perpetually wonders what the urbane Helena thought of Foote's exile.

. . .

One of the manifestations of Foote's class consciousness in the West is a clear divide between her kind of people with "background" and everyone else, white or otherwise. "The other" for Foote even included native-born American whites who did not share her specific values and norms. On at least two separate occasions she wrote to Helena Gilder that she did not like the attitude even of Chicago or Chicagoans. "Hy," she cries, using Gilder's nickname, "I *dont* [*sic*] like Chicago! I respect it, but I dont wish to be intimate. It doesn't 'understand'" (April 4, 1889). In addition, Darlis Miller notes that "although [Foote] voiced compassion for the hard-working poor, she criticized unions and had little understanding of the 'common sort,' people she believed to be crude or uncultivated" (270). Foote distanced herself from them or depicted them stereotypically, usually keeping members of different classes within their assigned roles and hierarchies. In this way, there is little class or ethnic conflict in her fiction, although she did choose to tackle labor unrest in *Coeur d'Alene*, set during the famous Idaho mining massacre. From the start, however, Foote's sympathies are clearly with the mine owners, not the striking miners. In a letter to her editor in Boston, Clarence Clough Buel, she dismissed the strike leaders as disreputable, Irish, and outside agitators, referring to "their impudence" (February 26, 1893).

Although underprivileged or merely uncultured Anglos got short shrift in Foote's fiction and letters, her attitude toward people of different ethnicities and races was not much worse. Much has been made in recent years of westering white women's attitudes—fearful, condescending, and even friendly— toward the Native Americans, Hispanics, Chinese, and African Americans whom they encountered on the frontier. Such ethnic or cultural populations were far outside Foote's sheltered social purview. She made patronizing remarks about Irish, Cornish, Italian, and German immigrants, as well as Jews and Catholics, but rarely went out of her way to insult anyone particularly. She was too polite for that—perhaps too much a lady. Such "types" were part of the scenery to her. Her exclusivity ruled out interaction as peers with people of a different color, and her mention of non-Anglo, ethnic populations was occasional and never in depth. Her attitude can be contrasted with Louise Clapp's (Dame Shirley) energetic enjoyment of the boisterous multicultural stew that was the gold rush mining camps in California or Mary Austin's respectful research and emulation of Native Americans in the California desert.[6] Foote made scant mention of the sort of cross-cultural exchanges celebrated by Bret Harte, Clemens, Cather, Mari Sandoz, and to some extent Laura Ingalls Wilder.

Foote only infrequently alluded to the waves of immigration during the late nineteenth century in her writings, and she did not address the institutional racism against Native Americans, Hispanics, or African Americans. In "The Trumpeter" the hapless Meta is unremittingly dense about the Anglo world, even though the girl is half-Scottish and has been raised in an Anglo household. In an 1892 novel, *The Chosen Valley*, Foote is still calling a well-to-do half-English, half-Spanish woman raised in California "mixed blood" (106).[7] And in *The Prodigal*, Foote is downright insulting when she dismisses protagonist Clunie's half-Hispanic former belle from the South Seas, Concha, as "a pretty piece of degeneracy, a child of Nature in the fatal transition stage" (70). Around the same time, in "Pilgrims to Mecca," when the narrator describes the "supreme and dainty elegance" of a charming society girl, we hear that "her resemblance to the ordinary full-fleshed type of Pacific coast belle was that of a portrait by Romney—possibly engraved by Cole—to a photograph of some *reina de la fiesta*." Perhaps this last comment struck Foote as being too racist, because the narrator then adds, "This was Mrs. Valentin's exaggerated way of putting it to herself" (*A Touch of Sun* 150). The slur on Hispanics is only slightly diminished.

Foote has an impassioned set piece in her early novel *The Last Assembly Ball* criticizing the unjust western treatment of the Chinese, but ironically the defense is prompted by anti-Chinese laws that prevent Leadville townspeople from hiring them as domestics. The deft Chinese cook Ito in "A Touch of Sun" is a paragon, working thoughtfully and efficiently to make everyone comfortable in a blistering California heat wave. But we learn nothing about his personality, only those of his mine manager masters. Foote wrote to Helena at one point how nice it was that their Chinese cook in Idaho stayed professionally distant from the family and did not bother her with his own troubles—if he had any, she added (April 18, 1887). The fact that Foote usually avoided dealing with class or ethnic conflict in her fiction serves to validate the existing power systems. Her views reflect the social Darwinism in the air that often was used to valorize race, "blood," and the supremacy of Anglo culture.

Nineteenth-century African American activism and writing receive not even a nod in Foote's fiction, yet in her youth she had been part of progressive evenings of discussion at the Hallock Farm by the Hudson with the likes of Frederick Douglass as well as activists Ernestine L. Rose and Susan B. Anthony. Foote does not seem to have carried this progressive streak with her into adult life. Her condescending tone toward "the other" was in line with *Century* readers, and her attitudes toward different ethnicities and classes, though narrow, were not unusual for her era, even in the West. Charles Fletcher Lummis, California booster and cultural activist, editor of the *Los Angeles Times* and later *Land of Sunshine,* praised the Los Angeles of his time, saying that "the ignorant, hopelessly un-American type of foreigner which infests and largely controls Eastern cities is almost unknown here" (Lukacs 16). Owen Wister also responded to immigrants with a blistering attack, calling them "hordes of encroaching alien vermin, that turn our cities to Babels and our citizenship to a hybrid farce" (n.p.). So much for multiculturalism in 1895. Many in the late-nineteenth-century upper and middle classes apparently "saw polyglot America as a social nightmare," and since Foote's stories lacked portrayals of that threat, they may have made restful, if blinkered, reading (Brodhead 166).

Chapter Two

Literary Allusions in Foote's Leadville Novels

"It Seemed a Playground for the Centaurs"

Foote's first three novels are set in Leadville, Colorado, in its silver boom days. She spent long summers there with her husband in 1879 and 1880, and observed firsthand how, as she termed it, a "crude community of transplanted lives" in the West quickly evolved from somewhat class-free exuberance into typical hierarchical strata (*The Led-Horse* 22). She did not disapprove of this inevitable consolidation, although she seems to have enjoyed the informality early on. As many have observed, she was a woman who did not want to shake off her background, and in the face of social fluidity she looked to the past for models. Foote's recurrent use of chivalric and epic allusions in the Leadville novels perpetuated upper-middle-class eastern social norms in a new setting.

When Foote lived in Leadville, she was, in her own words, one of the "'protected' women of that time," meeting only what she termed the "sifted pickings" of the boomtown, those whom her husband thought suitable for polite society (quoted in Davidson 123). Yet perhaps due to her "protected" status, she had the detachment and leisure to observe the circumstances of class in the West as shrewdly as any realist or naturalist. After the first summer she wrote to Helena:

> All this side of it is amusing but vulgar, or would be if there [were] not so much boyishness about it; but the sweetness and romance and pathos of many of the stories of men and women there one cannot weary of. You often speak of people being so human—there are many of that kind in a place like Leadville. The ride over the range seems to jolt the crust off people. Affectation is almost impossible or at all events quite unnecessary where we all begin at the roots of society again and build on a solid basis. There is no concerning what you are in a place like that. [Fall 1879]

Such sentiments notwithstanding, Foote set about writing tales that demonstrate how conventional social norms governed much of Leadville. She also perceived how emerging national capitalism dictated many aspects of personal life in Leadville, but no doubt due to her sheltered upbringing and literary bent she began her novelistic career with pretty tales steeped in the preindustrial tropes of chivalric romance and ancient epic.

...

The Leadville texts are *The Led-Horse Claim: A Romance of a Mining Camp* (1882), *John Bodewin's Testimony* (1886), and *The Last Assembly Ball* (1889). *The Last Assembly Ball* focuses on class issues overtly, but the two prior Leadville books also deal with them. The novels were serialized in the New York–based *Century* magazine and then published a year or two afterward, most by Houghton Mifflin in Boston. In each of the three Leadville novels, Foote deftly outlines the social hierarchy of the town and situates her genteel characters clearly within it, as if she wants to be sure that her readers will accurately read the class allegiances, conflicts, and occasional faux pas recorded in the narratives. Like Charlotte Perkins Gilman in the didactic 1903 essays in *The Home: Its Work and Influence,* Foote believed that beauty and taste are absolutes—and that the upper classes have a responsibility to teach the lower classes how to live properly. Two of the Leadville novels involve genteel girls coming west and in the end marrying eastern men who manage the mines; the third, a more sophisticated novel, serves as a warning to young eastern men that if they foolishly marry beneath their class in the West, only death can resolve such a transgression.

Foote's first venture into the novel, *The Led-Horse Claim,* can be caricatured as "Romeo and Juliet Survive Boomtown." In it, ingenue Cecil Conrath has come out from the East to join her brother, the nefarious whiskey-drinking superintendent of the Shoshone mine. She is too innocent or undiscerning to see faults in her brother and becomes interested in attractive George Hilgard, who manages a neighboring and rival mine, the Led-Horse. Brother Conrath is secretly digging deep tunnels into Led-Horse ore, and when Hilgard and an associate, after fruitlessly trying diplomacy, confront him with guns underground, Conrath is killed. Cecil sadly returns to the East, as does Hilgard, who was fired for his actions and must look for work. As luck would have it, both stay at the same hotel in New York City, and when Hilgard falls grievously ill Cecil and her aunt nurse him. But in spite of her attraction to her Leadville suitor, Cecil rejects him, since she blames him for her brother's death. Both leave the city to visit family, who, again fortuitously, live in the same part of upstate New York. The couple is reunited by accident, resolve their misgivings, and marry. A life in the West is their chosen lot, to the dismay of Cecil's insular grandmother, left alone in her grand house on the Hudson River.

Foote's next Leadville venture, *John Bodewin's Testimony*, has a similar mining dispute and romantic couple as its focus. John Bodewin is a mining expert and surveyor, and Josephine Newbold is the innocent daughter of a man who believes he owns the Eagle Bird mine. Bodewin refuses to testify in court to prove that Mr. Newbold does indeed own the mine and not hard-drinking, immoral Colonel Billy Harkins. It is suspected that Harkins had the boundary stakes for the Eagle Bird moved in order to access a particularly profitable lode of ore, and only Bodewin can prove it with his original surveyor's notes. Unknown to all, Harkins once saved Bodewin's sister from scandal, and conscientious Bodewin feels a debt to the disreputable Harkins. As Bodewin comes under the spell of young Miss Newbold and hears the townspeople's gossip that his silence is being bought by Harkins, he finally agrees to testify, only to be kidnapped by some rustics hired by Harkins. Bodewin escapes with the help of the lovely rustic daughter, who dies in a mine accident trying to see her beloved former captive. Although Bodewin finally does testify, his reputation as a surveyor and honorable man is ruined, and it is only through the faith and determination of Miss Newbold that his name is cleared.

Foote ends *Bodewin* on as lyric and romantic a note as any of her fiction. The last picture of Bodewin and his demure bride is of their alighting at a remote desert train station as they prepare to start a new life in the West. The mistakes they made in Colorado are past. They now begin again, their former lives a dim shadow, with the "wind of the great Far West, soft, electric, and strong, blowing up through gates of the great mountain ranges, . . . [w]ind of prophesy and of hope, of tireless energy and desire" blowing them to a bright future (344). In classic American fashion, they are given the chance (or the illusion) of a new life by starting over elsewhere, as Foote and her husband did several times themselves.

For her third and final Leadville novel, *The Last Assembly Ball*, Foote delves deeply into subtle class jockeying in Leadville, as Benay Blend and others have noted. The plot centers on a properly reared young eastern man, Frank Embry, who falls for the pretty housemaid Milly in his boardinghouse, marries her on impulse, and tries, unsuccessfully, to present her to Leadville society at a local ball. That evening, trying to defend Milly's good name, Frank dies in a pistol duel. *The Last Assembly Ball* is the darkest of the three Leadville novels in tone, yet it has interesting features, the best of which is not the protagonists but Mrs. Fanny Dansken, the young man's landlady and the maid's employer. Both she and Milly end up with fortunate marriages at the end of the ostensible tragedy.

• • •

One of the most obvious assertions of class sensibilities in these early Leadville novels is Foote's use of literary, often chivalric allusion. She resorts to it frequently in the texts, whereas there are fewer references in later novels and stories. This affectation connects the tales and their local western settings to the broader European tradition she and her eastern audiences would have known, using the allusions as pegs upon which to hang western experiences. Foote's links to the Arthurian tradition are essentially shallow, however. She does not use chivalric allusions to explore deeper questions about the nature of courage, for example, though the presence of such allusions somehow raises the bar for upright western male behavior. Rather, Foote's Leadville novels appropriate the trappings of myth and epic to situate the West within an established and to her immutable cultural and class framework. The effect, as Lynn Cothern notes, is that Foote "naturalizes" the class disparities around her "by glossing them in romantic terms." Similarly, on the trip to Mexico with her husband around the time she wrote the Leadville novels, Foote used feudal and medieval terms to describe Mexico. Her husband and his fellow mining engineers were "noble gentlemen," and the local laborers reverted "back into the middle ages" when the jobs were finished ("Becoming Western" 8).

Foote was not the first writer on American soil to use Old World frameworks to describe the New World, just a slightly incongruous one. Yet since she was popular during her own era, her audience must have appreciated what now comes off as forced. Owen Wister asserted in an 1895 piece in *Harper's,* "The Evolution of the Cow-Puncher," that "the knight and the cowboy are nothing but the same Saxon of different environments, the nobleman in London and the nobleman in Texas," thus tying the use of chivalric tropes to glorification of Anglos and the detriment of immigrants. Regardless of how incongruous medieval allusions about Colorado mining seem now, Foote perceived a credible historical parallel between the young men of good families vying for fortunes in the wilderness and young noblemen centuries earlier fighting for love and honor. Wister claimed that "Destiny tried her latest experiment upon the Saxon ... [and] his modern guise fell away and showed again the medieval man. It was no new type, no product of the frontier, but just the original kernel of the nut with the shell broken" (n.p.). The illustration for Wister's article, by Frederic Remington, is of a lanky cowboy surrounded by shades of famous knights from medieval European history. Foote herself illustrated the Leadville novels, and it is a loss that she did not think to draw such a striking image too, since it would have complemented her texts so well. As it was, she felt this mythological tie, as she noted in a letter to her best friend, Helena de Kay Gilder, after her first summer in Leadville: "All this seems part of the endless repetition of History, bringing back phases of human life and progress. These men are like the mediaeval knights—or would be if they were of good blood. Their code is much the same. I am not speaking of cattle herders or sheep herders but of the frontier type" (January 20, 1880).

The Led-Horse Claim has more allusions than later novels, with its feuding-mines story line and echoes of Shakespeare's *Romeo and Juliet*. Foote used fewer literary references in *John Bodewin's Testimony* and foregrounded a slightly more realistic western scenario. The last Leadville novel, *The Last Assembly Ball*, centers on a precarious social situation almost entirely, while chivalric parallels are only in the background. Its plot, however, is based at least partially on the Geraint and Enid story in Tennyson's Arthurian "Idylls of the King." Interestingly, the Idaho short story written during this time, "A Cloud on the Mountain," utilizes Arthurian allusions more successfully than any of Foote's novels, despite the mismatch of exquisite Pre-Raphaelite medievalism and dusty, rural Idaho. "Cloud" not only roughly parallels Tennyson's "The Lady of Shallot" but also sustains a complex texture of subtle chivalric allusions and authentic western details.

We need to bear in mind, of course, that Foote's is a *Victorian* and fictional view of chivalry, a chivalry as seen through the romanticizing eyes of Sir Walter Scott and Alfred, Lord Tennyson, among others. For familiar historical reasons that are beyond the scope of the present discussion, the appropriation of the medieval by the nineteenth-century British, from John Keats to Edward Burne-Jones, reflects a Hellenic, golden-age view of that, in fact, primitive era. So when the terms *chivalric, medieval,* or *Arthurian* are used to describe Foote's Leadville, one must bear in mind the rosy and self-consciously literary filter through which she conceived of this epoch. As Wister noted in the 1895 piece about the artistic appropriation of medieval knights, "In the chronicles of romance we hear none of his curses or obscenity; the clash of his armor rings mellow and heroic down the ages into our modern ears" (n.p.).

Janet Floyd accurately asserts that the chivalric allusions in the Leadville romances serve only to point up just how disconnected Foote's heroes are from the ethos of private love and adoration that is associated with true chivalry. If Foote introduced the courtly love motifs to underscore or emphasize her couples' bliss and deep emotional connection, it falls flat, Floyd avers, since the stories are presented to the reader with little intimacy or passion ("Mining the West"). One might also add that since the males are working for wages in technological, capitalistic endeavors, any chivalry can be only superficial at best since their world is in fact the "land of the bottom line," in contemporary songwriter John Gorka's phrase.[1] Foote knows this. The opening paragraph of her first novel dryly explains that "the olive-leaf of Eastern capital" finances or quits mining enterprises in dependent places like Leadville on its own whims (*The Led-Horse* 9); indeed, a bolt from the blue later shuts down Hilgard's mine in the form of a telegram from the syndicate. Modern financial realities rear their ugly heads and undercut the Arthurian idealism. The net result is that Foote again straddles the fence between fantasy and reality—destabilizing each. Perhaps she toyed with a sense of the medieval and grand epic in a western boomtown to gloss over the quotidian nature of the facts, especially at the beginning of her exile from the East when she still felt the force of the myth of the great West. She may have hesitated to depict a topic as unromantic as extraction engineering on its own merits. Later, when she understood more fully the challenges of professional engineers in the West, the novels are more factual, and she felt less need to pretty them up with fanciful overlays.

In any event, Foote's chivalric allusions, while undercutting the realism of the Leadville novels, serve to reinforce the class and interpersonal connections of the protagonists. At the beginning of *The Led-Horse Claim*, the narrator notes that "in the less heroic time in which his lot was cast, . . . Hilgard's excess of good looks was a positive inconvenience" (22). Despite this claim, however, Foote wants to portray him as a mining knight in shining armor. She compares Hilgard to the medieval French hero Henry of Navarre and also to royalty, claiming that he has a soul of purple (22, 24). The other young men of Leadville are also cast in this vein. When Foote compares the older men of the new boomtown, "who had come with a slightly shaken faith in themselves," with the younger untried and naturally more optimistic men, she refers to the young men as "knights of the virgin shield" (12).

Sometimes Foote drops facts in our path—the heroine's eyes are gray, like those celebrated in medieval and Renaissance poetry and painting; the hero's middle name, inexplicably but suggestively, is Tristram. When set alongside an older, jaded character, Hilgard is described as having "unstained armor and unquenched ardor of life" (73). His friend the Doctor once remarks how unfair it is that some morally repugnant men never want for women, whereas "chivalrous hearts like yours and mine haven't so much as a rag of a favor to stick in our caps!" (74–75). Hilgard's mine and its territory are said to be a "kingdom"

(101). The heroine, Cecil, thinks to herself that Hilgard has "knightly integrity," and Conrath's father refers to him as "the knight of the Led-Horse" (167, 235). Even within the logic of Foote's stories, however, these Leadville mine managers are not warriors but merely prep school lads newly graduated from mining colleges, out on their own in the world for the first time.

The effect of Foote's odd combination of profuse chivalric allusions and clear-eyed explanations of the business of mining serves to uphold what Peter Antelyes calls "the decorum of hierarchy and privilege." Since Foote's literary allusions validate the canonical readings of the upper middle class of her era, a reader is encouraged to emulate that class and perhaps "participate in the drives of self-interest and mobility" central to its success (xiv). Foote is obviously infected with "the Sir Walter disease," as Samuel Clemens terms southern writers' obsession with duels, chivalry, and "the jejune romanticism of an absurd past that is dead, and out of charity ought to be buried" (quoted in Ridgely 105). In nineteenth-century southern literature, such harking back to feudal aspects of the past resulted in a validation of social inequities, and to a lesser degree the same is true for Foote's appropriation of medieval trappings and tropes.

. . .

In addition to medieval references, the Leadville novels also include mythological allusions. Adding a similar erudite veneer, they have the same jarring effect on the realistic tone, with images ranging from plausible to obscure. In the beginning of *The Led-Horse Claim*, when Miss Conrath is out for a lone horseback ride near Leadville, she is saved from a stumble by the quick-witted Hilgard, who happens to be nearby. As he hands her riding whip back to her, the narrator tells us that his head "might have been modeled for the head of a young Jason at the time his personal appearance did him such good service at the court of King Æetes" (19). Thus, Foote valorizes the idea that blood tells, that her hero Hilgard is a prince among men, not only due to his upbringing but also on a more primal level because of his natural attributes and "keen instinct" (24). Foote's reference to Hilgard's heroic presence is only one of many indicating that she believes physiognomy and blood background count for much. In this era, the lingering effects of phrenology and other racially based pseudosciences thrived, encouraging people to assess a person's intelligence, character, and even soul on physiognomy. Lest it be thought that such transparently classist and racist ideas had lost favor by Foote's era, note that Joseph

Conrad's *Heart of Darkness*, published twenty years after *The Led-Horse Claim*, depicts an amateur phrenologist as only slightly behind the times.

In several texts, Foote consciously notes that she is giving a local habitation if not a name to the unstoried western regions she writes about. In *John Bodewin's Testimony*, the narrator compares the Arkansas River, which begins near Leadville, with Arethusa of Roman mythology. This is an interesting allusion, because it brings up a number of themes in Foote's work from this decade. The hero and heroine are out riding horses with friends in the pristine western landscape and come to a stream, which the narrator then characterizes mythologically: "The snow-born Arethusa was not swifter-footed or more musical than this unwritten, unsung Arkansas of the high valleys, not a day's journey from its cradle" (135). After Foote, of course, the humble Arkansas is no longer unsung.

Another issue raised in Foote's use of this seemingly charming classical allusion is a feminist one. The Arethusa of Roman legend is not "snow-born" at all but rather "rape-born," since Diana changes the wood nymph Arethusa into a fountain in order that she will not be ravished by a lustful stream pursuing her. Given Foote's excruciatingly chaste lovers riding along the Arkansas, her Roman allusion is either inappropriate or at the very least confusing. Bodewin is indeed pursuing a nymph, but he is not aggressive about it; in fact, the plot would have picked up considerably if he had behaved in epic fashion and acted on his impulses. As it is, he is a restrained eastern gentleman, and his equally proper nymph, the dark Josephine, has no need to be metamorphosed.

In other instances, too, Foote's mythological suggestions obfuscate instead of illuminate the story. Two of Foote's own granddaughters, raised in Massachusetts, admitted that it had been difficult for them to follow their grandmother's train of thought in her writing when she was at her most indirect and allusive, which she certainly is in some sections of the Leadville novels (Swift interview). In musical, artistic, or literary texts, allusions succeed when they supplement a theme or, inversely, when they ironically or perversely oppose it. But with Foote's references, one often just has the feeling of dislocation. In the middle of a prosaic passage about Colorado miners, the reference to Hilgard as Jason of the Argonauts is a surprise. And one wonders how Hilgard's physical beauty relates to the mythical Jason's, or how his actions parallel the Greek youth's adventures. Perhaps Foote wants us to believe that Hilgard's exploits, presaged by his noble head, enact a germinal American mythology. Mythology may have been the "crop which the Old World bore before its soil was exhausted," as Henry David Thoreau observes in "Walking" (n.p.), but Foote and others such as Washington Irving attempted to sow and harvest new North American myths using ancient seeds. This tendency comes naturally out of their education and reading. But it is also a badge of elitism. Reading poet Edith Thomas, Foote herself notes that Thomas is hampered by too much distracting classism. She wrote to Helena that Thomas has "a little want of color, perhaps—but I fancy she does not let herself go. She employs her classisms, perhaps, out of instinctive reserve, but I think she could well afford to be more direct, realistic—not that she is not exquisitely *true*. What I mean is—the cry of the Human. One hears it in her poems usually veiled in a beautiful Greek myth or image. The influence of this part of the continent is Hebrew not Greek" (January 8, 1888). Note Foote's dialectic, her Arnoldian paradigm about the sweetness and light of Hellenism and the darkness of so-called Hebraism, as well as her negative attitude toward what the western United States has to offer.

Like Thomas, Foote had "instinctive reserve, [and] could well afford to be more direct" and less allusive, for the mythologies of both Old and New Worlds meld together, as they did for much of educated nineteenth-century America. Foote wrote to Helena that when she first saw the expansive, high-altitude plain of South Park, Colorado, "it seemed a playground for the Centaurs—so vast, so brilliant, so free and utterly unspoilable" (May 12, 1879). Yet Foote's references, if heartfelt here, are usually superficial. The American West awaited the depth of Willa Cather, who, with a background of European reading and a major in classics at college, went one step further and created mythic and archetypal characters and situations that grew realistically out of western soil. Her rich characters fertilized the soil and give us a New World crop of archetype and myth.

If a present-day reader wonders why Foote added certain literary or epic allusions to these romances, since they sometimes contribute only dissonance and often do not fit with the overall theme of a story, Foote herself undercut some of her chivalric and literary tropes. Wallace Stegner's assertion about her honesty is again confirmed. Foote could not take chivalry and its attendant baggage entirely seriously in her own era, even as she revered it in her favorite authors from earlier times. Jessica G. Rabin notes that at this time the nineteenth-century romance "was on its way out, unable realistically to keep alive the belief in individual power in the face of a fast-paced industrialized, urbanized, materialistic, capitalistic world" (40). In *The Last Assembly Ball*, Frank ruefully remarks on this fact. He realizes that his impulsive, seemingly chivalric

actions are based on an outmoded code that has no relation to his 1880s western reality, but he still feels somehow trapped in the logic of the old ideals.
When he muses about his fate and the impending duel on his last night alive,
he calls to mind historical precedents for such folly but obtains no solace from
them. Even as "he thought of Andrea del Sarto, of Lydgate, of all the men who
had wrecked their lives in such frail craft as this, . . . he could not find the comfort of a prototype, either in romantic reality or in realistic romance. He was
no Andrea, no Lydgate; he was not even a youth who had 'lived'; he was merely
the husband of Milly" (192). Foote's antiheroic moment here—Frank's wry self-
consciousness—acknowledges just how implausible the situation is that she has
written her character into. And indeed at the end of her last Leadville novel,
Foote decided to let her mannered literary models recede into the background.
In an essay comparing Foote to Bret Harte, Janet Floyd asserts that Foote's use
of chivalric and "Arthurian idealism" in the Leadville novels underscores the
"irrelevance of such ideals to a modern imperial nation" ("Mining the West"
213).

True for Foote, since after *The Last Assembly Ball* her themes began to reflect
the modern world more. By this time, Foote was living in Idaho and facing a
rather naturalistic future, as funding and hope gave out for her husband's grand
irrigation schemes. *The Fate of a Voice,* a novella published in the same volume
as *The Last Assembly Ball* and set in Idaho, is the story of a woman whose artistic
gift is irrevocably lost after her marriage in the western wilds. Foote may have
jettisoned the chivalric and epic because whereas such tropes might succeed in
youthful, optimistic Leadville, they would not in the dusty Boise River valley.
Foote's protagonists remain genteel but no longer have to stand in for brave
knights and fair ladies of the corral. From this point on, Foote had her fanciful
moments but never again drew as derivatively or naively on literary precedents.
She found her voice, which still validated eastern social traditions in western
settings but did so with more authentic matter and less art.

Foote's Victorian uses of chivalry and epic, conflated with the spell of the
American West, must have glamorized Colorado for some readers. They add
heroic dimensions to the often dreary and dangerous world of pioneer drudgery and mineral extraction, of women aging prematurely and men living in
drafty tents at ten thousand feet, far from home and family. Foote sets out to
depict her male protagonists as noble individuals like those in the romances
and adventure stories she idolized, but even as she ostensibly presents a heroic

situation and a romantic plot, she keeps an attentive reader aware that eastern capital, business interests, and privileged mining college graduates are, in fact, controlling and changing the vast, seemingly mythic West.

...

Thus, literary and mythic ornaments dot the surface of Foote's Leadville novels, but underneath, bottom-line market forces influence her characters' behavior. Foote juggles reality with her literary impulses as she depicts both her own new class of professional exiles and the other to her less interesting classes beneath them. Modern, liberalizing forces in the boomtown, as well as what Foote calls the "restless crude striving mass of beings" (MHF to HKG, June 13, [1880]), are kept in check by her characters' eastern sensibilities. These can be defined as the literary background, social mores, and cultural standards for the upper middle class along the eastern seaboard. A matron in *The Chosen Valley* (1892) explains how this plays out practically: "A man should go east for his education, his accent, and his wife. He may go west for his fortune, perhaps" (107). The East is a world where patriarchy and tradition rule, and where women are supposed to be angels of various sorts in the house and the lower classes know their place. The social classes in both the East and the West did undergo changes after the Civil War, due to immigration and new manufacturing wealth, but the new urban professional middle class adopted many of the affectations of the old aristocratic elite, although they streamlined and modernized many of them.

Historically and in fiction, easterners who came west often discovered that habits and class distinctions appropriate in the East had to be reinterpreted for their new region. Foote and her protagonists resist adapting to the West and instead judge western society through eastern eyes. How shall we react to that? As Renato Rosaldo notes about anthropologists, the best one can do when describing a new culture is to acknowledge one's cultural position and use its admittedly ethnocentric terms as accurately as possible. Thus, even though Foote is more of a local colorist than an embedded regionalist, her vision can be just as useful to historians as diaries or more humble texts for the light it sheds on the social construction of the West. Benay Blend believes that Foote's "social criticism . . . perceptively undercut distorted eastern notions about the West and its society," but I see Foote's criticism of her eastern world as occasional and not systemic (quoted in Etulain, "Mary Hallock Foote" 147). Foote lays out the specific follies of eastern capitalists who manage western mines, but she none-theless depicts Leadville society almost entirely through the eyes of eastern notions of stratification and decorum. James H. Maguire accurately notes that Foote portrays the West as "a picturesque cultural vacuum" (44). Raised with a love of history and rootedness, she felt justified in overlaying the West with eastern sensibilities since she thought of it as an "historic vacuum" (*A Victorian Gentlewoman* 211). At one point in Idaho, Foote wrote to Helena: "Richard ought to come west to know the worth of his editorial work. The magazine [*Century*] is the light of the world out here" (January 10, 1886).

Western sensibilities may seem harder to define, but even now can be conceived of as being more open-minded and freewheeling, with an added feature of being more immediately practical than proper eastern customs. In 1964 Leo Marx articulated the conventional wisdom by asserting that "moving west means casting off European attitudes and rigid social forms and urban ways" (238). This simple formula has been complicated by more recent scholarship, including Brian Roberts's *American Alchemy: The California Gold Rush and Middle-Class Culture* (2000), which posits that the "cult of respectability" was both accepted and cheerfully defied by eager new westerners (15). As a beginning novelist, Foote stuck to the social conventions and literary tropes she learned in her Hudson River upbringing. And although she was not uncritical about the impact eastern culture and capital were having on the West, in the end her style and content served to make eastern ways seem the norm in the West for *Century* readers.

A useful contrast to Foote's novels are Isabella Bird's 1873 carefree, solo travels in Colorado depicted in *A Lady's Life in the Rocky Mountains*. The very British Bird celebrates the region's newness and freedoms, enjoying the lack of established hierarchies and conventions. Foote would have little of this. She kept a narrow social set, which in Leadville was made up of the educated and talented from the East and Europe. They were men "who are too good for saloons and variety Theatres," she noted to Helena. "There are some very fine men out here—all the finer that there is every opportunity to be spoiled. Of course many are spoiled but I know only the nice ones, personally. Arthur has a way of keeping people at a distance which is a valuable accomplishment in a place like this" (June 13, [1880]). The spoiled ones are kept at arm's length in the Leadville novels, too. Foote condescends, terming them "bronzed-faced, hairy-throated men," "adventurers" (*John Bodewin's* 30), "the mud, the weeds, and the driftwood" (*The Led-Horse* 12) or giving them local-color dialects that distinguish them from gentlefolk. Playing devil's advocate, Dr. Godfrey in *The Led-Horse Claim* states at a Leadville ball, "Here, there is no classification. You have to pick your way among all the people who are crowding you, elbow to elbow" (91). But in fact and in Foote's fiction, the lines remained pretty firmly drawn. Foote gave lip service to the chaotic nature of the social situation in Leadville, but she did not let the apparently flexible social situation influence her disapproval if her protagonists choose socially inappropriate marriage partners. Frank Embry quickly pays for this error in judgment with his life. The warning is clear.

. . .

The way in which Foote herself initially came to know the West accounts for further features of her class consciousness and aloofness from her neighbors. There were no arduous covered-wagon treks or homesteading with locust plagues for Foote. Her personal experience of the West took for granted rail transportation, towns where food and firewood could be purchased, and at least occasional visits back to the East. In addition, she had immersed herself in British and American writers such as Scott, Cooper, Stevenson, Kipling, Hawthorne, and Emerson. Thus, she saw the West, at first at least, through the lens of nineteenth-century imperialism and boosterism. This explains in part why Foote's voice is so different from those in the diaries and novels of women pioneers and homesteaders. In addition to her better education, Foote had more options—though actually only a few more—than the women who drudged in sod houses or ministered to miners. Soon after the Leadville days, she made (just) enough money to afford a governess and a cook in her remote households in Idaho and California; she corresponded with literati from New York and elsewhere. She even came up with the means for a trial separation from her husband at one point, and realized that if she chose to, she could support her three children by herself.

The characters in most of Foote's novels reflect these professional and peripatetic experiences in the West and make casual mobility seem the norm, not the exception. Many diaries and autobiographies by westering women such as Anne Ellis's *Life of an Ordinary Woman* (1929), and indeed later autobiographical novels such as Mari Sandoz's *Old Jules* (1962), stress the hard and irrevocable nature of a move west, but Foote's Leadville characters, especially the males, are not marooned. Taking Walter Nugent's demographic characterizations of western frontiers, Leadville is a Type II: predominantly young and male, seeking not settlement but resource extraction and fast wealth. A gentlewoman like Foote had a unique perspective as a sheltered observer, even if her propriety prevented her from investigating it fully. Nugent's Type I western population is like those depicted in Laura Ingalls Wilder's *Little House* series: it has family units and is more evenly divided between males and females. Leadville, on the other hand, swarmed with predominantly unmarried male job holders on site for the short term, enjoying the prosperity that mining provided and able to move on to other projects when the silver veins dried up. Like "ski bums" of later eras, Foote's protagonists are college educated, only temporarily camping out for fun and profit in Colorado. In fact, after Francis Parkman's grand tour of the West in 1846, such an American substitute for the European grand tour did become more fashionable.

Although Foote's young miners have not made fortunes in the West yet, they are not so destitute that they cannot travel back to the East for one reason or another. Hilgard in *The Led-Horse Claim* has the financial backing of his company to return to New York, even though he goes back in disgrace. Once there, he can afford to stay at a hotel respectable enough for genteel ladies such as Cecil and her aunt to be there, too. Frank and his dilettante colleagues at the boardinghouse in *The Last Assembly Ball* are in Leadville to try their soft hands at placer mining until something better comes along. With their backgrounds and educations, they have mobility and choices. It is clear that the young people in Foote's novels enjoy what the fussy Hudson River grandmother in *The Led-Horse Claim* disparagingly refers to as "this rushing back and forth, thousands of miles at a stretch," across the continent (271). Since Foote cherished her own visits to the East, and since the Leadville novels were written somewhat later when her traveling was curtailed by financial straits, perhaps she stressed the mobility of her characters in compensation for her own lack of it. For whatever reason, the mobility of professional classes in the West is a feature of Foote's fiction.

. . .

Foote's ideas on class are similar to those detailed in California-born Gertrude Atherton's 1898 novel, *The Californians*. For her, the United States in the 1830s was

> more or less bound together by the conventions it had inherited from the great civilisations that begat it. These conventions exist today only in men of the highest breeding, those with six or eight generations behind them of refinement, consequence, and fastidiousness of association. In these men, the representatives of an aristocracy

that is in danger of being crippled and perhaps swamped by plutocracy, exists the convention which forces the most deplorable degenerate of old-world aristocracy to manifest himself a gentleman in every crucial test. So thoroughly did Trennahan comprehend these facts, so profound was his contempt for the second-rate men of his country, that he was almost self-conscious about his honor. (243)

Less haughty but similarly steadfast are Foote's gentlemen mine managers and the men they were modeled on, Foote's husband and colleagues. She felt they elevated the social standards of Leadville against the "second-rate" masses arriving in town, declaring in her autobiography that in Leadville she and her husband "lived on the crust of much that lay beneath" (*A Victorian Gentlewoman* 197).

The sometimes righteous propriety and untainted morality of Foote's protagonists may seem outdated to later readers. In Foote's eyes, however, such correct and moral behavior held back the tide of social chaos flooding the West. In *The Last Assembly Ball*, she even goes so far as to justify class hierarchies by asserting that life with them is in fact less restrictive: "Middle age has decided, or has learned to dispense with many things which youth continues to fash [sic] itself about; and the older societies, with all their perpetuated grooves and deep-rooted complexities, are freer and more cheerful than the new" (5–6). Foote was proud to say that the young men of distinction she knew in Leadville were "all so true to their own background . . . so young in experience but morally so sound" (*A Victorian Gentlewoman* 199). She thus took her stand with older social structures against the newer, more colloquial culture that was creeping, with industrialization and immigration, into the North American population.

· · ·

Although the literacy rate for white adults was 90 percent in the first part of the nineteenth century, those who made editorial decisions, as well as those who had the time to read for pleasure, were generally upper middle class. And if they were not, they aspired to be. Since her audience of the emerging professional class inclined to gentility, Foote could assume they shared her belief in the superiority and cultural worthiness of the upper classes. With the narrator of Cather's *Lost Lady*, she believed that "a fortunate and privileged class was an axiomatic fact in the social order" (12–13). This is more apparent in the Leadville novels than later, when Foote became less insistent on the blue blood of her characters. Still, the upper class in Foote's Leadville novels is represented by the members of the *working* upper middle class, and not by individuals even more privileged, such as her friends Richard and Helena Gilder, who kept great houses, vacationed in Newport, and entertained presidents. Foote's more humble elite are her stories' protagonists: young men of "good" eastern families and the proper but not actually aristocratic gentlewomen whom they woo. The narrators present these men and women as different from and better than others on the Colorado frontier due to their sense of decorum, expensive or tasteful ways of dressing, moral rectitude, excellent manners, and bright expectations for the future. Foote was a member of and a believer in what Gertrude Atherton maliciously called the "aristocratic middle class" in the United States (*The Aristocrats* 142).

Even though it was her own income, and not that of her inconsistent husband, that maintained the family's upper-middle-class status, Foote was content to stay in a dependent female role her whole life. Some nineteenth-century women writers and activists rued the fact that women often perpetuated class distinctions as much as men, even though in the larger political sense they did not create them. But Foote believed that this civilizing was part of women's mission. By this light we understand, therefore, why the supersensitive ladies at the ball in *The Led-Horse Claim* are the first to leave the room when Milly the servant is presented to them as an equal. The men linger longer in the face of her sheer physical beauty; they are not as sensitive to the appearance of impropriety as the women. As one of Foote's favorite authors, Sir Walter Scott, has the narrator humorously note in the 1819 *Ivanhoe*, "It was of course amongst [the lesser gentry] that the most frequent disputes for precedence occurred" (90). Foote knows this when she has the provincial ladies in Leadville snub Milly.

In Foote's writings, members of the higher classes are generally from the New World—they are not titled Europeans. For the American-born elites in her stories, acceptance by society in New York or Washington is the apogee; Europe is not vital to their success. Foote was thus more self-sufficiently American in outlook than authors whose purview insisted on a European context of culture, refinement, and class, such as Atherton, James, Wharton, or even in some contexts Alcott and Cather. No one goes to or comes from European technical colleges or finishing schools in Foote's novels although the great mining schools were flourishing in Germany at that time. Foote was actually acquainted with some European-educated men in Leadville, since the silver boom had drawn them, but she did not include these "types" in her Leadville novels. This provincialism narrowed Foote's scope, yet may have set her audience at ease, since European travel was still out of the reach of most of the reading public at this time. *Century* and other elite magazines certainly had their share of articles about the titled personages, great houses, quaint customs, and charming cities of Europe, but at this time American national sentiment was also rising for a United States that was able to create its own culture independent of its European legacy.

As we have seen, Foote observed that when societies first formed in a new town, social interactions were somewhat fluid, but quite soon the strata settled out according to region and background. As utopian and western scholar Robert Hine points out, the myth of opportunity and classlessness was often just that. In the case of Leadville, society quickly became an "oligarchy," although Foote notes with her usual irony that it was "under conditions, it must be owned, that made the renaissance something of a burlesque" (*The Last Assembly Ball* 38).

This rapid class making was in part driven by the effects of the Civil War. Foote notices that the dispossessed yet still aristocratic southern young men in Leadville "brought with them the feudal feeling and the need for personal distinction," and their northern counterparts were often "bred with the same exclusiveness" (*The Last Assembly Ball* 38). She relates how quickly members of these new societies established standards as rigid as those from where they originated. The small, informal dances at Mrs. Dansken's boardinghouse in *The Last Assembly Ball* enlarged to "Assemblies" at the local hotel, and "before autumn much of the simplicity had departed. The day of competition and of preferences had begun.... There were other changes, showing how in the newest society the old experiments are repeated in the sequence history has made us familiar with" (37–38). This aside points up both Foote's detached irony and her acceptance of the status quo. She did not particularly want the region to allow new experiments in social relations, which women such as Bird and Mary Austin celebrate. As Blend puts it, for Foote the West was essentially "a cultural colony of the East" (89). When Foote first came to San Francisco in 1876, she was uneasy with the idea that rewards and distinction might be meted out differently in a different region (MHF to HKG, December 7, 1876).

In Foote's writings as in real life, the upper classes tend to have more family backing than those less well off, as well as a longer view of generations and families. These societal connections add an import and special drama to their lives and indeed their deaths. This is evident in the treatment of Conrath's body after he is killed in *The Led-Horse Claim,* when his fellow Masons close ranks and arrange as festive a funeral and burial as the grim little town can provide. The narrator remarks that "whatever their indifference of faithlessness to their eastern ties during life, the men of Conrath's rank on the frontier confidently expected those ties to contract in the extreme moment, and restore them to their earlier associations" (193). "Earlier associations" continue to aid the unpleasant Conrath even after death, for when Conrath Sr. finally hears of his son's death (he had been away on a winter cruise to Cuba), he arranges for the body to be exhumed and shipped back to the East, where it is reburied in the Conrath family plot. In the end, for the Conrath family, "all was forgotten save the good they had known of him"—a fortuitous rehabilitation of a shabby life by means of ready cash and family amnesia (297). We are reminded again of Edith Wharton's *Sanctuary,* in which Kate Orme draws the blinds "on the ugly side of things" (325).

Family influence has perhaps a less beneficent role in *The Last Assembly Ball,* where Frank propels himself to a reckless death after he envisions his proper parents receiving news of his marriage to a servant. The framed photograph of Frank's mother in his Leadville boardinghouse bedroom further serves to remind him of his shame when he speaks of it to his new wife, Milly. Frank's family is the sort of family Foote approved of. In her *Reminiscences,* Foote recalls a moment in Leadville when she was looking at a friend's photographs of his eastern family. She remembers thinking, she says, that "they were lovely faces, types of the very best sort of people anywhere" (*A Victorian Gentlewoman* 199). In his room Frank is first embarrassed to remember that Milly knows his personal possessions in her capacity as housemaid and then, as he tries to envision Milly's reaction to his mother, feels hopeless, "as if he should never again speak of his mother" (192). The propriety manifest in Frank's "very best sort of people" mother has a remote yet terrible influence on her son, standing as she does for class exclusivity.

As in James Fenimore Cooper's 1827 book, *The Prairie,* Frank Embry and other elite characters in Foote's work have an emotional reticence and discretion that less restrained individuals like the voluble Mrs. Denny in *John Bodewin's Testimony* lack. This is manifest in the oddly restrained passion between the purported lovers in the novels and in both Hilgard's and Bodewin's stubborn refusal to speak to others about their professional and personal troubles. As Wallace Stegner dryly notes in *Angle of Repose,* the Foote-like character, the young Susan Burling Ward, and her best friend, the Helena-like Augusta, may not have known at first which of them the Richard Gilder–like character, Thomas, was really wooing, since "if you are genteel enough, that sort of imprecision is possible" (45). Whether true or not for Foote and her friends, it certainly happens in Howells's *Silas Lapham*. It is sometimes difficult for the modern reader to tell exactly what Foote's well-bred characters are, in fact, thinking, since the narrator is discreet even with the reader. Mary Poovey calls this "strategies of indirection," and asserts that many nineteenth-century female authors practiced it (42). Purportedly, they chose not to participate in the dominant male fiction modes that spoke directly about facts, emotions, and situations. Susan K. Harris explains that they chose instead to write more obliquely, assuming "that readers will . . . 'fill in' the outline they have sketched" (32). Foote often preferred this indirect approach, in both her fiction and her letters, setting quite a challenge for later readers to read between the lines. This feature of Foote's method of characterization also reflects her ideals about class, since emotional restraint and personal reticence are virtues of the genteel. Foote wrote at one point to Helena that although Helen Hunt Jackson's poems have "more color and passion" than Edith Thomas's, she feels that "the west had not a good effect upon her art; she took up its sorrows and needs too passionately, for perfect Art" (January 8, 1888).

. . .

The middle class has more freedom of morality and fewer genteel restrictions of movement than the elite in Foote's novels, and she condescends to them accordingly. They are the usually nameless shopkeepers, miners, or wives who appear onstage as necessary for the main plot and the heroes' and heroines' needs. Such middle-class men dutifully carry Conrath's body from the mine in *The Led-Horse Claim*, they boorishly stare and thus taint the unclaimed body of Babe in *John Bodewin's Testimony*, and they attend the Assembly Ball and do not leave in disapproval when Milly is presented as if she were a proper lady.

The women in Foote's middle class lack the financial or family resources that, as Foote herself termed it in a letter, "protected" women enjoy, and as such they may act or dress gauchely or make other unfortunate aesthetic choices in life (Davidson 123). Mrs. Denny in *The Led-Horse Claim* and Milly Robinson in *The Last Assembly Ball* fit this bill. Mrs. Denny's faults are that she shows too much unrestrained vivacity and is provincially thrilled at what she deems to be the cosmopolitan nature of the Younger Sons Ball in Leadville. The narrator calls it "laughable" how little it took to be thought civilized in Leadville (20), but as Gertrude Atherton points out, "there is really no reason why a new country should not take itself seriously" (*The Californians* 54).

Milly may be considered middle class because even though she works as a housemaid, her landlady reveals that she was not born a servant—"she is just one of the chances of the place," she informs her boarders (52–53). And middle-class girls have to take chances and live by their wits, if, as happened to Milly, they have to support themselves and a baby when their husbands desert them. With no one to advise her, Milly's natural spinelessness, like Conrath's lack of moral compass, gets her into trouble. She had initially allowed those at her first job in Leadville to mistake her for being unmarried (since her baby had died), and later she permits the well-bred Frank's attentions. Because no one in transient Leadville knows Milly's personal history, there are no external constraints to prevent her from drifting into a mismatched alliance. Milly, like Conrath, might have lived a life without incident back in a settled town where she and her family history and status were better known. The difference that social class can make becomes apparent when she and Conrath drift from propriety, however. After death, the disreputable Conrath is actively rehabilitated by his friends and family. After her embarrassment, Milly lives in obscurity, nursing the sick, but her beauty and meekness—classic tools of women's upward mobility—soon effect her somewhat miraculous escape from Leadville via marriage to a Montana rancher. Milly's unclassified status has its positive side, however, since she has no inconveniently coarse family, as does Babe in *John Bodewin's Testimony* or the Colorado heroine in Hope Williams Sykes's *Second Hoeing* (1935). In Sykes's novel the protagonist is dismayed to realize that her moneyed suitor expects her to spurn her lowly sugar beet–growing family if she marries him; she decides to stay a spinster with them rather than follow her lover into deracinated upward mobility.

The prosperous rancher who falls ill in Leadville and ends up marrying the hapless Milly at the end of *The Last Assembly Ball* is one of the first socially neutral middle-class western characters in Foote's writing. Perforce, he is a sketchy character—all we know of him is that he is "a big stock-raiser," wears a beaver coat with a diamond stick pin, and falls for Milly (212). But except that Foote seems to indicate that diamond stick pins are somewhat flashy by her Hudson Valley sartorial standards, the rancher is both respectable yet authentically of the West, without having been given eastern antecedents in the usual Foote way. This represents a growth in Foote's experience of western social settings. A middle class without an immediate eastern context is beginning to exist for Foote's characters, even if in her life she did not want to associate socially with such people. Consciously or unconsciously, the effect of depicting the West this way promoted settlement and tourism in the West. Foote's West could be grafted onto the East—Milly and Sir Lancelot ride off into the sunset.

In general, Foote's middle-class characters lack not only the quick intelligence and moral delicacy of her upper-middle-class protagonists but also the picturesque simplicity and hint of roughness of her lower classes. Members of the middle class crowd the provincial Leadville streets with their lack of urban poise and disregard for correct reticence. They buy the imitation lace in the burgeoning shop windows and make dinners noisy at even the nicest hotel in town, she notes in letters. The ladies try to dress and act in what they conceive of as a refined manner, even as they are quietly ignored or snubbed by the true eastern elite. But in the end, these upstarts often achieve a comfortable angle of repose in the West, and the elite are left wondering what happened. At the end of Foote's final Leadville novel, *The Last Assembly Ball*, three ordinary middle-class people—Milly, her rancher, and the intrepid Mrs. Dansken—find love and security in the West, while the elite boy Frank, despite his friends and family in high places, lies dead after an avoidable duel.

. . .

In her fiction, Foote used lower-class characters only for specific effect as "types"—a favorite term in her letters and fiction. She preferred to focus on genteel types and presented only rough or crude people as negligible foils for her proper protagonists. The lower class is stereotypically colorful but never developed in Foote's writing. The narrator in *The Led-Horse Claim* alludes to the hardiness and coarseness of German and Irish immigrants, as do Foote's letters from that era. In *John Bodewin's Testimony*, Sammis and the chorus of roughnecks around the mine manager's porch are as unrealistic as the hammy pirates in Gilbert and Sullivan's *Pirates of Penzance*, as they artificially set the scene of the novel with folksy dialect. Use of dialect itself is a class indicator in Foote's writings, as it often is in regionalist and local colorists. Babe's family, the squalid Keesners in *John Bodewin's Testimony*, speaks in dialect but is less charming than Sammis's crowd. Interestingly, the most class conscious of Foote's novels, *The Last Assembly Ball*, lacks members of the lower class. The novel's crucial distinctions are between those on either end of the wide middle class.

Foote does not mention African Americans or Hispanics in the Leadville novels, but she defends the Chinese. Like some other nineteenth-century female authors, Foote apparently felt safe putting into Mrs. Dansken's mouth some spirited criticism of the established powers and unpalatable social truths about regional prejudice. The "intrepid" landlady criticizes the prohibition of Chinese workers in the town limits of Leadville, a ubiquitous western practice that Foote commented on in several later texts and in letters. Mrs. Dansken is anxious to find an inexpensive domestic servant and is not interested in the social or mining costs of imported labor. Later, she complains that she is all but forced to hire the good-looking Milly as a housemaid, because there are no other workers available.

When Foote lived in Idaho she liked and admired the Chinese cooks her family retained—they even exchanged presents at Christmas—but of course she did not socialize with them. In *The Last Assembly Ball,* it is dryly noted that domestic help was hard to come by in the first days of the silver boom, because few women had arrived yet and also because, in the waggish quip of Foote's narrator, "Chinese labor had been excluded from this camp of idealists" (17). By "idealists" here I take Foote to mean that the miners had an "ideal" to keep wages high, but it is an oblique reference and may have other interpretations. Yet in *The Last Assembly Ball* at least Foote openly addresses the pervasive fact of Asian discrimination in the West. Perhaps because of her early contact with Chinese immigrants in California and her subsequent knowledge of them in Idaho, she defends their right to work and live in America, although only as servants. In many western regions, and especially in mining communities, ordinances decreed not only that the Chinese live quite separate from Anglo settlements but also that they not mine profitable areas. Only after a vein was played out were Chinese miners allowed in. In 1878 Leadville's silver mogul Horace Tabor had tried unsuccessfully in the face of local resistance to import a gang of Chinese men for his Matchless Mine, and by 1879 the founder of the *Leadville Daily Chronicle* could smugly assert that "no Chinaman had ever dared to set foot in Leadville" (Carlyle Channing Davis quoted in R. Lee 295). The national Chinese Exclusion Act was passed in 1882, barring further immigration. Foote's modest tirade in her 1889 novel, then, echoed some of the contemporary western political debates, albeit a bit belatedly.

Portrait of Mary Hallock taken around 1874, two years before her marriage. At this time she was a popular illustrator, doing work for *Century* magazine, as well as for books by Henry Wadsworth Longfellow and Bret Harte. Reproduced by permission of the Huntington Library, San Marino, California.

"At the foot of the pass." Foote's illustration for her first Leadville, Colorado, novel, *The Led-Horse Claim* (1882). For her initial trip to Leadville in 1879, Foote's husband, Arthur, drove them in a carriage up the Old Stage Road, still visible along the South Fork of the Arkansas River. November 1882, *Century*. Courtesy of the Denver Public Library.

"Between daylight and dark." Foote's illustration of the lovers parting in *The Led-Horse Claim*. This shows Foote at her most sentimental, but accurately depicts the blasted, high-altitude landscape around Leadville, Colorado. The need for fuel and mine scaffolding had denuded much of the area. January 1883, *Century*. Courtesy of the Denver Public Library.

"There were sounds which might have been miles away." Foote's illustration of Cecil Conrath visiting the mine in *The Led-Horse Claim*. Foote ventured down into one of her husband's mines to see the darkness and hear the deep rumblings for herself, despite a superstition that women were bad luck there. To make her illustrations, Foote carved on wooden blocks in the West and then sent them to *Century* in New York for engraving. December 1882, *Century*. Courtesy of the Denver Public Library.

"The engineer's mate." A lady of the world with her elaborate belongings looks out over the western wastes. This image is on the cover of Foote's autobiography, *A Victorian Gentlewoman in the Far West* (1972). It poignantly depicts the isolation of a polished woman in a featureless landscape with a rough laborer nearby, who may be of help with the baggage but is hardly compatible company. May 1895, *Century*. Courtesy of the Denver Public Library.

"The cabin by the ditch" in Leadville. Eastern and western luminaries visited the Footes in their small cabin for evenings of congenial talk, including U.S. Geological Survey director Clarence King and author Helen Hunt Jackson. October 1879, *Scribner's Monthly*. Reproduced by permission of the Huntington Library, San Marino, California.

"Dream horses." Foote's illustration of Polly on her pony in Idaho. The model was Foote's daughter Betty, who loved horses and would beg her mother to draw them. The Foote children had an English governess for their lessons while living in remote Boise Canyon. November 1888, *St. Nicholas*. Courtesy of the Denver Public Library.

"Afternoon at a ranch." Foote's illustration of daughter Betty napping on a hot Idaho afternoon. As Melody Graulich notes, the objects shown in the sketch indicate Foote's cosmopolitan taste—Japanese lantern, hammock, and decorative vase with an artful dried plant arrangement. August 1889, *Century*. Courtesy of the Denver Public Library.

Portrait of the accomplished and beautiful Helena de Kay Gilder at home in New York City, probably taken in the 1870s after her marriage to Richard Watson Gilder. She held glittering evening salons and worked to found the Art Students League in the city. Courtesy of the Foote family.

"A pretty girl in the West." Note the same desert porch setting as in the illustration of Betty napping. Courtesy of the Department of Special Collections and University Archives, Stanford University Libraries. Drawing: 1888–1889, *Century*. Courtesy of the Library of Congress, Washington, D.C., P&P CAI LC-USZ 62-39630.

Mary Hallock Foote in the mid-1870s. Foote often described the clothes she and others wore in the West in letters to Helena Gilder. She enjoyed elaborate clothes in her youth but related to Gilder that when she lived in the canyon ten miles from Boise, she appreciated being able to dress more informally. Courtesy of the Foote family.

"Between the desert and the sown." Foote's illustration of a dainty and dependent woman by an irrigation ditch in Idaho, created for Foote's novel *Between the Desert and the Sown* and run in a *Century* piece entitled "The Conquest of Arid America." The plight of educated and cultured women and men who "get left" in the rural West became one of Foote's themes when her husband's irrigation schemes failed in Idaho and the family was stranded there for more than ten years. May 1895, *Century*. Courtesy of the Library of Congress, Washington, D.C., P&P CAI LC-USZ 62-39631.

"And the spreading waters below." Foote's illustration of a lonely stretch of Idaho with Arthur Foote's irrigation ditch offering promise to the desolate, arid land. Foote's legacy is one of blighted but dogged hope in the absence of cultural touchstones and in the face of a vast region indifferent to humans. October 1892, *Century*. Courtesy of the Denver Public Library.

The Foote family in Boise, ca. 1894–1895. *Back row:* Mary Hallock Foote, her sister Bessie Sherman, governess Nellie Linton, Bessie's daughter Mary Birney Sherman, and Foote's children, Agnes (with short hair after a bout with scarlet fever), Betty, and Arthur B. Foote. Mary's husband, Arthur D. Foote, is absent from the picture, as is Bessie's husband, John Sherman, who died in 1891. Courtesy of the Foote family.

Gender Roles in the Leadville Novels

"More Delicate, More Sympathetic, and Especially More Moral"

In spite of the proscribed class strictures that Foote depicts in her Leadville fiction, new social possibilities opened up there. In these first works we see some new home-grown western character types and a few instances of successful upward mobility as well. The various classes rub up against each other on the busy streets, and even with Foote's allusive and literary tone, fresh possibilities arise from the jumble of transplanted individuals. A look at the gender roles that Foote allows shows her growth, for both eastern and western characters.

Western historian Ida Rae Egli asserts that as nineteenth-century social norms came west, many of them were "aimed at controlling women" (88), but Mary Hallock Foote did not resent this; she wanted everyone socially controlled, regardless of sex or background. One critic notes that Foote's novels use the power of feminine social expectations and domesticity to exert order over the "disorderly classes of the West" (Blend 89). Indeed, proper women could set the tone and improve the social chaos of boomtowns, even if they did not participate much in its more raucous social events. Melody Graulich may be correct when she says that in Foote's early novels the "woman's story" is "held captive" by the "male's text," but in Foote's eyes, if a woman had a public "story" it eroded her aloof class position (46). Women were allowed to do less in the public realm than men were, but for Foote, this was how civilized society should be. A proper lady had her name in the newspaper only three times: at her birth, her marriage, and her death.

Foote had a career, and so had more publicity than this in her own life, but was never comfortable with it. She occasionally allowed that her choice of subject matter was circumscribed because she was a woman, but as Lee Ann Johnson notes, she "questioned but did not shirk the feminine role dictated by genteel tradition" (32). In a letter to one of her editors, Foote explained this situation: "I hate that air of knowingness in a woman's work—the case of me who knows the bad old world pretty well, and might say more an' if she would.

Yet an Artist to be a great Artist must know all there is to know about life, and no woman can know all there is about this life out here, unless she has a husband who spares nothing in his talk, and my husband is not one of that sort, I'm thankful to say" (MHF to Andrew Anthony, 1894).[1] Women were to be thus separate from the world, and if their art suffered, so be it.

Foote admiringly described her mother as "an exquisite gentlewoman un- spotted from the world" (quoted in Armstrong 138). That seems to have been the rarefied model for her pale and moralistic heroines in the Leadville novels. Women of a certain class are not of this world; to be on display or to be un- shielded from the common people is to risk vulgarity. When Foote first trav- eled to Leadville, her husband hired a two-horse buggy and drove her himself the many miles from the train terminus at Webster, Colorado, rather than sub- ject her to a stagecoach and the perils apparently rife on public transportation. She explains that she approved of this extravagance, since "that is the price of Romance: to have allowed his wife to come in by stage in company with drunk- enness and vice, or anything else that might happen, would have been realism" (*A Victorian Gentlewoman* 172). Thus, Foote may not been as apologetic as she sounded in 1922, answering queries from a Colorado historian by explaining that she was "one of the 'protected' women of that time" and hence did not see the more sordid side of Leadville's boomtown days (qtd. in Davidson 123).

In *Last Assembly Ball*, Foote states the now often-quoted Footism that "when an Eastern woman goes West, she parts at one wrench with family, clan, traditions, clique, cult, and all that has hitherto enabled her to merge with her outlines—the support, the explanation, the excuse, should she need one, for her personality" (39). This statement stirringly asserts the need women have for a social background to their lives, as opposed to the traditionally more autono- mous men. Few critics analyze this statement in light of class, however. In the same passage, Foote goes on to note that this newly western and now exposed woman "will conform to any restrictions that will secure her in this immunity from general observation, which implies general criticism" (40). Her mother's being "unspotted from the world" is thus not just a comment on her mother's moral fiber but also a class marker. Only in this light can we understand why it is that in *John Bodewin's Testimony* the proper Josephine Newbold, who is a stranger to the local mountain girl, Babe, tries to prevent Babe's body from being on public display after she dies in an accident. While alone viewing the body, Josephine has "an almost hysterical sensation to think of the crowds that to-morrow would press around this form of sacred maidenhood, and stare at its beauty, and wonder at its history" (265). Josephine is not merely sorry that Babe's friends or family have not claimed the body (since they do not yet know of her death); she wants to avoid what in the end happens: Babe's body lies publicly at the undertakers, and, upon hearing of her beauty, the miners of Leadville troop past to have a last voyeuristic look.

This public display of an unattended female body would have been a scandal for any woman or man from a genteel family, which is why Conrath's fellow Masons quickly arrange his lodge burial when his family is not forthcoming in *The Led-Horse Claim*. But especially for women, any sort of publicity is not appropriate if they want to be considered respectable. Like some contemporary fundamentalist religious adherents, Foote claims that in fact the private obscurity her kind of women desire is "emancipating." She also notes that entrée to an exclusive social set is naturally "somewhat jealously extended, and only to those who can be relied on to preserve" these privileges (*The Last Assembly Ball* 40). Such sentiments no doubt help create the minute stratification in Leadville—actual and fictional—that forms the backdrop for *The Led-Horse Claim* and *John Bodewin's Testimony* and is more carefully detailed in *The Last Assembly Ball*.

. . .

The moral and passionless aristocratic but still middle-class heroines in Foote's first two Leadville novels are scarcely to be distinguished from each other. James Maguire notes that in her novels Foote "bring[s] to life the experiences of the Gibson girl *deracinée*, uprooted from New York salons and New England cottages" (44). This is especially true in the Leadville novels. Foote's pale heroines are not exactly to the manor born or *pukka sahib* (eternally upper class), but even if they are from as western a place as Kansas City, they at least model demure and ladylike behavior; they have finish and polish, morality and manners. Foote felt that manners were a sign of a true aristocrat. In her brief travels into essentially feudal Mexico just before she started writing the Leadville novels, she was deeply impressed at the centuries-old ceremonies and gracious households of her wealthy hosts, and she noted approvingly that Mexicans of all classes had good manners, even though she found the treatment of poor women brutal (*A Victorian Gentlewoman* 214–15, 220). Cecil's shy reserve in *Led-Horse Claim* and Josephine's confident choice of appropriate clothes for her father's court date in *Bodewin* serve to place the young women as people of distinction.

We first see the demure Miss Cecil Conrath in *The Led-Horse Claim* when she encounters some laboring miners on her afternoon ride near Leadville, and is pointedly said to appear "indifferent to their respectfully curious glances." She is such a well-bred damsel that although "she had a dimly appreciative eye for the fine curves of their powerful backs,... they were not present to her consciousness" (17). If they *had* been present to her consciousness, we would have known at once that she was possibly prurient—not truly respectable. As it is, Foote may be making a dubious foray into sensuality by letting Cecil appreciate their musculature at all. But Miss Conrath is otherwise nonsexual, which ensures that, in the end, she will attain a gentleman husband. Another genteel aspect of Cecil's makeup is her physical and emotional sensitivity. As in James Fenimore Cooper's 1827 novel, *The Prairie,* the lower-class women (and men) are hardier than the upper. When Cecil's dissolute brother is killed in the mine, her maid Molly spares her devastated mistress any decision making as well as any visits from well-wishers at the cottage. It is related without disparagement that Cecil is prostrated and made useless by her grief.

The heroine of *John Bodewin's Testimony,* Josephine Newbold, is of the same type as Miss Conrath in *The Led-Horse Claim,* though as her name suggests, she has a little more spunk. A mildly astute reader knows the outcome of *John Bodewin's Testimony* from the very beginning, since Miss Newbold is first described as a "young lady," and her father a "gentleman," which tips us off instantly that this young woman is a worthy love interest for the dignified Bodewin (12). Miss Newbold, interestingly, is every inch a lady in spite of her midwestern background. In the nineteenth century the whole country naturally looked to the East and to Europe for standards for etiquette (see Kasson), and although regional differences for appropriate behavior were emerging in the nineteenth century, the standard was still that of the eastern metropolises of New York, Boston, and Philadelphia. Thus, John Bodewin exhibits initial disdain for any girl like Miss Newbold who has been brought up in Kansas City, because he has prejudices about midwestern social training and manners. In William Dean Howells's *Chance Acquaintance* (1873), a proper Bostonian cannot prevent himself from being condescending and snobby with a non-Bostonian girl, and not surprisingly their romance falters. Bodewin, however, genteelly described as "a native of one of the little [Long Island] Sound cities of Connecticut"—like Foote's husband—is pleasantly surprised that Miss Newbold has poise and "a delicate head," though she comes from Kansas City (14). Written nine years before Oscar Wilde's *Importance of Being Earnest,* this phrase echoes arch Lady

Bracknell's pleasure at discovering the "distinct social possibilities" of Cecily's profile, although Wilde is parodying the phrenology of gentility and Foote is not (quoted in Corrigan 456).

Cooper brings a schema of social class to life in *The Prairie* that resembles Foote's, at least in her Leadville novels. The more elite people in Cooper's novel are from a region settled for centuries, whereas the lowest on the scale are new settlers of undistinguished origins. Cooper's hilarious invention, Dr. Obed Bat, has the last word about social stratification in the West. In one particularly ludicrous example of the scientist's many attempts to categorize the various species in the West, Bat greets a character with, "Ay, I remember you well, young man. You are of the *class,* Mammalia; *order,* primates; *genus,* Homo; *species,* Kentucky" (112). In her own efforts at social taxonomy, Foote takes pains to inform the reader of significant characters' origins—it means something upper class if they are from Connecticut; it means something less determinate if from Denver or Kansas City.

Foote herself was as unsuited to the adventurous, uncivilized western lifestyle as her heroines, even as she came to accept and even love aspects of it over the years. As she notes about herself in her autobiography, "No girl ever wanted less to 'go West' with any man, or paid a man a greater compliment by doing so" (*A Victorian Gentlewoman* 114). Her personal difficulties with the region affect the credibility of her female characters' ability to adapt to life there. The reserved heroines in the first two novels are as hopelessly out of place as Foote was in crude western towns—"superfluous," as Miss Newbold gaily admits about herself (*John Bodewin's Testimony* 35). As if to compensate for these unrealistic creations, in the next novel, *The Last Assembly Ball,* Foote gives the reader the practical Mrs. Dansken, a more authentic western character, though one who warns her young gentlemen boarders about the social problems inherent in romances between men and women of different regional and class backgrounds. Interestingly, in Foote's drawings of Leadville for her books as well as for Ernest Ingersoll's 1879 "Camp of the Carbonates" in *Scribner's,* Foote depicts only the very genteel sort of women who were her heroines in the Leadville books. Never doing any work, they lounge about with fourteen thousand–foot peaks as a backdrop, reading a book or taking a quiet stroll with well-dressed swains. Foote refrains from presenting illustrations of ordinary women like Mrs. Dansken, perhaps because they would detract from the fiction that the West was a playground for well-bred easterners. Also, they would not have been either as elegant as upper-class ingenues or as picturesque as lower-class exotics. *Century* and *Scribner's* would not have wanted illustrations of lower-class women of any stripe, one would suspect.

. . .

Foote is somewhat ambiguous about women like Mrs. Dansken in *The Last Assembly Ball*, condescending to her while at the same time giving the plain-speaking landlady her due. In our first glimpse of her, the narrator describes her as an "intrepid little widow of—let us say Denver, not to be personal" (17). This may make the reader wonder what the status of widows from Denver is and what Foote may be implying. "Not to be personal" perhaps indicates that Mrs. Dansken is anonymous, coming as she does from a place where it is impossible, for Foote at least, to "place" her socially. Women of what Foote called "good breeding"—in other words, women who had had a sheltered up-bringing—would have shuddered to be called the epithets Foote uses for Mrs. Dansken: she is "honest, shrewd," and a "merry, capable, honest little woman" (32) with "rowdy little ways" (211). This is surely damning with faint praise, but serves to alert eastern readers that the landlady is a social nobody and that they do not have to take her actions as blueprints for their own or mistake them for social perfection. Further, Foote has made it clear in the novel that whatever impromptu social set Leadville can muster does not particularly count in the eastern social hierarchy. At one point, a slightly vulgar matron, Mrs. Denny, observes that Miss Conrath "keeps her head very well for a girl who has been out so little," and the aristocratic Hilgard cannily responds, "Do you suppose a young girl from the East would call this being 'out'?" (47).

Nonetheless, a shrewd pippin like Mrs. Dansken is the most positive exam-ple of the female middle class in Foote's Leadville novels. She is an energetic shift from the conventional, pliant ingenues of romance to a more realistically rendered and mature female type. She differs from the younger, more docile characters most markedly in that she is not too refined for the West. The Misses Conrath and Newbold are last seen landing in western wastes with their new husbands, but their uneasy relation to Leadville disavows an easy, acclimated future on the frontier. Foote knew that truly aristocratic ladies and gentlemen could only be tourists in the West. Her friends Helena and Richard Gilder, for example, could never have lived in remote Leadville, as Foote's letters to them make clear. Foote held out a faint hope that they might be interested in va-cationing in the region, but it seems as if she knew that was a rather remote possibility.

Foote respects Mrs. Dansken, even as she makes fun of the widow's success-ful attempts at gentility in her boardinghouse. She approves of Mrs. Dansken's deference to her tenants' "standards, presumably higher than her own," as the narrator condescendingly describes them. Foote tells us that Mrs. Dansken, with "no artistic principles to bother her," learns good taste from her privileged eastern boarders. Luckily for her, since "she was nothing but a good imitator . . . [s]he did not attempt too much, and so she never failed in the discouraging and pitiable manner of more imaginative decorators" (27). Foote disliked the awkward pretensions of the locals in the western places she lived, particularly in Boise, preferring such people to leave matters of taste to those raised with more cultural exposure.

Mrs. Dansken's honest and straightforward way of getting her living after widowhood merits Foote's approval. Foote's own beautiful, beloved, and hard-working sister Bessie Sherman had started a boardinghouse in Boise around this time after Arthur's first financial failure bankrupted his and her families. Interestingly, this did not degrade Bessie's class status for Foote; she respected her efforts. Like Bessie, the landlady in *Last Assembly* is methodical and unpre-tentious, but Foote particularly respects Mrs. Dansken because she does not at-tempt to act above herself. Foote scorned the indeterminate social conditions in western towns, where one could call oneself "Colonel" or "Doctor" with little regard for the usually expensive and exclusive institutions that conferred those titles. Unlike these pretenders "in a land of gratuitous titles" (*John Bodewin's Testimony* 131), however, Mrs. Dansken "knew what she was in the land of in-flated values, where pippins were as good as pineapples so long as the latter were not obtainable; but she had no desire to pass for anything other than the honest, shrewd little pippin she was" (31–32). Like novelist Ellen Glasgow in *The Miller of Old Church* (1911), Foote felt that rapid upward mobility is a bad idea. Glasgow's narrator dislikes the miller in the novel because he "showed the disturbing effects of a freedom which had resulted from too rapid a change in economic conditions rather than from the more gradual evolution of class" (42). In Foote's novel, Mrs. Dansken's unassuming qualities are rewarded, and in the end she beguiles one of her well-brought-up young boarders to the ex-tent that he marries her and settles in the West.

Thus, even in her early novels, Foote wisely begins to create female protago-nists who have some refinement but are not so civilized as to be downright appalled by Leadville's provincial living conditions. Mrs. Dansken represents a shift to a more realistically rendered female type. More than carefully reared eastern girls who cavort in charming riding habits and blush at a stranger's gaze, the women who actually succeeded in the West had the personalities and class backgrounds of the fictional Mrs. Fanny Dansken or the hardworking real-life Augusta Tabor, the first Mrs. Horace Tabor. In *Led-Horse,* the narrator notes somewhat condescendingly that "it is said that the first woman of the camp [Leadville] crossed the range on foot with her husband, a German miner, and helped him set up the 'poor Lar' of the pine-board shanty during the early snows of the first autumn" (12). In her autobiography, Foote further articulates what in the novel goes unspoken about the wife in question, that she "had walked in with her man over the pass and helped him carry their goods. It would be a German wife when it came to carrying goods" (*A Victorian Gentlewoman* 166). It is difficult to mistake Foote's condescension to this sort of immigrant woman, exhibited in the mention of what she felt was a "common" nationality, and the strong, unladylike, and indeed pack-animal behaviors detailed. A lady could never have walked to Leadville or carried goods for trade, let alone turned carpenter in the freezing weather. One must be hungry and work hard to succeed in a frontier economy, and one must not mind the absence of middle- (or upper-) class comforts and nuances. With Mrs. Denny and the Irish immigrant Molly in *The Led-Horse Claim* and Mrs. Dansken and Milly in *The Last Assembly Ball,* Foote demonstrates just what sort of women could make it in the West. All are women of undistinguished background who do not have family status or undue nostalgia for their places of origin. As far as the reader knows, they left their homes because there was little opportunity and never looked back. Mrs. Dansken, in particular, is pleased to have set up her little boardinghouse business in Leadville and hence to reap the financial and social rewards from her own astute initiative. Her careful re-creation of genteel furnishings signals to the reader that she cannot have originated in the upper class. When her tenant Hugh wisely ends up marrying her, even though she is older and not as well bred as he, he thinks to himself that she is a more suitable partner for "his wandering Western life than a delicately bred, supersensitive, romantic girl from the more carefully weeded ranks of society" (211). Still, Foote feels she must add that careful and rational justification for an interclass marriage.

From a class perspective, the most interesting part of *The Last Assembly Ball* may be Mrs. Dansken's protracted misgivings about the possibly complicated social situation if she hires the beautiful Milly as a housemaid for her eastern boarders instead of an old woman or a Chinese immigrant. She makes her young tenants promise to avoid fraternization and advises them, "Behave yourselves, my dear boys, and go home and marry your own girls, to the happiness of all concerned." Mrs. Dansken somewhat obliquely explains why western girls will not do socially in the East: "Because there are women enough there already—women who are acclimated, body and soul. And how does it end? You forsake your East for the sake of your wife, or your wife for the sake of your East!" (34). Foote thus even discourages mixing up regional and cultural populations, since apparently the results can threaten the status quo that she so believes in. In *The Chosen Valley*, published three years later, Foote presents an interregional marriage where the wife—ironically, California born—lives in Europe by choice while her husband toils in a remote canyon in Idaho. The message to readers is: Stick with your own kind, and society will be run along safe and predictable lines. Step out of line, and you may end up shunned or dead.

A precursor to middle-class Mrs. Dansken is Mrs. Denny in the earlier novel *The Led-Horse Claim*, whom Hilgard scorns for few reasons except that the lady is perhaps a little hearty and unsophisticated. To her, a ball at a new hotel in Leadville represents real society, and when she blithely gushes, "I don't know what you would call being 'out' if this is n't," Hilgard is embarrassed and notes to himself, "There was a fatality about women of this kind, he had observed, and vaguely questioned whether, as related to social brutality in man, they represented cause or effect" (48). Foote has made sure to describe Mrs. Denny so that we see that she is aging quickly in this harsh ten thousand–foot climate, Foote's "altitude of heartbreak," as if that were somehow an indication of her lack of well-bred background. Nonetheless, it was not uncommon for popular American authors of the era to condescend to any "commonness" in immigrants or in native-born Americans, as a way of confirming their own gentility (see Motz and Browne).

. . .

Despite her overt upholding of upper-class standards, then, Foote allowed that less elite values often succeeded better in the West. A nonstandard interpretation of *The Last Assembly Ball* story line illustrates this. I aver that Foote has it both ways with the romance formula in *The Last Assembly Ball*, though not all critics who read the novel would agree. Maguire asserts that Foote's structure "emphasizes the grimly realistic ending" of the novel, but it is my view that aside from the naive and unlucky Frank getting himself killed in an unnecessary duel, the story has a happily realistic ending, for the female characters at least (16). In classic American tradition, the waiflike Milly moves onward and upward from the mistakes of her early life. She acquires a profession (nursing), gains some respect in the community as a result, and, after facilitating the convalescence of a prosperous Montana rancher, goes there with him as his wife. Similarly, Mrs. Dansken achieves a husband, one younger than herself and from the East. The opportunities for resourceful women thus open up in this novel, whereas Foote's ostensible hero dies because he insists on sticking to outmoded eastern or Old World standards of decorum and honor.

Most critics take the melodramatic plot of *The Last Assembly Ball* at face value and thus miss its class and feminist ramifications. Foote's first biographer, however, correctly identifies the novel's main issue as being "the dangers inherent in a shortsighted allegiance to the East" (L. Johnson 71). The rhetoric of the text sets the reader up for a grand tragedy, from the opening pages where the narrator holds forth about the "demands upon self-restraint" in a society like that of early Leadville, "which has no methods, which is yet in the stage of fermentation," to the last chapter, where the narrator laments, "Poor Frank, alas! had given occasion for all the family prophets who had ever doubted him to say, 'I told you so'"(5, 213). Foote's chapter titles also encourage a reader to agree to a tragic trajectory for the story: "Part I. The Situation" and "Part II. The Situation Developed" are followed by the climactic "Part III. The Catastrophe." Despite such formal markers of tragedy, however, the novel can be viewed as having a positive ending for the nonelite and for women. Frank's death at the end is not any kind of catastrophe. He has behaved like a shortsighted, if gallant, fool throughout the tale. Foote makes it clear that he does not love Milly—he just feels sorry for her and finds her beautiful—nor does she love him.

Susan K. Harris notes that nineteenth-century women readers read on two levels, discerning subtexts that others might miss. Accordingly, I think some would have understood *The Last Assembly Ball* to indicate that conventionally and publicly, the plot centers on Frank, the male protagonist who is fatally punished for violating eastern norms. But using Harris's terminology, our "Janus-faced" nineteenth-century readers also would detect the other more concealed message in the novel: that middle-class women's options were enlarging, at least in the West (19). Such readers might feel encouraged that even though Milly makes some mistakes in the world away from parents and support systems, she ends up not only alive but prosperous, too. In fact, the "Catastrophe" chapter turns on the scandalous revelation to all in the town that Milly was married before, was abandoned by her husband elsewhere, and had a baby who later died in the Leadville hospital. This is socially unacceptable enough apparently, but what really offends the standard-bearers of Leadville society is that when Milly first gets a job in the town, she passively lets her employers think that she is unmarried, instead of explaining her embarrassing and all but widowed state to them. It matters not that soon after her arrival in the town she learns that her husband has, indeed, died. To misrepresent oneself as a virgin was a serious offense. The conventional Leadville middle class and the few elite, too, are wedded to respectability and feel that Milly has transgressed too many codes with her egregious omissions: she must be royally snubbed. She herself feels guilty for not having been totally honest. But it is an opening up of class restrictions in the romance genre that Milly is not ruined but thrives after her shame is revealed. In real life, poor but beautiful western women sometimes married well and lived their lives in luxury. Foote's formulaic plot purports to term what happens to foolish Frank a catastrophe, but insightful readers know better. They know an artful compromise has been made and that new possibilities for women have opened up for non-"superfluous" women like Milly and Mrs. Dansken.

...

Like James Fenimore Cooper, Foote rewards only steadfast, hardworking types with upward class movement, and she avoids the rags-to-riches western stories that journalists and local colorists detailed. This is ironic, since Foote had the flamboyant real-life silver kings and queens of Leadville as possible subjects. Horace Tabor had just started keeping adulterous company with Elizabeth "Baby Doe" McCourt during Foote's second summer in Leadville. Tabor's scandalous divorce and subsequent social snubbing three years later may in fact have helped inspire the theme of *The Last Assembly Ball*, the disapprobation of a socially unsanctioned liaison.

At any rate, Foote disregards the authentic and mercurial celebrities from Leadville's boomtown streets and for upward mobility instead presents humble and worthy characters such as Molly, the loyal servant of the Conraths in *The Led-Horse Claim*. She rises to the middle class at the end of the novel when her honest timberman husband is promoted to night foreman of the newly consolidated Led-Horse–Shoshone mine. Molly is an old-fashioned kind of family retainer who exhibits deference and sympathy for her mistress and has no independent life outside her role as cook and maid. She is an unproblematic and simple character and as such elicits respect from the narrator.

Like her depiction of the devoted servants Molly in *The Led-Horse Claim* and old Ann Matthews in *The Last Assembly Ball*, Foote paints a sympathetic portrait of Babe Keesner, the faithful mountain maiden in *John Bodewin's Testimony*. With her peasant vigor and naive emotions, Babe is an Ántonia character, but unlike Willa Cather's archetypal earth mother, Babe cannot find a suitable role in Foote's class-conscious West. Babe is honest and faithful to the hero but, as she herself sadly acknowledges, is no kind of suitable match for him. Even though she has a heart of gold and saves Bodewin's life, after she realizes he is in love with someone else she still wants only his happiness and lets him go. Babe's lack of social background dooms her love, and Foote somewhat arbitrarily kills her off. Someone of Bodewin's own social class, Miss Newbold, who is a less energetic and resourceful character than Babe, gets to marry him and share his respectable life as the wife of a mine manager.

Bodewin's condescension toward Babe reveals Foote's dismissive attitude toward lower-class women, as evidenced earlier by her treatment of the immigrant German wife. Although the hero Bodewin feels sorry when Babe dies, earlier in the story he has revealed his patriarchal attitude toward her: "He would have had [Babe] come and go before his absent gaze in her beauty that was so satisfying in its strength and completeness, and be no more a problem than the sunlight on the wall" (213). Even though he admires Babe's exquisite exterior, noting that she had "nymph-like proportions" and "was to the eye perfect," Bodewin knows, as does his friend Hillbury, that she is "of a class from which he could not take a wife" (200–201, 196). When Hillbury mistakenly believes that Bodewin has had a dalliance with Babe, he outrageously refers to his friend as one of "the living dead" (197). But Babe knows her station and is no real threat to the social order. She accepts her negligible status and in a heroic if misguided gesture walks many miles to town from her mountain home in order to merely glimpse the woman Bodewin does love, "the chosen one," as she poignantly calls her. "After that," the narrator adds, "whatever came to her, it would be easy to bear" (236). Thus, in addition to validating an elite male dismissal of Babe and her ilk, Foote also presents a lowly character who is pathetically content with her lack of respect and options in the world.

· · ·

In the Leadville novels, Foote presents the reader with three types and classes of men, but only the upper echelon is given any in-depth treatment. There are the rough miners, the slightly disreputable friends of eastern men of refinement, and finally the professional eastern managers and surveyors themselves. The readers of *Century* get a glimpse of the Wild West kept in check by proper gentlemen. The lowly anonymous miners in the novels serve to swell the crowds, add local color, and fill the reader in on background details. The only lower-class men who are at all fleshed out are Babe's hillbilly father and brother in *John Bodewin's Testimony*, where hints of casual violence and lack of morality place them irredeemably beyond the pale. Foote did not want to depict too much sordidness, since to display such knowledge would be unladylike,[2] and her always precarious realism suffers as a result of this self-imposed gentility. A safe middle ground between lower and upper classes are the down-at-heel, "shipwrecked" friends of the upright managers such as the Doctor in *The Led-Horse Claim* or the nameless respectable men at the last assembly ball. Foote does not give them much personality, however, and saves her focus for the professional eastern men.

In his examination of the popularity of turn-of-the-century cultural icons Theodore Roosevelt, Frederic Remington, and Owen Wister, G. Edward White asserts that "as technological and financial triumphs, coupled with a vast increase in population of an increasingly mixed ethnic nature, made white Anglo-Saxon America, in the eyes of the native born, both the glorious and most threatened nation in the world, the role of masculinity, individualism, and gentlemanliness became of crucial interest" (197). In this vein, Foote emphasizes gentlemanliness in her western heroes, though they are capable of virile western action if circumstances demand it. On some level she is defending Anglo-Saxon America years before Wister and Roosevelt did, albeit with less xenophobia. Foote's male characters are not the dime-novel western come-from-nowhere, man-with-a-gun loners but are instead very much tied to the eastern sensibilities of their upbringing. With the refinement of Wister's 1902 Virginian, they have a more professional role to play in the West. As most are mining engineers, they are connected to eastern power structures by education and career choice.

In Foote's Leadville novels the legendary lawlessness of the West—the sensational subject of western male writers—is mostly kept in check by legal sanctions and the stalwart behavior of Foote's aristocratic heroes. And by presenting Leadville as safer than it actually was, Foote subtly encouraged settlement or tourism to *Century* readers. Centering on respectable character types kept her books decorous and publishable in family magazines in the 1880s. Even though Foote's narrator calls Leadville's streets "turbulent" and we observe that her heroes are forced to use pistols occasionally, these details are just window dressing (*The Led-Horse* 14). Instead, Foote makes Leadville one of Walter Nugent's mostly male "Type II" frontiers, friendly and understandable. In *The Led-Horse Claim*, the narrator says that the maiden Cecil does not have much personal freedom to walk or ride by herself, but in fact the novel opens with her riding solo. Later she manages to rendezvous alone with the hero at a remote location. After the mine war heats up, Cecil is told to stay indoors, but the conflict is portrayed as an isolated feud—a fearsome level of violence in the town as a whole is not emphasized. In *The Last Assembly Ball*, Leadville's boomtown turmoil takes a back seat to decorating middle-class homes and jockeying for prestige, whereas the pistol duel at the end is presented as a ludicrous anomaly dreamed up by a naive youth with his head in the medieval clouds.

We see Foote distance herself from rough-and-tumble western fiction self-consciously in *John Bodewin's Testimony*, where the heroine's father notes that John Bodewin, though indeed being "one of the types of the place, [is] . . . [n]ot the red-flannel shirt and revolver style, but something a little more subtle" (36). Later, after Bodewin has been abducted at gunpoint and has made no effort to resist his captors, the narrator feels an explanation is in order for such submissive behavior. After all, this is the Wild West, and perhaps even *Century* readers might be disappointed in a hero who meekly submits to oafs with revolvers. But Foote is determined to demonstrate that an introspective, astute hero is better than the conventional shoot-first, ask-questions-later type. She challenges macho constructions of masculinity by gentrifying the West:

> Bodewin took off the handkerchief from his eyes and looked about him with keen interest. He was turning a new page of his experience, which was likely to prove exciting, if not instructive. . . . Bodewin's courage was of a deliberate and philosophic kind. He was too indifferent to danger to seek it, nor was he possessed by that necessity to fight under any provocation which belongs to the men of the "game" variety. He was game in a somewhat different sense. He had remained quiet when he found himself disarmed, with a pistol at each ear, nor from fear of the pistols, but from an objection to an illogical suicide. His blood had been cool enough to let his mind work, and to Bodewin's mind to have invited death at such hands, and in such a manner, would have been supremely objectless and silly. (177–78)

"His blood had been cool enough to let his mind work"—this is Foote's new gentleman hero who will win out over the outlaws rumored to control the West and make it safe for *Century* readers. As Maguire notes, "Society apparently did exist in the West in the late seventies; though rules suited the frontier

situation, decorum consisted of far more than a claim and a gun" (15).[3] Foote's
men (and women) stick to decorum and avoid the gun. With Theodore Roosevelt, Foote believed that "beauty, refinement, grace are excellent qualities in a
man, as in a nation," but disagreed with him that this should "come in second
. . . to the great virile virtues—the virtues of courage, energy, and daring," as
T. R. admiringly described Owen Wister's fiction (quoted in White 197). Foote's
goal was always refinement; her male heroes succeed in the West without gratuitous shows of violence. As her friend Helena Gilder wrote years later, Foote
was "more delicate, more sympathetic, and especially more moral" than the
other authors of western fiction ("Author Illustrators" 342). Foote's male (and
female) protagonists are moral to the degree of priggishness and folly in some
cases, but they are never coarse. They may lose a little shine in the "turbulent"
streets of Leadville, but as she said many years later about one chastened male,
"He was still good to look at; and to look the man that we would be goes along
way toward feeling that we are that man" (MHF to [Benjamin Holt Ticknor?]
[ca. 1885–1895]).[4]

When she sets the scene in *The Last Assembly Ball*, Foote presents one view
of what happens to social classes in exile, asserting on the first page that "as a
matter of experience, no society is so puzzling in its relations, so exacting in its
demands upon self-restraint, as one which has no methods, which is yet in the
stage of fermentation" (5). She undercuts these ideas of fluidity in the novel but
does set up a tension about whether these properly raised young men will stand
the test. Foote admired her seemingly steadfast husband and the sophisticated
colleagues of their small Leadville circle for their strength of moral character in
the face of Leadville's temptations and pressures. When she later endeavored to
describe the atmosphere of Leadville, she noted that her husband was "the sort
of man it was safe to go to Leadville with; it would have been a regrettable experience to have gone there, that summer, with some men" (*A Victorian Gentlewoman* 174). Her early heroes are based on him and the friends they welcomed
nightly in lively salons in their tiny log cabin by an irrigation ditch. It was the
cultured traits of these men, in addition to more literary sources, that inspired
Foote to create the young, morally rigid transplants in the novels.

Although we as readers from a later century might prefer to read about the
sorts of men it was *not* safe to go to Leadville with, Foote refused to focus on
unsavory types and brought them into her novels only as necessary foils for
the very decent heroes. A representative passage demonstrates this attitude,
as the narrator of *The Led-Horse Claim* explains the optimism that certain

well-heeled men brought to Leadville: "It was, perhaps, this immense, though undisciplined, force of sanguine youth which saved the city. The dangerous elements of the camp—the mud, the weeds, and the driftwood which would have choked a more sluggish current—were floated and swept onward by its strong tide. The new board sidewalks resounded to the clean step of many an indomitable, bright-faced boy, cadet of some good Eastern family, and neophyte in the business of earning a living, with a joyous belief in his own abilities" (12). Leadville would be intolerable and not respectable, it is clear, without the cleansing influence of youth, money, family ties, privilege, and the predictable, conventional behavior that follows from the possession of such assets. The *Century* reader can picture him- or herself walking alongside these likable and unthreatening characters. Foote's narrators constantly confirm—more or less overtly—that her eastern protagonists are refined and civilized people who just happen, for legitimate reasons, to be sojourning in Colorado. Foote's heroes have plenty of what she calls "background"—in other words, an upper-middle-class upbringing and education. Proof of this can be seen when John Bodewin, riding along by himself near Leadville, comes upon a man and woman who are obviously a gentleman and a lady. Wanting to impress "the fair woman in the forest," as he terms her to himself, he makes "a hasty restoration of his hat from the *angle of comfort* on a hot afternoon with the sun on the back of one's neck, to the *level of decorum* under all circumstances" (13; emphasis added). This simple gesture, however, signifies much, for as Susan Goodman notes about Howells, Foote comprehended "the political and commercial significance of manners . . . [and] understood that the tipping of a hat brim might betray an entire system of power" (quoted in Rubin n.p.).

Century readers, demographically largely indistinguishable from such characters, would find nothing off-putting about a western society in which the *punctilios* of eastern etiquette were so rigidly observed. Such readers thus would probably have conceived of western expansion as its more lofty promoters would have wished, as a bringing of civilization to savage and empty lands. Indeed, an 1893 review in *Critic* asserted that it was "a patriotic duty to extend . . . felicitations to Mrs. Foote" for her forays into western fiction ("Literature" 379). If we accept John Kasson's assertion that "established codes of behavior have often served in unacknowledged ways as checks against a fully democratic order and in support of special interests, institutions of privilege, and structures of domination," we can see that Foote's depiction of the subtleties for gentlewomen and gentlemen served to uphold eastern class values and, further, was part of the assimilation of the West by the eastern United States (3). As Foote describes it in *John Bodewin's Testimony,* by facing down the raucous sidewalks and questionable morals in Leadville, Foote's upper-crust heroes, men who are "liable to turn up almost anywhere, those fellows—at the swell clubs in New York or London, or the President's receptions," socially transform "that unpeopled land which has no history except the records written in fire, in ice, and in water" (38, 30).

. . .

Foote's early fiction presents sometimes unrealistic and often allusive romances set in a tantalizing western locale. Due to her authorial inexperience and conservative principles, as well as the publishing pressures on her to honor gentility, she stuck to conventional gender roles and happy-ending plots. In the margins of stories depicting eastern-educated mining professionals clumsily wooing visiting gentlewomen, however, Foote conveyed the subtle changes in class expectations and possibilities that western expansion had created. Her depictions of deserved upward mobility, if rare, modestly began to break the mold for her mannered eastern protagonists. A new breed of self-made person arose, the westerner. Social changes were afoot in the West, and even Foote could not deny them. The words of Rainer Maria Rilke echo for us in peripatetic Mary Hallock Foote's two-mile-high sojourn in the West: "Beware, wanderer, the road is walking too."

Class for the Kids

The themes of Foote's children's stories center around simple child's playtimes, yet because of her tone they validate social hierarchies and pride in family background, just as in the adult texts. Generational continuity became an increasingly important concern for Foote in her life, as did the function of family in the perpetuation of class and the inculcation of gentility. Reflecting her own situation, most of Foote's children's stories touch on the exiled nature of, in her own words, "little Eastern children, transplanted in their babyhood to the far West, [who] have to leave behind them grandfathers and grandmothers, and all the dear old places associated with those best friends of childhood" (*The Little* 120). Foote explores what it means for a child to grow up apart from entrenched geographic and cultural touchstones. Her child characters exhibit refined behavior and usually are secluded from the sordid world, which was often the goal of middle- and upper-class parents at the time.

All sixteen of Foote's children's stories were first published in *St. Nicholas* magazine for children between 1878 and 1897, and though nine were later published as Houghton Mifflin's *The Little Fig-Tree Stories* in 1899, seven others remain uncollected. Almost all of them are set in either of two settings, her own green Hudson Valley or the arid canyons of Idaho, east of Boise. She lovingly and sentimentally describes "Grandfather's Farm" in the Hudson Valley, which had become run-down and was sold in 1889, and she makes picturesque Idaho canyons the setting for the unplotted idylls and slight adventures of "little Eastern children" living there. In most of her stories, she fosters "the genteel performance" in children, her recurring themes subtly reinforcing social class (Gatewood 182). But Foote steers clear of the moralistic and didactic impulses that nineteenth-century children's writers often exhibited. In this way her children's stories seem more modern and less dated than some of her adult fiction.

The topics of Foote's children's stories focus on exactly the kinds of "cultural capital" that Pierre Bourdieu asserts keep those born into the upper classes in them (*Distinction* 57). By writing for national family and children's magazines about genteel activities, Foote managed to keep her own family solvent, somewhat in the way that Harriet Beecher Stowe, *Little Colonel* author Annie Fellows Johnston, and Louisa May Alcott did in similarly dire financial straits. Like Marmee and her impoverished but hardworking daughters in Alcott's autobiographical *Little Women,* Foote had the education, skills, and connections to maintain family advantages and opportunities. She was not about to let their cultural capital drift off into the Idaho bluffs that her misguided husband spent eleven years trying to irrigate. Particularly during the Idaho years, Foote resourcefully and sometimes desperately traded on her cultural capital to bring in the essential checks from the East.

. . .

As transportation and communications improved in the United States in the late nineteenth century, social life changed. In rural areas and small towns, people had known most everyone and their relative positions, something Foote was comfortable with. In the West and in cities, however, connections and clear-cut roles mutated, as "continuity, community, and manageable scale" became confused or lost. Foote responded to these "dislocations" by withdrawing and not risking her identity and that of her family to unknown forces (Ohmann 205). This holds true in her portrayal of children. Her young people do not make friends with different sorts of children and thus learn new, less insular ways, as those in some of Alcott's stories do, for example.[1] Foote's child protagonists live remote from possibly unsettling new social dynamics, either in a tranquil world of yesterday in the "Grandfather's Farm" stories or in isolated contentment in the rural West.

Foote critics mention her children's stories fleetingly, if at all. James Maguire does not discuss her children's stories other than to categorize them as "mostly sentimental sketches or moral fables" (26). Melody Graulich, in the *Legacy* profile of Foote, correctly states that "Foote introduced children to a West quite different from the wild territory of Beadle Dime Novels" but does not go into detail (45). Graulich may have meant that even the less well-heeled children in Foote's stories are too dainty and sheltered to fit into the genre of mass-produced frontier dime novels. Rodman Paul, editor of Foote's autobiography, and Lee Ann Johnson and Darlis Miller, authors of the two Foote biographies, briefly mention the origins of some of the children's stories but do not dwell on their class implications.[2] Yet from the first, Mary Hallock Foote foregrounds assumptions about class and gentility in her children's stories, as did most other

St. Nicholas writers. These assumptions are usually coded in the details of the stories and not explicitly spelled out, for as a twentieth-century Yale alumnus and gentleman farmer from Connecticut notes, "one isn't supposed to talk of such things" (Birmingham 251). Child readers presumably would have picked up knowledge of taste, behavior, and their place in the existing hierarchy more subtly. They would have learned to read between the lines, hearing what is said and not said, observing who are the protagonists and who the supporting cast.

St. Nicholas

The leading children's magazine of its day, *St. Nicholas* had a readership that was primarily upper middle and upper class.[3] The magazine catered to discriminating readers and published the best in children's literature between 1873 and 1940. Alongside Foote were stories by Alcott (for whom Foote illustrated "Under the Lilacs"),[4] Elizabeth Stuart Phelps, Frances Hodgson Burnett, Mark Twain (Samuel Clemens), Rudyard Kipling, Howard Pyle, and editors Mabel Mapes Dodge and Frank Stockton, among others. *St. Nicholas* was not as classist as children's fare in Britain, much of which in the middle nineteenth century was either "drawing room" tales marketed to upper-class children or "cottage" tales acquainting lower-class children with their humble place in the world (Gillian Avery in Butts 42). Even British hymnals of the nineteenth century subtly prepared upper- and lower-class children for productive lives within their birth classes (Adey 88). In the United States, class differences had never been as dramatic as in Britain, but fears of European immigration, new industrial wealth, and western expansion brought class to the fore. It also created new markets for children's magazines. The arrival of generally unskilled, non-English-speaking immigrants prompted many Anglo-Americans to consolidate their power and status by means of exclusive social clubs, private colleges, and the rhetoric and ideology of family background (P. Hall 182). As Richard Ohmann notes, "Internalizing these norms counted as building character, highly prized in itself and also invaluable as a transgenerational expression of family worth" (161).

Being an elite publication, *St. Nicholas* validated the existing class system and other ethnic, racial, and gender hierarchies, although there were gestures toward equality for girls, as well as stories modeling compassion for the poor. The new emerging professional middle class in the United States was well represented, and was taught how to blend into the ruling class. To be sure, the ostensible subject matter in *St. Nicholas* was often heroes, folklore, and travel adventures, and not the minutiae of social hierarchy. Yet issues of class subtly and not so subtly permeated the magazine, from rivalries between old and new money summering on the shores of the Atlantic (see Davis) to stirring accounts of the lives of European royalty and fairy tales with princes and princesses of the blood marrying their own kind.

An assumption of comfort attends most of the fare in *St. Nicholas*. Child protagonists usually attend boarding school or female seminaries.[5] And many of the children in the stories have long summer vacations—that their families can afford such luxuries is taken for granted. Thus, as Alice Wellington Rollins depicts eastern children vacationing at their uncle's ranch in Kansas, she can blithely observe, only partially tongue in cheek, "Of the delights of visiting that [haying] camp, I forbear to write, lest those of you who—poor things!—are obliged to spend the summer at Newport or Mount Desert should have your simple pleasures spoiled for you by comparison" (70). Foote's stories also assume some of this elite background, though she sets her pieces in upstate New York or in Idaho, far from eastern watering holes and polite society.

. . .

To people of Foote's social status, the proper sort of upwardly mobile aspirant had a humble, unaggressive attitude rather than the confident, cocky attitude of the hired hand made good who snatched the Foote farm forever away from its gentry. Two examples in *St. Nicholas* magazine for children model how poor people might improve their lot without upsetting the delicate sensibilities of their social superiors. In Alcott's "Jack and Jill," Jill's mother is an English widow, "who had seen better days, but said nothing about them," and who takes any work she can to support and educate her daughter. When Jill is injured in a sledding accident, her mother says to herself, "She'll win through, please Heaven, and I'll see my lass a gentlewoman yet, thanks to the good friend in yonder, who will never let her want for care" (94). Jill's mother is grateful to her kind, rich neighbors who take pity on their humble situation, help her daughter, and scatter largess on them as they see fit. Like in *Little Women,* a rich neighbor makes life bearable in times of crisis for a deserving poor but cultivated family.

Another instance of humble upward mobility in *St. Nicholas* is in a remarkable piece by Olive Thorne Miller called "A Summer Home for Poor Children," which describes the energetic if condescending efforts to give impoverished children a week in the country once a year—perhaps a precursor to the *New York Times*'s Fresh Air Fund. A little poor girl's wholesome day is described, and the benefactors hope that after being fed and clothed properly for six days, "the poor little thing, tossing afterwards on a heap of rags, may long so much for a return of these comforts that she will resolve to learn all she can, and so better her condition." The optimistic narrator then continues, "Thank heaven! Ways of learning to be good scholars and good workers are now open in our cities to all poor little girls, so that even the most destitute may hope to be able, in time, to earn comforts and even luxuries for themselves" (648).

The key feature of these deserving poor folk is their willingness to accept slow improvement in their lot, usually by means of education or menial work. Mary Hallock Foote had no use for those who attempted to climb the social scale hurriedly without becoming educated in both culture and taste. She mentioned in letters to Helena that she herself simply would not return pretentious social calls in Leadville, and she made fun of the unsophisticated tastes of the women of Boise (June 12, 1880; January 5, 1885). Those who set out to emulate proper poise and customs deliberately by reading one of the many etiquette books of the period might have elicited Foote's polite derision, but she at least might have approved of the books' using the manners and customs of her eastern background as the "standard" (Kasson 6).

Early California and Colorado Stories

Foote's western children's stories are mostly accounts of daily life as told to a young eastern audience, the readers of *St. Nicholas*. But even as we read the perhaps too cheerful descriptions of life in the exotic West, we can see how Foote distances herself from it and is conflicted by how to portray it. One of her early stories, "A 'Muchacho' of the Mexican Camp," is a profile of one little Estaban Avilla in the desert mining camp of New Almaden, California. On the one hand, Foote makes a point to explain interesting and unfamiliar western terms and situations—relating the characteristics of the child's exotic pet horned toad, teaching the reader that *casa* is *house* in Spanish, and depicting the excitement of the mine children as they run to greet the daily stagecoach. But she unconsciously shows herself to be the materfamilias when, encountering the child Estaban on a ramble one day, she somewhat imperiously orders him to retrieve her sketching chair and then pays him to sit for her because she finds him and his horned toad picturesque. In the text, the narrator-artist, obviously Foote herself, then speculates on how this Mexican boy will spend his pay, and predicts that, due to his ethnic heritage, he will be more generous and less saving with it than a Cornish boy living there would be. According to women's historian Sandra L. Myres, this sort of racist condescension was common in California at this time for Anglos toward Hispanics, as well as for Hispanics toward Anglos.

Foote's racism is in line with the attitudes of other *St. Nicholas* authors. Almost anyone who is not Anglo-Saxon in culture or race is either cheerfully exotic or darkly degenerate. A *St. Nicholas* piece on a Chinese boy living in China breezily relates quaint ancient Chinese customs but then purports to show how Christianity has improved the lives of ordinary Chinese people (Wingate). A discussion of a photographic portrait of a Paiute woman and her two small children, however, calls them "rather poor creatures," and laments that they are bereft of useful culture. It is explained to the young reader, however, that "white missionaries have exerted such a good influence" that the Native Americans may soon be able to change their old ways and get in step with mainstream American society ("An Indian Mother" 29).

Foote's New Almaden "Muchacho" sketch also evidences her concern about family origins and the importance of placing and stratifying people, even in the West. As Richard W. Etulain states, "Unlike other women regionalists such as Mary Austin and Willa Cather, Foote rarely uses settings to picture a frontier West vigorously shaping character over time. Rather, she utilizes western scenes to make comparisons with a static eastern society and culture" (*Re-imagining* 13). Revisionist historians of the West such as Patricia Nelson Limerick note that this is not unusual and aver that eastern values and prejudices went west with the wagons. In "Muchacho," the narrator categorizes the camp children, whose fathers are day-laboring miners, by their country of origin. Like most western mining towns, New Almaden was carefully divided into ghettoes, in this case Cornish, Anglo, Mexican, and Chinese, and Foote is merely recording the norms of the time and place. She relates a significant exchange in which she asks a little Anglo girl about her background. The child becomes confused and asserts that she is not Cornish or indeed "'Merican" but actually *English*, even though she was born "down to San Jose." Foote relates that another little Anglo girl then pipes up that she is not sure *where* she comes from, only that it is "in a kind 'o brown house back there" (81). This ignorance is perhaps significant to Foote.

She chose to include a moment like this because being rooted was so important to her, and she thought of these mining urchins as a different sort of creature from anyone in her own family: whatever their ethnicity, they were picturesque but uncivilized, with no background. Respectable class status for Foote involved family and ties rooted to a stable core, and this was not to be found (for her) in the West. Foote had her first child soon after this story was written and was to keep her three children out of contact with local children for most of their youth. It troubled her that these California camp children in "Muchacho" lacked any notion of heritage and permanence. Soon after Foote wrote the piece, she and her husband moved to Santa Cruz, where she wrote to Helena Gilder that her new baby "is greatly admired *here*—but I consider that there is no competition here. There isn't a well-bred child in the place scarcely—you know what I mean" (Fall 1877). When Foote first moved from New York State, she naturally believed that social standing meant connection to the East. Although some critics feel she later became westernized, a strong case can be made that her views on society and class persisted with only minor emendations during her many subsequent years in the West.

. . .

The three "Grandfather's Farm" sketches, collected in *The Little Fig-Tree Stories,* reflect Foote's concern as a parent that her children were growing up rootless westerners and might not end up sharing her respect, nostalgia, and reverence for the settled and cultured East. The Foote farm in Milton, New York, which had been in the family for five generations, was sold a year or two before Foote wrote the sketches. Like Stowe, Cather, and Henry James, among others, Foote felt that a civilized epoch in American history was vanishing as her parents' generation dwindled. With James she had "a dread of vulgarity, and even a theory that it was increasing in the society that surrounded [her]" (*Washington Square* 38). In writing these stories, Foote honored a part of herself along with the past, in this case the Hudson Valley and its Quaker traditions. In the first of the three pieces, "The Gates on Grandfather's Farm," she frankly states, "For the sake of these younger ones, deprived of their natural right to the possession of grandparents, the mother used to tell everything she could put into words and that the children could understand about the old Eastern home where her own childhood was spent, in entire unconsciousness of any such fate as that is involved in the words 'Gone West'" (120–21). Foote's choice of language in this passage indicates the disaffection she felt at having to live in the West. Yet because this was to be a children's text, she tries to keep an upbeat tone. After her deprecating remarks about the "natural right" of children to grandparents and the "fate as that which is involved in the words 'Gone West,'" she lightens her tone: "The catalogue of grandfather's gates always pleased the children, because in the cañon there were no gates, but the great rock gate of the cañon itself, out of which the river ran shouting and clapping its hands like a child out of a dark room into the sunlight, and into which the sun took a last peep at night under the red curtain of the sunset" (121). These sentiments sound more like what we might expect in nineteenth-century children's fare, with her implausible explanation of why her children might request to hear about *gates,* of all incongruous and nonfascinating things, and her charming depiction, like those in Robert Louis Stevenson's *Child's Garden of Verses* (1885), of the river acting like a cheerful child and the sun peeping playfully under a curtain.

The Grandfather's Farm stories present a picture of an old and stable family whose history gives it a sense of importance, especially when Foote leaves the frame narratives of the sketches and plunges into descriptions not only of grandfather's gates but also his sheep and their nurture, the farmhouse attic and its treasures, the customs of the farm, the artifacts in the guest bedroom, and even the family graveyard. Cather's loving portrayal of Old Mrs. Harris's "comfortable rambling old house" back in Tennessee has the same ring of history and gentility (*Obscure Destinies* n.p.). As Klaus Eder notes, "What separates 'real' classes of people is ability to justify the legitimacy of one's own culture. . . . [T]hose who can better justify have the better chance of prevailing" (92). As Foote describes farm ways and family customs and documents the storied associations of "all the dear old places" of her own youth, she reclaims and indeed elevates the significance of her family history (120). In a *St. Nicholas* story by Alcott, a girl guilelessly declares about her father, whose ancestors were English gentry, "He's only a farmer now, but it's nice to know we were somebody two or three hundred years ago" ("An Old-Fashioned Thanksgiving" 8). Foote indeed felt that she and her people were "somebody," and that their gentle and civilized ways should be documented and, she hoped, emulated. In her Grandfather's Farm stories, then, she makes, in Cather's description of Annie Fields's house, a "place where the past lived on—where it was protected and cherished, had sanctuary from the noisy push of the present" (*Not Under Forty* 61).

Changes in American manufacturing, transportation, and communications—the very changes that allowed Foote's husband to move west to work, as well as made it possible for Foote herself to heavily supplement his wages by writing for magazines whose editorial offices and indeed readership were thousands of miles away—came from the same forces that made the charming, self-contained, self-sufficient world of the Hallock family farm obsolete. After one can cheaply buy manufactured household items, such as soap, candles, foodstuffs, and clothes, many of the elaborate and time-consuming tasks of a farm, so picturesque to those not doing them, are no longer as necessary.[6]

Manufacturing advances aside, there may have been a more feminine reason Foote might have cataloged her family's artifacts so reverently: her family's respectability and lineage were bound up in them. Jean Gordon and Jan McArthur explain that in earlier less mass-produced times, because "household objects were scarce and passed on from generation to generation, they could have multiple layers of meaning for the women who looked after them." Harriet Beecher Stowe notes this in *The Pearl of Orr's Island:* "Every plate, knife, fork, spoon, cup, or glass was as intimate . . . as instinct with home feeling, as if it had a soul" (both quoted in Motz and Browne 30). This love of family objects was part of the woman's sphere in this era, genteel or otherwise. As a well-connected twentieth-century matron put it: "There must be continuity in a family, and when there is continuity in the things it treasures it is even better" (quoted in Birmingham 293). A simple yet telling example of this is in *The Chosen Valley,* where the narrator makes a point to explain that a certain glass tumbler has survived untold years in an irrigation camp due to the conscientiousness of a loyal family housekeeper.

...

One of the prime functions of cultural fare like *St. Nicholas* was to help form the taste of children. In this Foote excelled, especially in the Grandfather's Farm sketches, since her topic was "the unmodernized picturesque," in Richard H. Brodhead's phrase (163). She accurately felt that, if not trained in discernment, children would not be able to appreciate the things that made the way of life in the Hudson Valley superior to that in rural Idaho. Sociological research finds that taste is indeed quite specific; it relates to one's historical and sociological position, as one Bourdieu critic explains (Lucy Burke in Ardis and Lewis, *Women's Experience*). In many ways—for example, the description in "The Garret at Grandfather's" of the semiannual house cleaning and seasonal storage changes in the attic—we see Foote's respect for an organized household, one that retains handed-down objects in order to sustain future generations. Another story meanders through Grandfather's guest room, listing and describing everything in it, indicating that, like the elderly, transplanted French father in Cather's *Shadows on the Rock,* Foote disliked change and innovation. In her eyes, conservative housekeepers like her mother, whose linen styles and "mantel's treasures never varied or changed places," were valued role models (*The Little* 172). Foote's loving catalogs of her parents' farm both confirm her own class position as well as instruct the young in how to carry it forth. The lists of objects that Foote chooses to share with her children and the *St. Nicholas* audience—itself a subset of what her ancestors and family chose to save—reveal her tastes and priorities. From her word pictures of the farm's prosaic inventory, Foote demonstrates that worn objects such as tools or clothes—all originally of good quality—should be admired for their stalwart service and, accordingly, carefully maintained as long as possible.

How would this have gone over with *St. Nicholas* readers? Since the emerging upper middle class did not need to live a slow, cyclical farm life and preferred buying the new mass-produced household goods to making them, these glimpses into the recent past would have been pleasant period pieces, ones that might have caused parents to smile, remembering the routines and the hard work of their youth. Family magazines liked to run this sort of nostalgic story in what Brodhead calls their "monthly renewed public imagining of old-fashioned social worlds." Quaint regional customs and people who did not yet fit into complicated contemporary life became "a symbol of union with the pre-modern chosen at the moment of separation from it," and as such made the modern reader feel his or her superior fitness to rule (in Dimock and Gilmore 155). In *House of Mirth* (1905), Edith Wharton has Lily Bart discover that the traditions of her well-born but now poor family are irrelevant in the changing world, but Foote never fully acknowledged that irrelevance, even if in her more lucid moments she suspected it. As an old woman she wore a lace Quaker cap and still used the quaint "Thees" and "Thous" with intimates—clearly, she was never ready to jettison her roots (E. Gardiner personal interview).

Like Vladimir Nabokov, who admitted that he made a "careful reconstruction of my artificial but beautifully exact Russian world," Foote deliberately re-created a perfect world from her own nostalgic memories (quoted in Seidel 167). Her eulogy for her tradition's tasteful Bourdieuian "everyday choices of everyday life" served to console her and at least tried to influence a new generation (*Distinction* 5–6). Foote's imaginative facsimile of an exiled place may seem more important and more real—to her and to the reader—than the original. As James Clifford notes, "*Objets trouvés* are not just occasions for reverie. This they surely are, but they are also signs of vanishing worlds," certainly true for the Hallock attic and other relics from Grandfather's Farm (157). Whether because she felt the loss of the farm keenly when writing the Grandfather's Farm sketches or whether she became so caught up in what for her was a pleasant nostalgic activity, the places and artifacts from Milton are depicted with a sustained level of emotional intensity rare for Foote. As she validated the material culture of her beloved "long-settled communities" along the Hudson, in the process she left for her descendants and for later readers the *feeling* of tradition (*The Little* 135). This is perhaps as useful, or as damaging, as actually having ancestral houses, heirloom mantel ornaments, and old lace still in the family.

Idaho Stories

The Idaho sketches in *The Little Fig-Tree Stories* portray the mild escapades of the Foote children, thinly disguised as "Jack" and "Polly," as they play in the canyon that is their home and world. We hear about a stray lamb that the children tried (and failed) to nurse back to health, Polly's love for horses, Jack's visit to a nearby miner's claim, autumn activities in the canyon, and the family's weeklong fishing expedition down the Boise River. The children of these tales drift through their exploits with the unconsciousness of real children; they do not act lonely or exiled in the canyon—Foote merely walks them through simple canyon-based activities. They have little unique personality, but perhaps this is useful. As with the generic dime novels of the era, Foote's unidiosyncratic children's stories allow readers to project themselves into a safe western scene and live a western fantasy. Since Foote depicts generic western landscapes and generic children as protagonists, the reader has the freedom to fill in the details. It is only in the sometimes wistful, sometimes disparaging, and often eastward-looking comments of the narrator-mother that the reader discerns that this is not your average pioneer family from the Little Stone House in the Canyon. The materfamilias narrator never lets the reader forget that Jack and Polly are part of a cultured eastern family, albeit temporarily in exile.

And indeed the children in the Idaho stories do not do much work at the ranch. They have a few unspecified duties but are mostly free to play. This situation is similar to most story backdrops in *St. Nicholas,* but not accurate about the United States in general and the West in particular. Children's historian Anne Scott MacLeod notes that children of the early nineteenth century "were more often than not working members of their families and communities," and although Foote's stories are written decades later, living conditions in the West would have reflected an earlier era (131). Gillian Avery asserts that nineteenth-century American children were more independent and mature than British children due to the lack of a servant class in America; children learned about work and the real world early (in Richardson 24). Elliot West notes that children's perceptions were "deepened by work, play, and exploration" in the West, but Jack and Polly frolic and amuse themselves, enacting their upper-middle-class status and having none of the interesting work of western pioneering that, for example, Laura Ingalls Wilder depicts in her *Little House* series (252). And they are clearly a different class of being from the shabby but savvy boy and his dispirited, dislocated mother who turn up in the canyon in Foote's story "A Four-Leaved Clover in the Desert" (1894)

The years in Idaho (1884–1895) were Foote's most difficult, living as she and her family did usually ten miles outside the provincial capital, Boise, with the specter of financial uncertainty and even ruin always hovering. Foote wrote out of dire necessity in this decade, and as a result the themes of exile and precarious class position are ever present in both her children's and her adult texts. Although Foote's family situation was, as her biographers and critics have noted, not unlike the isolated and family-oriented farm of her childhood, Foote deeply regretted being so far from the cultural center of her universe, New York. She appreciated some aspects of the West, but would have preferred to "choose her country," as she phrases it for a heroine in a later novel, *The Royal Americans* (1910) (119). With the money Foote made in Idaho, she not only supplemented (and usually surpassed) her husband's irregular salary but also kept a Chinese cook and sent her boy off to an eastern preparatory school. She also paid to have an educated British spinster, who was the daughter of her art school mentor (and incidentally the stepdaughter of English journalist Eliza Lynn Linton), tutor her children so that they would not have to go to the local Boise schools. Rodman Paul comments that the Foote household was "of surprising proportions for a family of precarious means" (introduction to *A Victorian Gentlewoman* 26). Like her own depiction in "A Cloud on the Mountain" of Mrs. Tully, an unhappy eastern mother making do in Idaho, Foote never forgot her own "former standards of comfort and gentility: for [she] had been a woman of some social pretensions, in the small Eastern village where she was born" (*In Exile* 156).

Foote's narrators' descriptions of western places often start out defensively, as they take the time to explain the lack of lineage and hence respectability of the wild, raw land. In a description of the complicated geology of Idaho in "An Idaho Picnic" (1887), the narrator feels she has to defend her exiled home from the possible criticism that it is not fit subject matter for literature. She remarks that "the river as it flows past the camp is still very young and inexperienced," and in addition, "Its canons [*sic*] have never echoed to a locomotive's scream; it knows not towns or villages; not even a telegraph pole has ever been reared on its banks." But, she continues, "Young and provincial as it is, it has an ancestral history very ancient and respectable, if mystery and tragedy and years of reticence can give dignity to a family history" (*The Little* 55–56). Here Foote adopts the same strategy with this western subject as she later did with the arid California orchard in "The Flower of the Almond and the Fruit of the Fig." By consciously coupling aspects of her western locale with traditional attributes of high social class—reticence, respectability, and dignified family history—she brings the concept of class into new territories. And Foote apparently enjoys her technical knowledge in this regard, noting that whereas "the river's story has been patiently recorded on the tablets of the black basalt bluffs that face each other across its channel, . . . [t]heir language it is not given everybody to read" (56). She then launches into an extensive geologic "sequence of events" that accounts for the unusual land forms in the region.

Note the use, typical of Foote, of the term *tablets* for what the mythic history of the canyon is written on. In the same passage she describes the prehistoric lava eruption in the canyon as "a battle between the heavens and the earth" (56). She often makes Old and New Testament references and parallels such as this, in both her children's and her adult texts. At one point she notes that Idaho is a "strange, biblical land," capable of inspiring poets (quoted in Pearson 52). In her era Foote's use of biblical and other more obscure literary references connected her western material to mainstream culture, although often now the more obscure quotes and allusions confound her meaning.

Not surprisingly, many *St. Nicholas* writers writing about the West also used the East as a cultural touchstone, but they reveled in the newness of the West and usually painted more glowing pictures. Alice Wellington Rollins has an eastern boy on a Kansas vacation note that even though "he had not been berrying and he had not had a sail, . . . he believed he had done everything else that a boy could do to have a good time" (69). A normal vacation, it is implied, takes place by the eastern seashore, and even though young Fred is satisfied with his holiday, he feels he must defend its exoticness and westernness.

Similarly, on multiple levels, Foote's western children's stories identify the

East as superior to the West, despite nods to the uniqueness of the western experience. In a non–Jack and Polly story set in an Idaho canyon similar to theirs, a local doctor's beautiful new horse is described as being from "grass country" and is "no cayuse, nor mustang, nor scraggy Texas pony" ("A Four-Leaved" 644). Idaho was never Foote's favorite place. Thoroughbreds, it is implied, come from the East, and the doctor's "noble mare" has class: "She was kind and graceful and intelligent, as a thoroughbred should be" (645). In contrast, the generally hapless and history-less "desert settlers" in the story are thus described: "Most of them had been unfortunate in one way or another; and many were merely restless men who never stayed in any place, but tried all climates and ways of getting a living, always hoping to find a way of getting one without working for it." Keep in mind that this bitterness and cynicism is exhibited in a *children's* story. Then Foote shifts her gaze from the rabble to her story's protagonists: "But the best of [the desert settlers] were, like Hester's father, men to whom difficulties have a certain attraction; strong, hopeful men of their hands, with courage to conquer a home out of the desolate waste places" (644). This paean to Hester's father is quite positive, yet the phraseology seems a bit too pat. Foote *tells* us with clichés instead of *showing* us what a laudable pioneer the man is. In one of her novels Foote says about a similar character that he "showed in his striking person that union of good blood with hard conditions so often seen in the old-young graduates of the life schools of the West" (quoted in Etulain, *Re-imagining* 13).

Such glimmers of optimism are rare in Foote concerning the effect of the West on a person's character. More often than not capable men become "shipwrecked" in the West. Hester's sturdy father turns out to be more western oriented than her mother, who misses the East and shuns contact with impoverished local squatters, fearing they will teach her child coarse language or give her diseases. The uneducated squatter boy, however, assisted by Hester's father, saves the day and finds water in the dry canyon. This only partially undercuts the ringing elitist, pro-East sentiments that lace the story, from the noble mare's lineage to the unappealing descriptions of the dusty landscape and the mother's suspicion of vagrant settlers.

···

Foote was not alone in keeping concerns about social class visible in her children's stories. Class lurks in most stories of the era, not surprisingly with female writers seeming more concerned about social niceties than the males. Men often wrote travel and adventure sagas, which focus the reader outward. It is easier to put aside the nuances of Victorian respectability in Rudyard Kipling's or Robert Louis Stevenson's tales from abroad or Twain's midwestern exploits, let alone in western novel series for boys, with escapades in canyons; battles against Indians, floods, and rustlers; and life-or-death circumstances with prairie fires and howling blizzards. The often nationalistic and sometimes racist American male fare was a far cry from the generally tamer stories by women writers, which tend to depict more domestic subjects, with the attendant social context and class consciousness.

An early adult short story by Foote, "In Exile," explains these differing priorities, particularly as they apply to the West. A young eastern schoolmistress and an eastern mining engineer who meet while living in a remote part of California concur that it is rare for women to be content in new isolated areas of settlement. All the uprooting to the West, and the freedom associated with it, they note, "is a man's idea of happiness . . . [since] most women require a background of family and friends and congenial surroundings" (15, 17–18). As has been noted, some western women adapted happily to western deracination, but Foote did not. For personal reasons, then, as well as to distinguish herself from male adventurers and dime-novel stereotypes, Foote sticks to stay-at-home tales of domesticated eastern and western children.

Although she perpetuated social class distinctions in her stories, Foote avoided the "lessons" and moralizing favored by Alcott and earlier-nineteenth-century, often Christian-themed, sentimentalists on both sides of the Atlantic. Alcott, Burnett, Johnston, and many others often designed tales that put children of the upper class in contact with ones less fortunate. Depending on the story, a message is frequently imparted about helping the poor, and just as often the less well-heeled children have important lessons to teach their social superiors. Without that moral high ground or noblesse oblige mentality, and without the psychological complexity of Twain or, later, Kenneth Grahame, for example, Foote and her narrator sometimes fall back on mere description of backdrops. And even though the digressive narrator-mother may seem fussy and distracting to present-day sensibilities, she is less pious than many other children's narrators. Her refreshing lack of didacticism, however, also leaves her a bit faceless. She generally keeps the reader engaged, with her meticulous details of running a nineteenth-century farm or setting up western mining claims, but her accounts can seem flat and leave the reader wanting more emotional engagement. Foote's children's stories did serve a function, however—

aside from keeping Foote's own family solvent—of introducing a polite western vision to the *St. Nicholas* crowd, even if the vision was more two-dimensional than three and more mannered than realistic.

Merely by setting her texts in the West, Foote was in the process of creating what Washington Irving referred to as "storied and poetical associations" of her chosen region (10). And she went out of her way to let eastern readers situate themselves in this new landscape, such as in "A 'Muchacho' of the Mexican Camp," where she makes a point to educate her juvenile audience about things western. One of the most rewarding aspects of Foote's writing in exile was sharing her impressions with friends and those who she felt would appreciate the strangeness or beauty she observed around her. Her first piece for *Scribner's* was in fact a patchwork of her letters that her friends the Gilders put together. This lifelong letter and fiction writing became a form of power for Foote, not only economic power but also power to control what others might think about her life or the West, or even about mining and irrigation engineering. Being a protected woman, she did not want her western details too gritty, and she knew that to some degree her adult and child audiences wanted to be shielded similarly. They wanted charming local color details, and she provided them.

Like countless other travel, colonial, and exiled writers, Foote wrote with confidence, knowing that few had the knowledge to contradict her. She seemed to enjoy this cultural superiority in "Muchacho," and in the Idaho sketches, too—deftly explaining the layout of an irrigation engineer's base camp, what domestic and unbroken animals are colloquially termed on the range, and what a "typical" Chinese miner might wear. In a telling comment to her editor at *Century,* when the question came up about the western station stops in a story for adults set entirely on a train ride, Foote remarked cavalierly that "I tried to change that, but it involves too many other changes, and does not give him enough time on the sleeper with the girl: and nobody knows where Pocatello is" (MHF to RWG, November 23, 1893). She was the first to bring some kind of muse into the western region, and although she did not want to settle in Idaho in particular, once there she seemed to get an obscure sort of pleasure out of sending back her exclusive version of it.

Because Foote has strong reasons to defend her cultural capital and the status it conferred, she rarely criticized the system that in fact perpetuated much social inequality. Her "status anxiety" kept her from any sustained social disparagement. Other children's writers, such as Burnett on the other hand, often had characters who empathize with the impoverished and the kinds of inappropriate behavior that poverty sometimes prompts. In Burnett's charming "Editha's Burglar" from *St. Nicholas,* privileged young Editha innocently muses to her father that perhaps the reason burglars burgle is because "they can't help not having had advantages" (in Frye 230). The burglar who eventually breaks into Editha's house is so startled by her sympathy for his underprivileged plight that he does not harm her and desists from taking her mother's things because she requests it of him. Although in the end Burnett upheld the class status quo in "Editha," as well as in her other children's stories, she at least asked some Dickensian questions about economic inequities, inherited wealth, and class opportunities.

Foote did not ask such questions in her stories, although she shared Burnett's belief in "character" as being a crucial personal attribute. The closest Foote got to questioning class assumptions was in "A Four-Leaved Clover in the Desert," where a resourceful but indigent squatter boy in Idaho, who has been snubbed by a snobbish eastern wife, finds a hidden spring that saves their arid community. The boy's success can be read as a criticism by Foote of the woman's, and Foote's own, snobbery, although elitism in general and eastern-centric attitudes are validated in the story as a whole. Foote's views on class, in her children's stories and elsewhere, were comparable to Alcott's a generation earlier in that they both believed that class divisions were real and valid, that birth and background mattered, and that social hierarchy needed to be respected.

When writing for children, some western authors became caught up in romantic rustic fantasies, but Foote could do this convincingly only about the East. Her Grandfather's Farm stories present a lovely vision of ordered rural life in upstate New York, where in the old Quaker saying, "Many hands make light work," and family history makes the homestead breathe reassurance and love. But once in the West, Foote could not keep the vision going: her backgrounds in Leadville or Idaho seem less interesting. They lack the traditions and storied associations of the Hudson, and come off like mere travelogues or pastiches. Even in her generally mellow autobiography Foote calls her Boise days "darkest Idaho!" continuing with the descriptor: "thousands of acres of desert empty of history" (*A Victorian Gentlewoman* 265). The Idaho children's stories are more realistic and, aptly, grimmer in tone than others, as they soberly present child protagonists having unremarkable sojourns in dry, unloving, and unstoried places.

Louisa May Alcott, on the other hand, wrote of uncultured girls and boys living joyous, honest, innocent lives in rural backwaters; often the elite folk in their milieu are unhappy, duplicitous, inauthentic, or bored. Alcott's rustics bring new American energy to elites: in "The Princess and the Brownie," a feckless princess learns from a poor peasant's daughter that hard work and a simple diet improve one's quality of life and character, and in "Baa, Baa," two country girls show by their compassion to thirsty sheep being transported by railway that they are better people than the careless, greedy adults in charge of the stock company. Foote's child characters do not usually play the sentimental Victorian role that Alcott liked—that of the youth teaching adults by way of moral example—but unless situated in Foote's Hudson River setting, her kids simply are not part of any social or class system. This reflects how Foote's family may have felt when they lived in the Idaho canyon some miles east of Boise. In the Idaho novels her adults are aware of class and social proprieties, as is her children's narrator, but not surprisingly the children themselves are not.

· · ·

Although Foote's fictional children never stray from gentility and the assurance of family background, they are not truly privileged. They are, of course, shielded from the harsh facts of life that make *Tom Sawyer* or *Huck Finn* so interesting. But unlike the aristocratic if sometimes temporarily impoverished children in Burnett's *Little Lord Fauntleroy* or *A Little Princess* or Annie Fellows Johnston's southern *Little Colonel* series, Foote's little ladies and gentlemen are really only middle class. She portrays a very proper world, but one without the trappings of real wealth or social position. Her children do not have the rigorous lessons, busy social life, or exotic travel that the true elite could offer their children, the world that Helena Gilder's children, for example, would have known. Often one gets the feeling reading about elite children from this era that they will soon follow in their parents' successful career paths as captains of industry or landed gentry living off their holdings. Despite their exclusivity, Foote's child protagonists are not being groomed for this leadership path. On some level, of course, they are complicit in the American White Man's Burden to subdue the West or to promote national hegemony, but Foote engaged in little of the jingoistic, imperialistic rhetoric that so offends revisionist critics (see especially Singh).

How Foote managed to maintain her own children's gentility in the wilds of Idaho or California would have been interesting reading—after all, the family had a Chinese cook and an English governess much of the time. These themes are not a focus in her children's fiction, however, or in her adult books, either. A story about how the well-educated governess found rural Idaho in the

1880s might have been particularly apropos for *St. Nicholas* readers. In a story for adults, "The Harshaw Bride," Foote describes how her private educational arrangements probably strike the locals in Boise: "We are hardly up to the resident-governess idea as yet. It is thought to be wanting in public spirit for parents not to patronize the local schools. If they are not good enough for the rich families, the poor families feel injured, and want to know the reason why" (*A Touch of Sun* 207).

Nonetheless, Foote's views on elite education were not monolithic, and it is gratifying that in a story in the same collection, we read criticism of exactly such an exclusive western education. In "A Touch of Sun," heiress Miss Benedet, who was raised according to her mother's cranky ideas of perfection and somewhat like the Foote children but richer, explains, "I was not allowed to play with ordinary children; they might have spoiled my accent or told me stories that would have made me afraid of the dark; and while the perfect child was waited for, I had only my nurses. I was not allowed to go to school, of course. Schools are for ordinary children. When I was past the governess age I had tutors, exceptional beings, imported like my frocks" (44). Here Foote cleverly disparages the way she would have liked to bring up her own children, and has the repressed teenage Miss Benedet finally break out of such suffocation and try to elope with a cowboy ranch hand. Foote seemed to realize that youngsters will rebel if they are treated like hothouse flowers and not allowed ordinary playmates and nonelite experiences. Even so she keeps her fictional children segregated from the local kids—whether poor whites in the East or poor pioneers in the West—but it is not clear what advantage this gives them other than to be respectable enough to appear in *St. Nicholas*.

．．．

The complexities of social class that made British and eastern American nineteenth-century novels so interesting "had a deadening effect on children's books," and only the best authors like Burnett or Alcott managed to include them effectively, if not always perfectly realistically (Gillian Avery in Butts 42). Foote's class tags in "Menhaden Sketches: Summer at Christmas-Time" make this point. The narrator presents a modest but uneducated sea captain who finds himself among leisured summer people after his boat is wrecked near their beach hotel on Long Island. The young seaman is described as having a "high-bred line" to his head, despite his lowly status (123). Foote must have felt that it would be inappropriate in a children's story to explain more fully the tensions between a stranded, inarticulate man of the sea rooming in a boardinghouse with families on vacation—sharing the hallways, seeing them take their daily swim on the beach where he works daily to rebuild his vessel. Nonetheless, a character in the story soberly observes, "The contrast must have been rather cruel between his own outlook and the easy, graceful, summer holiday life of his entertainers [the summer people]" (122). The narrator dryly notes that the captain would not know what to do at the multiple-course dinners at the hotel. Children reading the story might sense from this that the captain is a different sort of person from the vacationers, yet really not understand the reason for the narrator's kind condescension. In another story, set at Grandfather's Farm, Foote describes a traveling organ grinder's polite deference to small children and the few pennies they give him, but she does not explain why the narrator discreetly notes that, unlike these children, some people find organ grinders "a nuisance" (*The Little* 130).

Foote is more successful when she confronts class head-on, as she does describing the segregated ethnic neighborhoods in a California mining town in "A 'Muchacho' of the Mexican Camp" or animating transparently class-conscious trees in "The Flower of the Almond and the Fruit of the Fig." In this story, class and perhaps also ethnic hierarchies are transplanted to western settings. In the spirit of "The Fir Tree" by Hans Christian Andersen and "The Silver Party" by Alcott, the story presents sentient household artifacts and paints a pretty Victorian tableau replete with class rivalry, pious moralizing, and stern judgment. Darlis Miller dismisses the tale as "insubstantial" (189). Lest we think that Foote's views were utterly anachronistic for her day, she wrote to her publisher that this story had been one of her most popular stories, inspiring letters from fans. "Many persons who don't remember the other stories speak to me of this one," she boasted (MHF to Houghton Mifflin, June 28, 1899).[7] In "The Flower of the Almond," Foote gives characterizations and speech to an orchard of trees in arid northern California. It is spring, and when the young, foolish almond trees flower before the last frost has passed, older trees look on and discuss the wise and foolish habits as well as the lineage of the various species planted on the hillside. We can see Mary Hallock Foote laying out her views on heredity, tradition, and regional differences as she puts anachronistic sentiments into the "mouths" of these exiled western trees. Recall that by this time she had lived more than twenty-five years in the West.

Much like the class-conscious sterling and plate silverware in Alcott's "Silver Party," the orchard trees in Foote's story quarrel and chat about their fellows, debating whether the almond trees should have bloomed so early. The almonds claim that their eastern forebears had always bloomed this early, and that it had done them no harm—ignoring the fact that they themselves dwell in a very different climate from their ancestors. This adherence to regional tradition reflects a concern that troubled Foote throughout much of her time in the West. She altered her eastern customs only very slowly—Wallace Stegner suggests not at all (*Angle* 85).

Although Foote could not entirely embrace the West and its different expectations, she could create characters that could. When the prim Normandy pear tree, who the narrator carefully tells us "bore one of the oldest names in France," validates the almonds' imprudent yet traditional blooming schedule by stating that "inherited tendencies are strong in people of good blood," the feisty, nonelitist crab apple tree pipes up that the pear tree is old-fashioned and inappropriate to hark back to Europe and the Bible for validation of traditions (*The Little* 2). "We go back to the 'Mayflower,'—that is far enough for us," the crab apple says, supporting a new and distinctly American set of standards, albeit elite ones (2–3). Of course, in this exchange, the characters and the narrator assume that it is appropriate for eastern American customs to dictate western horticultural practice. Nevertheless, we see that Foote champions, in theory at least, the making of new cultural touchstones, even as she clearly adheres to traditional notions of class roles in other aspects of the tale.

In writing a text as mannered and full of moral arguments about lineage and its relation to redemption as "The Flower of the Almond," Foote at once elevates her material into the high genre of allegory and fable and makes "storied and poetical associations" for the dry foothills of northern California (Irving 10). As Darlis Miller notes, the elitist tone of the tale relegates it to a mere period piece for later readers, but nonetheless Foote's devotion to things eastern and her concern with social status were perhaps shared by many of the parents who paid for *St. Nicholas* subscriptions. Foote called it one of her "so-called successes," noting that it was "a great favorite with [her] California friends" (MHF to Houghton Mifflin, June 28, 1899).[8]

Children in the West

St. Nicholas stories and set pieces often extolled the natural beauty and interesting challenges for young people in the West, but Foote, though she nodded to these themes, stood her provincial eastern ground and judged them by the

East. Willa Cather explains that as a child she preferred the Nebraska frontier with its many immigrants to her stratified Virginia birthplace, since "struggle appeals to a child more than comfort or picturesqueness, because it is dramatic. No child with a spark of generosity could have kept from throwing herself heart and soul into the fight these people were making to master the language, to master the soil, to hold their land and to get ahead in the world. . . . [T]he life of every family was like that of the Swiss Family Robinson" (quoted in Porter 53). Although Foote could empathize sometimes on an intellectual level with the fight the settlers were putting up, she could not do so enough to re-create their joys and sorrows, their challenges and victories. Their crude attempts at civilizing the West did not stir her deeply, as we know from her lack of interest in most of the inhabitants of Boise, and later Grass Valley. She made friends with a few of the military and political people in Boise, and supported the local library, in fact, but as she lived aloof from the locals, she, too, kept her characters aloof from them in her writing.

It is ironic that by distancing her child protagonists from the local riffraff in order to maintain her and their class advantage, Foote denied the reader much interesting local flavor, particularly of the West. Most *St. Nicholas* authors writing about the West in the 1880s and 1890s made more of an attempt at plot than Foote, although simple travelogues like hers or descriptions of vacation trips were common also. Like Foote, many writers assumed the superiority of eastern ways and were careful to situate their child protagonists as children of patrician ranchers or large landowners. The West was portrayed as exotic and wild, to be tamed by or as a playground for civilized easterners. Edward Marshall's 1894 "Locoed," for example, depicts two well-mannered girls on a ranch in Texas, one an unassuming invalid, who are treated like royalty by the local cowboys and live a life of leisure.

Foote's stories make no claims for the wholesome rural western life. Contrast this attitude with Cather or with Laura Ingalls Wilder's lively autobiographical books, which show an appreciation for the spunk of the settlers, their practical activities to keep the family safe and fed, and the details of their various attempts—which we now know were generally unsuccessful in Pa Ingalls's case—to succeed in the West. But perhaps for Foote such daily struggles were so dispiriting to her adult sensibilities that although she dealt more candidly with them in her novels, she could not make herself broach such realism to kids. It is our loss, for stories about how her husband and his partners planned and built irrigation ditches, how she nursed her own children through scarlet fever, or how their antics made her sometimes precarious life bearable would have been unique and could have driven home the lessons of class continuation better than the often predictable, somewhat bland tales she did write.

Foote's West is not the fascinating, ever changing place that Cather and Wilder depict, since try as she might, Foote could not imagine how a cultivated person, young or old, might find contentment there. In the short story for adults, "A Cloud on the Mountain," stolid, hapless teenager Ruth Mary loves the West and is satisfied to watch her river drift by, but she is not a character a reader would care to identify with, whether the reader is from Boston or Boise. Ruth Mary is depicted sympathetically, but she is no role model for how a thoughtful, civilized child might find imaginative stimulation in the West, happily free of the restrictive, eastern codes. Foote could not seem to create a western child of high or low family background or any ethnicity to whom our hearts go out and from whom we might learn about the beauties and challenges of the West. She also showed little appreciation for the land's original inhabitants, an appreciation that James Fenimore Cooper, Mary Austin, or Rudyard Kipling transmitted.

Yet even as she did not depict a rounded picture of the fabric of western life, Foote performed a different function, one that modeled how the new professional middle class might now interact with its children. The narrator-mother in the Idaho stories has the time and leisure to appreciate and encourage creative play in her children. They cavort about like kids in a modern playground, not having to stay spotlessly Victorian like Johnston's exuberant Little Colonel, who is constantly scolded for mussing her pinafore. Both the narrator and the parents in the stories clearly enjoy the children's imaginations. This indulgent attitude is more typical of the middle and upper classes of this era than of the hardworking lower class. The virtues of "play," born, perhaps incongruously, of both industrialization and literary Romanticism, were progressively applied to children, adults, and even animals in the nineteenth century. Families were smaller, parents had more time and money to nurture them, and as a result children had longer, less work-filled childhoods. This new middle class's gentler ways of raising kids, its "injunctions and practices," were a "recipe for family and class distinction through the enactment of gentility" (Ohmann 161). Thus, although Foote's somewhat generic children drifting through their domestic days make for unexciting reading, their lack of tasks or constraints does attest to their social status.

. . .

An interesting aspect of Foote's children's stories is in the narrator-mother's frequent digressions on various topics, from western isolation and aridity to social context or the lack thereof. The narrator-mother in the stories is a constant presence, now smiling at the children's exploits, now giving the reader background about Grandfather's Farm or Idaho geology. Her asides reveal, among other things, Foote's ambiguous attitude toward her adopted region and her insistence on class distinction. The narrator mediates the experiences for the reader, addressing class and hierarchy issues of which her child characters and child readers are unaware. In one story, in a quintessential Foote gesture, the narrator equates greenness and the "well wooded and watered" landscape in the East with civilization and proper social hierarchy (*The Little* 17). The arid and unstoried West suffers in comparison. Parents reading *St. Nicholas*, who it might be argued were as important an audience as the children, would have probably shared Foote's class stance and most probably her eastern-centric gaze as well.

Another characteristic example of these mediating tangents is found in "An Idaho Picnic," where the narrator-mother explains why it is better for her child and the family to live ten miles from town: here there are "no mosquitoes, no peddlers, no tramps, no book agents, [and] no undesirable neighbor's children, whom one cannot scare away as one may the neighbor's dogs and chickens" (*The Little* 45). This bald statement reflects Foote's own situation. When the Footes moved to Boise in 1884, it was just over twenty years old, serving as a supply center for local mining and, soon, forestry interests. Not unexpectedly, it was a plain, unpolished place with little of the refinement or culture that Foote craved. The isolation that Foote chose for her children and family—and it was her wish to live ten miles from "the commoness [*sic*] of the Boise atmosphere"—is reflected in the seemingly lonely lives of the children in Foote's Idaho sketches (*A Victorian Gentlewoman* 4). Rather than expose herself or her own children to the tedious, if well-meaning, local society, Foote preferred the little world in the canyon of her family, her husband's colleagues, and the domestic help. Yet the narrator's dismissal of western social life is abrupt and incongruous in a story ostensibly about a pleasant picnic. Not infrequently, Foote was quite autobiographical like this. One wonders what Richard and Helena Gilder, or other family members, thought, reading such bitter sentiments so publicly displayed. One also wonders if any "undesirable neighbor" in Boise ever got hold of a copy of that issue of *St. Nicholas*.

The narrator-mother's sometimes arch and sometimes off-topic detours are manifested variously. At one point she informs the reader what Jack's mother thinks about uncouth neighbors eking out a living in the dry canyon. In another story about the children's efforts to save a dying lamb trampled in a desert stampede, "The Lamb That Could N't Keep Up," the narrator begins the story with an apparently unrelated several-page paean to the gushing, plentiful water in the East and then adds a lament about the aridity in the West. Her fervent sermon argues that water means security and the ability to thrive—she cites the "ancestral planks" on top of an old well at Grandfather's Farm as proof that the copious water there sustained life for many generations (*The Little* 19). In contrast, she continues, aridity means privation, isolation, and not being able to put down roots as her grandfather and his grandfather before him had done.

Foote's relations with the West were complicated, and in time she came to love the dry wastes, but she never accepted them wholeheartedly. As Cather notes about the Nebraska landscape: "It's a queer thing about the flat country—it takes hold of you, or it leaves you perfectly cold. A great many people find it dull and monotonous; they like a church steeple, an old mill, a waterfall, country all touched up and furnished, like a German Christmas card" (quoted in Porter 54). Foote preferred the German Christmas card.

The relaxed, noncoercive parent-narrators in most of Foote's children's sketches are echoed by a loose, digressive style. Some of her children's stories even border on modernism in their digressive structure. They seems to have been a more experimental sort of endeavor for her than her genre-bound novel and adult short-story writing. Richard Watson Gilder and Robert Johnson, the editors of *Century* magazine, demanded rewrites and emendations—as her correspondence with them attests. But given the various styles and genres of Foote's children's stories, it seems that she had more flexibility with *St. Nicholas*. Her highly autobiographical and often rambling sketches were accepted by its editors and readers. She apparently felt freer both to try new forms and to let go of her more structured genres. She wrote to Helena and Richard Gilder that it was a more serious thing to write for an adult magazine than for "St. Nick" (D. Miller 51). This latitude is our gain, since these often nonlinear texts show Foote's candid views about her adopted region and the difficulty of maintaining cultural and social standards in what often seemed to her a vacuum. If she had found a publication venue with even fewer content and genre strictures than *St. Nicholas*, it would have been interesting to read more honest accounts of her views. Foote might have grown from her disgruntled asides in children's stories into a more insightful western realism with more psychological depth.

. . .

Whether it is a sketch about her Hudson River grandfather's attic or an account of a picnic in an Idaho canyon, Foote explores the challenges that western isolation brings to families and to children. Much of Foote's overt agenda deals with the complicated sorrow, guilt, superiority, and perhaps anger at her own and her children's isolation, and she determined to fill what she perceived as a lack in their lives by writing about her beloved and now all but vanished traditions. To do this, she underlay her stories with conservative ideas about history and social class, determined to validate and keep alive the eastern world and its hierarchy. The plots are not complex, nor the characters remarkable, but what remains are slices of mannered nineteenth-century life. Foote wanted to ensure that her children did not grow up like Ruth Mary in "A Cloud on the Mountain" and be happy little savages "haunted by no fleshpots of the past" who have "no misgivings about [their] home" (*In Exile* 157). In a letter to Helena, written when her children were aged six, ten, and fifteen, Foote worried that "while we are striving in exile in order that we may one day take our children home, they are striking deep roots into this alien soil and may not consent to call any other *home*" (quoted in Pearson 72).

Of Foote's two surviving children, her engineer son did make his life in the West, taking over management of the North Star Mine in Grass Valley after his father retired. Her daughter Betty, however, attended art school in Philadelphia, married a Harvard engineer from an eastern family, and later settled in Massachusetts. Elliot West asserts that although adult pioneers missed civilization terribly, their children, raised in the West, were often more content. Foote notes at the end of her autobiography, lyrically if somewhat wistfully, that her son and his children are indeed westerners: "The North Star House now has its own flock of children, little Californians to whom this place will always be home; its memories will haunt them as the desert wind and the sound of that cañon river rising to our windows at night has stayed with our own children all their lives" (*A Victorian Gentlewoman* 399). She seems to accept here that the precious East that she loved so well has receded into ancient history for her descendants and with it perhaps her version of civilization. In *The Valley Road*

(1915) the narrator asserts that "the understanding of one generation [does not] fit the needs of the next" (352). Remember Thoreau's similar observation: "One generation abandons the enterprises of another like stranded vessels" ("Economy," in *Walden* 64). Foote's children's stories attempt to bridge the geographical generation gap by transplanting privileged eastern ways to the remote West.

The Ground-Swell, the New Woman, and Social Class

"A Complete Revolt Against the Old Order"

Mary Hallock Foote's complicated relation to social class can be studied further by analyzing her last novel, *The Ground-Swell* (1919), which deals with the impact of early-twentieth-century feminism on a traditional family. The novel is narrated by a retired California mother, Mrs. Cope, who relates the successes and follies of her three grown children, especially of her older daughter, a twenty-six-year-old social worker. It is on this adult child and her world that I wish to focus. Katherine Cope, the energetic and unconventional daughter, is a quintessential New Woman—eschewing marriage and economic stability for a life devoted to work and ideals. Mrs. Cope's distress at her daughter's lifestyle enacts upper-middle-class expectations, expectations that only fleetingly register the many years of transatlantic feminist activism that preceded the era of the novel. Conservative Mrs. Cope sometimes seems to speak for conservative Foote, since we can find similar ideas in Foote's letters, autobiography, and other novels. At other times, Foote is probably playing devil's advocate when she puts truly anachronistic rhetoric into Mrs. Cope's mouth. But the creation of a character as appealing as daughter Katherine blunts complete condemnation of this new lifestyle and tentatively validates women's options despite a constant undertow of criticism. In this Foote performs cultural work similar to that of Catharine Beecher, Sarah Josepha Hale, Fanny Fern, and Margaret Fuller, who in many ways enlarged roles for women even as they preached traditional values.[1]

The term *New Woman* came to be used in the 1890s and early twentieth century to describe women who avoided or reinvented marriage and family life and strove to create autonomous lives for themselves working outside the home. In *The Ground-Swell*, Foote ambiguously presents a circle of college-educated women living either alone or with female roommates, doing social work and engaging in other progressive activities. The novel is an often disparaging yet simultaneously admiring portrayal of a feminist avant-garde in the 1910s. And realistically or not, Foote manages to introduce class into this lifestyle, since Katherine Cope and her colleagues live a pleasant, cultured life despite their work among the poor. I contrast attitudes about class in Foote's novel with fictional and nonfictional New Women of the era. This demonstrates that fictional work on the topic, especially Foote's, is trying to stabilize a fluid class situation that appears to have changed irrevocably due to the aftermath of the Civil War, improvements in transportation and communication technology, increased European immigration, and, finally, the onset of World War I. *The Ground-Swell* reveals much about shifting class lines and women's roles in this period.

From what can be gleaned from Foote's autobiography and letters, she did not approve of women's political independence on many fronts, but despite her often disapproving portrayal of Katherine and her set, the reader gets a glimpse of a thriving female community living and working in New York City in the 1910s. As Margaret Mead notes of this era, "We belonged to a generation of young women who felt extraordinarily free—free from the demand to marry unless we chose to do so" (quoted in Conway 295). Foote is a little belated on this subject, as New York had been a stage for female liberation and opportunity for a generation by the time she wrote *The Ground-Swell* (see Stansell).[2] Nevertheless, she reproduced a polite version of such groundbreaking circumstances; the protagonist Katherine's ideals and interests are in keeping with those of young women of her era and class. Foote seems to have been both appalled and fascinated by these changes, and she chose, not surprisingly, to ignore certain aspects of independent women's lives and to create for her characters a refined world that suited her own comfort level.

...

The Ground-Swell is typical of Foote's later novels, in that it is a story about generational dynamics in a western family. Over the years Foote's ideas on class grew in complexity, as her earlier simple romances between couples with an assumption of gentility evolved into more complicated plots that touch on social situations where gentility is less assured. *The Ground-Swell* focuses on an upper-middle-class family on the eve of World War I. Newly retired Colonel (now General) Cope and his wife camp out in comfort on the remote shores of northern California for a summer before they decide where to retire permanently. Of their three daughters, one is newly married and living in the Philippines, another is married to a dissolute but well-connected San Franciscan, and the third, Katherine Cope, is the New Woman. Katherine works with underprivileged women in a city program that is called, perhaps facetiously, Wiser Mothers and Better Babies. The matronly Mrs. Cope, although close to her daughter, is frustrated and perplexed by the young woman's freewheeling behavior. She wants Katherine and her well-bred friends to marry and produce bourgeois babies instead of rethinking women's roles. Mrs. Cope disapproves of their bohemian lifestyle, and no doubt would agree with a character in another of Foote's novels who declares, "I distrust any relation which is not counted natural by ordinary standards. It's unnatural for a young woman to give her best years to the children of another woman" (*Edith Bonham* 241).

At her mother's request, Katherine visits California for the summer, and while there has a mild flirtation with an earnest, self-educated local rancher, Tony Kayding, after her mother schemes to throw them together. Tony proposes, and Katherine not unkindly rejects him. In a separate development, Mrs. Cope inadvertently witnesses the semiaccidental death of the mistress of her San Francisco daughter's husband as the couple sport by the ocean. Mrs. Cope is appalled that her cowardly son-in-law lets his paramour fall to her death, and she suggests he leave the country and work for the war effort in Europe. The San Francisco daughter, who has been naive about her husband's philandering, carries on to look after her children alone.

The Copes leave California for the winter and come to Manhattan to visit Katherine, since she will neither marry nor settle with them in the West. There they get to know the other New Women. At the end of the visit, the couple is shocked and saddened to hear that Katherine wants to go to France to be a war nurse. The now penitent son-in-law returns to the States, confesses all to his wife, and goes off again to the war, this time in a more glamorous role as a pilot. Meanwhile, the loyal "shore-man" in California, Tony, has inherited a large tract of land. Unbeknownst to the elder Copes, he builds a dream house for them on their summer promontory, using the taste and connections of the San Francisco daughter. Word comes that Katherine has died of a fever in France, and that the bad son-in-law is redeeming himself by proving his mettle as an airman. The novel ends with plans for the daughter in the Philippines and her children to join the Copes in California after her husband, too, is called up to fight. The groundswell of the title thus refers to both the war and the changing roles for women. Immense global and social forces have arisen that affect everyone one way or another, even those like Mrs. Cope and Mary Hallock Foote, who would rather stay aloof from the pulse of ferment.

· · ·

Analyzing the historical and literary context of New Women biographies, organizations, and literature of this period reveals that Foote's New Women are more genteel than many of those real-life gritty New Women who worked and indeed fought for causes around the turn of the twentieth century. Nonetheless, Foote presents the new options for middle-class women by depicting a sympathetic character who cares as much about the larger world as she does about her insular, respectable family. Underlying the attitudes in the novel is Foote's usual insistence on decorum and her protagonists' class position. But she also toys with new ideas, even if the novel seems to end with an affirmation of the status quo. Through Mrs. Cope, Foote presents the conflicting pulls and emotions that a modern mother might have about her daughter's activist choices. For selfish reasons, Mrs. Cope wants Katherine near her, preferably married. But Mrs. Cope also appreciates Katherine's vibrant energy and independent spirit, recognizing that hers is a brave new world where the traditional trajectories of marriage and family lack appeal. As Susan B. Anthony explained it to African American activist Ida B. Wells, marriage was all right for some women, "but not women like you who had a special call for special work" (quoted in Gaines, "Black American" 79). To use a contemporary phrase of Dorothy Canfield Fisher's, Katherine is a "splendid, vital, fearless modern girl" (222). Such force of character causes as much anxiety as pride and love for Mrs. Cope, however, and, one suspects, for Foote.

Foote's insistence on the gentility of her New Women may be based in part on the fact that the character of Katherine Cope is probably drawn from two real women: Foote's beloved youngest daughter, Agnes, who died at seventeen of appendicitis, and a sister of her husband, who had a journalism career starting in the 1860s and married late, at the age of fifty-five. This sister is once quoted as saying she was "not a marrying man" (*A Victorian Gentlewoman* 159). Foote also no doubt drew on happy memories of her own independent and youthful three years in 1860s New York City, attending art school and living with well-to-do, worldly Quaker relatives. It does seem unlikely, though, that Foote would have wanted young Agnes, had she lived, to have been as liberal as the daughter in the novel. But like many turn-of-the-century female novelists, she explored the narrowness of traditional female lives and the more varied lifestyle options that new technology and social conditions had enabled. Like them, Foote worried about the rapid pace of change as she demonstrated the wrongheadedness of this innovative and newfangled thinking. Other authors who created New Women characters similar to Katherine Cope, such as Dorothy Canfield Fisher and Gertrude Atherton, also gave the reader an outward veneer of convention—often adding a pat romantic ending. As a group these authors present new possibilities as well as perceived limitations of respectable women's lives. As writer and editor of *Colored American Magazine* Pauline Hopkins noted, "Fiction is of great value to any people as a preserver of manners and customs—religious, political and social. It is a record of growth and development from generation to generation" (13–14).

Criticism on *The Ground-Swell*

Analyses of Mary Hallock Foote's writings have not foregrounded the New Woman issues in *The Ground-Swell*. James Maguire even avers that Katherine is unhappy in her lifestyle, saying that she "sacrifices all happiness in fear of any indulgences" in her "thankless altruistic quest in the East." Critics usually do not discuss the class overtones of Katherine's friends' jobs and living arrangements, Maguire merely characterizing the young women as "modern," "liberated," and "idealists" (43). Some find Katherine a more positive figure, yet they still come at her lifestyle with conventional assumptions about women's roles, asserting, for example, that the young women in the novel "suppress their femininity and replace it with commitment to an idea" (L. Johnson 149). Both Foote's first biographer, Lee Ann Johnson, and Melody Graulich do note that during Foote's career, her heroines progressed from helpless and innocent ingenues to more competent and worldly characters like Katherine. Cecil Conrath in *The Led-Horse Claim* and Josephine Newbold in *John Bodewin's Testimony* have little notion of worldly power or social issues or class position; they are pawns and incapable of independent action. Katherine Cope, on the other hand, astutely comprehends the intricacies of the world at the tender age of twenty-six, makes her own life choices, and deliberately steps outside of her gender and class expectations by working and not marrying. She is unlike her San Francisco sister, Cecily, who lacks the imagination to think outside the paradigm of social and economic status. Though not outright rejecting class strictures, Katherine lives as though they were not important. Nonetheless, Foote draws back from making Katherine personally incendiary; this very positive young woman is full of youthful optimism and experimentation, not scary radical fervor.

Both Katherine and her independent lifestyle represent a growth for Foote beyond the male-identified, romantic virgins that she depicted in her earlier novels, characters that she herself called a "silly sort of heroine" (quoted in

Davidson 123). Lee Ann Johnson happily notes that "Katherine Cope is thus a type of young woman conspicuously absent from Foote's previous fiction" and quotes a revealing 1894 letter from Foote in which she admitted, "My girls never have a 'career'; never do anything to advance the 'causes'; have not the missionary spirit; do not show any progressive spirit even as towards 'man.' . . . To be honest, I am a sad recreant in these matters of woman's place in the future—the near future:—in politics and the professions, and in everything conspicuously progressive" (149). Still, Foote's female characters do exhibit more personality and autonomy as her novels progress. Perhaps Foote wanted her heroines to have more autonomy than she did and not be forced to live where they do not want to. Once having chosen Arthur as her husband, Foote was obliged to follow him around the western wastes if she wanted to avoid the scandal of separation or divorce. Tellingly, a section of *The Royal Americans* (1910), published when Foote was sixty-three, is titled "Catherine Chooses Her Country." This young woman gets to decide her locale at least.

But as Foote discerns and as *The Ground-Swell* shows, increased autonomy in young women of marriageable age can give the traditional class system a jolt. In the novel, Mrs. Cope is the mouthpiece for convention and does comprehend, if not fully, just what a challenge Katherine's life choices are to conditions as they are. When Katherine decides to spend her "coming out" money to go to college instead and later wants to live and work a continent away from her parents, Mrs. Cope says that "it was a break in the family that to our view lacked the natural sequence of marriage." She and her husband "feared that [Katherine's] commitments would end in a complete revolt against the old order" (57). Foote's devotion to the "old order" is the subject of this book, and her insistence on its importance in the face of early-twentieth-century developments for women is the subject of this chapter. Even as Katherine Cope escapes from traditional marriage roles, however, she also exhibits the necessary decorum of her class. She does not drink alcohol or run around to parties, and her associates are young women of her own carefully bred ilk. There is none of the self-indulgent, reckless abandonment of Atherton's flappers or sophisticates in Katherine's sober New York City life.

Critics rarely fail to mention Foote's elite literary tastes and strict eastern-based views on proper behavior, but Richard Etulain comes closest to explaining Foote's class attitudes when he notes that she "worried that the newness, the openness, of the West might encourage a threatening individualism" (*Reimagining* 14). The threat of individualism is constantly voiced by Mrs. Cope in *The Ground-Swell,* as she ambivalently describes the ways in which Katherine and her New Woman friends cheerfully disregard tradition. As sociologist Kevin K. Gaines points out, "Marriage promised economic security" in this era and, further, was "closely associated with moral superiority" (*Uplifting* 78).

At first Mrs. Cope tries to interfere with Katherine's idealistic goals by putting her in the way of the attractive California local, Tony. But Katherine is steadfast in her lifestyle choice. She stoutly says to her parents, "I wrenched all your plans to pieces and took my own way" (195). The Copes—who have lived their lives for family and duty—wonder what the world is coming to and grasp for reassurance. Like the narrator in Henry James's *Bostonians,* they are troubled by newfangled ideas brought on by "people who disapproved of the marriage-tie . . . lady-doctors, lady-mediums, lady-editors, lady-preachers, lady-healers," in short, women who had "rescued themselves from a passive existence" (85, 86). Late in life Foote herself referred to the early feminists of her girlhood as "Freaks" (MHF to "Mrs. Sanborn," December 20, 1938).[3] But the engagingly normal Katherine takes autonomy for granted, and tries to reconcile the old and new dispensations. She ponders the question that Margary Latimer puts in the mouth of a young female character in "Guardian Angel" (1932), "Would a person be able to help toward a new world and marry too?" To this Latimer's older, more jaded female character answers, "Some think they can. . . . People claim it can be done" (121). Katherine never gets the chance to find out.

Historical New Women

Who and what was the New Woman? English novelist Sarah Grand and Ouida (Marie Louise de la Ramée) are generally thought to have coined the phrase in an 1894 exchange in *Nineteenth Century* and *North American Review,* although Carroll Smith-Rosenberg credits Henry James with popularizing the term.[4] The cultural pursuits of a "lady" in the late nineteenth and early twentieth centuries evolved for some into a broader, more political, and also more action-oriented bent toward social change. As Ellen Condliffe Lagemann observes, "An interest in art, literature, and music often became an interest in the social and educational value of culture." For example, ostensibly purely cultural activities such as Shakespeare clubs sometimes "were way stations to participation in social reform, good government campaigns," and other programs for immigrants and the urban poor (5). American women's activism during the Civil War, as well as technological advances and demographic growth around the turn of the twentieth century, set the stage for women to enter the educational system and the workforce outside the home. These newly educated women were generally from middle-class and white backgrounds, though some were upper class. Many working-class or immigrant girls climbed the organizational ladders in the New Women movement, too, due to brains, ability, and, usually, a well-connected female mentor. All these women did not join New Women clubs per se or write manifestos, and did not necessarily call themselves New Women. It was a term of convenience, often of derision, by journalists and novelists of the day, and is now shorthand for historians.

Middle-class Katherine Cope in *The Ground-Swell* belongs to the second generation of New Women, those who came of age in the twentieth century and had more freedom of expression and dress than the first generation. Historian Paula Blanchard asserts, by way of context, that all the friends of first-generation Sarah Orne Jewett (1849–1909) "were ladies in the strictest sense. They all, including those who agitated for suffrage or preached in public or founded schools and colleges for women, conformed without question to the current norms set for womanhood, putting family or church before work, dressing in irreproachable fashion with corsets and bustles, and gracefully deferring to gentlemen when custom required" (221). Foote would have liked this graciousness still to be extant in Katherine's time, but in fact only the very elite still adhered to such niceties.

Novelist and short-story writer Margaret Deland remarked in 1910 that even though New Women were highly scorned, there indeed existed "a prevailing discontent among women," and hence there had been "a change in what we might call the feminine ideal" (289). She continues that the malcontents were not just poor women: "It is the discontents of the woman of privilege, of woman of sane and sheltered life, which have real significance" (290). That a writer like Foote, from a sheltered if not sane life, would tackle the New Woman theme shows just how mainstream the transformation had become by 1919. As already noted, Foote was a bit late writing a novel with a New Woman theme, since controversy surrounding the role of woman had been a public and novelistic issue for at least a generation. Harriet Beecher Stowe herself declared as early as 1871 that "all that relates to the joint interest of man and woman has been thrown into the arena as an open question" (quoted in Hochman 116). In addition, earlier novelists, from Catharine Maria Sedgwick (1789–1867) to Fanny Fern (1811–1872), occasionally depicted unmarried women who create useful and happy lives for themselves. Elizabeth Stuart Phelps (1844–1911) explored whether a woman could be both married and have a career or talent and usually decided that the two were incompatible.[5]

These and other nineteenth-century writers talked a good deal about a woman's "dignity," a code word for respectability in middle- and upper-middle-class life. They attempted to show that women could be dignified even if unmarried, and that status did not necessarily reside in having a husband. Phelps, Atherton, and other later women writers with more of a realistic edge than Foote also faced up to the cultural roadblocks preventing women's economic autonomy and maintaining their dependence on men for social status. These stories become less an individual's struggle and more an analysis of the structural forces that prevented women's class autonomy.

In most cultures a woman's social status has been directly tied to her father's or husband's. *The Ground-Swell* narrator, Mrs. Cope, makes very clear that she believes a woman's life is almost meaningless without a husband. Indeed, for Foote, a woman's life has little legitimacy without the public sanction of a man's social identity. She relates in her autobiography that a beloved aunt from childhood was discouraged from marrying a man who was "not worthy of her" and ended up an old maid. Foote comments that if her aunt Phil had indeed married her inappropriate suitor, "her life would have been wrecked—still it would have been a life and there might have been children," as if that would have made all the difference (*A Victorian Gentlewoman* 85). As it was, the aunt lived in limbo, not really having a clear status. She doted on her siblings' children, and at one point loaned her entire inheritance to a male relative whose business venture failed. She was never paid back, Foote soberly informs her readers. The slightly pathetic role of an old maid has been a subject for much fiction, before and after Henry James's wry dismissal of Catherine Sloper, that she "became an admirable old maid" (*Washington Square* 203).

Not all New Women were politically radical or demanded the vote, though the suffragettes were considered New Women. In addition to suffrage, New Women worked for temperance leagues, immigrant and minority welfare, urban settlement houses, worker health and safety standards, unionization, birth control, reformed divorce laws, and education for women. They were the first female doctors, lawyers, public officials, and business entrepreneurs in the industrialized world. The term was in vogue from the mid-1890s onward, and was still being used in the 1920s, sometimes in the original meaning and sometimes more generally to refer to flappers—young women who worked outside the home, dressed somewhat immodestly by traditional standards, and smoked or drank in public. As Smith-Rosenberg puts it, "Successive generations of New Women followed each other, differing from each other in significant ways," with the early generation exhibiting more social commitment and the later more emphasis on personal or sexual fulfillment (177). Women banded together socially in order to underscore that they "belonged to a group of women for whom accomplishment . . . was not an aberration but a normal and enjoyable way of life" (Blanchard 222). In some ways, Foote's Katherine Cope is a perfect bridge between "true womanhood" and "new womanhood" (Mary P. Ryan in Freedman 518). She is feminine, genteel, and wants to work within the system to show the world how it may be reformed by thoughtful, selfless women. In many ways, her "domestic feminism" is a natural yet quietly revolutionary outgrowth of the widely held Victorian belief that women were the better and more moral nurturers (Giele 39).

During the Progressive Era, the informal New Women groups that flourished in the major cities of the United States and Great Britain, as well as in parts of Europe, were of mixed classes, albeit with a middle-class base. By contrast, leaders of official women's clubs were often upper middle class. Revisionist critics claim to have finally "reveal[ed] the classism, racism, and Eurocentrism of various feminist organizations and activists" during this time (Ardis and Lewis, *Women's Experience* 2). That women from like backgrounds tended to stick together cannot be denied, but there was also much idealism and cross-class contact in the various formal and informal New Women networks. Elizabeth Ammons acknowledges that women's clubs had a "class bias" and "many internal tensions . . . [and] falling out along class, race, and regional lines," but notes that they did get women working together "*as* women" (6). Kristin Mapel-Bloomberg says that women gathered together in "broad-minded social organizations" (n.p.). Clearly, some cross-class mingling was part of this new social movement.

Many New Women lived in Greenwich Village in its first bloom as a haven for the avant-garde. Within Greenwich Village, one organization that reflected this new thinking was the Heterodoxy Club, founded and maintained for more than twenty-five years by "unorthodox women," as Mabel Dodge Luhan termed them. It was, in the words of International Workers of the World organizer Elizabeth Gurley Flynn, "an experience of unbroken delight . . . a glimpse of the women of the future, big spirited, intellectually alert, devoid of the old 'femininity' which has been replaced by a wonderful freemasonry of women" (Luhan and Flynn quoted in Schwarz 1). The club met at inexpensive restaurants and other locales every two weeks for lunch and a debate or lecture. A glance at the biographies from the club's roster shows that women came from all over the United States and the world as well. From family backgrounds high, low, and in between, they were drawn beyond class to the freedom of this new lifestyle.[6]

There were African American New Women as well, generally arising out of the African American women's clubs formed in the late nineteenth century. They had a more complicated personal and social agenda, as elite black women had to deal with the dual oppression of race and gender. Anna Julia Cooper and other African American women activists criticized the Anglo women's movement for its self-centered snobbery, and a recent African American critic states more forcefully that "black feminism has evolved historically over centuries, outside traditional white feminine roles, white social institutions, and white feminist cultural theory" (Guy-Sheftall 1). This may be an overstatement, since there was certainly some cross-pollination between New Women of different ethnicities. Nonetheless, African American New Women had more on their minds than personal fulfillment, with antilynching campaigns, voter rights, social justice, and race advancement as important concerns of the day. Elizabeth Ammons notes that the black New Women were different from white in that they "were not the daughters of restless matrons rebelling against a restrictive Victorian ideal of True Womanhood," which is exactly what Katherine Cope is (7).

Although many in the public resented, or were at least confused or threatened by women's yearning for things that had hitherto not been appropriate in their traditionally private sphere, some of the media of the time embraced it. The *New York World* installed a column devoted to New Woman doings in the 1890s. In the same decade a magazine toothpaste ad sported a jaunty New Woman wearing pants, with the explanation, "The New Woman—whatever costume she may wear, will be particular about her teeth. Fashion decrees changes in wearing apparel, but it will always be fashionable to have the teeth white and the breath sweet" (Ohmann 205). Thus were the New Woman's radical politics defused, diffused, and co-opted by marketing, not unlike later advertising to the baby-boomer hippies in the 1960s. Much of the media at the turn of the twentieth century engaged in negative and defensive retrenching, however, with strident anti–New Woman journalism, editorials, and fiction appearing on both sides of the Atlantic.

The class implications of the New Woman revolution were subtle but far-reaching. New Women "reject[ed] the gentility of their mothers," which in turn "threatened, for some, the old lines of class, nationality, and above all, gender" (Freedman and Klaus 400; Sarah Wintle, introduction to Allen 11). Merely by their lifestyle choices New Women suggested that "people should question the social framework" (Senf xiv). Individual women's personal decisions about how to live their lives thus affected the social hierarchy and inheritance structures elaborately built up over centuries in European and American history. It seems like simple girlish idealism that Foote's Katherine Cope avoid or delay marriage and help underprivileged women and their children instead of raising her own family as her mother so fervently wishes. But the significance of this is not to be downplayed as mere youthful role-playing and experimentation. When women step out of the inheritance hierarchy of their class by choosing not to participate in its re-creation, a new class, a "third sex," comes into being, as Foote and other period writers termed such unconventional, wage-earning women. Katherine is "problematizing . . . the traditional middle-class family plot," in Susan Gilbert and Sandra Gubar's terminology (*The Norton Anthology* xv). In speaking of her daughter's circle, Mrs. Cope admits that "it is plain that such girls cannot marry under terms not obtainable short of a new planet, or this old one made over according to their ideas" (214–15). Even in Foote's mannerly portrayal, the radical nature of these young women's acts becomes apparent.

Fictional New Women

Educated and working women, and later New Women, were a popular subject for British and American novelists and playwrights from the 1870s into the first decades of the twentieth century. Fiction and plays about the New Woman often have more glamorous settings than real life, and tend to focus on the beautiful, accomplished daughters of the upper middle class. There are some exceptions, such as Edith Wharton's *Summer: A Novel* or Stephen Crane's *Maggie: A Girl of the Streets,* but these tales of the underclass generally portray just how difficult it was for an aspiring New Woman to become one if she lacked education, money, or mentoring. This negative approach to the subject may in fact have discouraged less well-heeled young women from leaving the patriarchal nest.

Initially, Britain led the way, as various sorts of fictional females make various attempts to renavigate and reinterpret the social and marital roles laid out for them. Dorothea Brooke in George Eliot's 1871 *Middlemarch* comes to grief when she follows her intellect instead of her heart and marries the pompous middle-aged scholar Casaubon. In some stories, such as Sarah Grand's *Heavenly Twins* (1894), the women do not succeed in their experimentation and die tragically or make passionless marriage compromises. Nervous Sue Bridehead in Thomas Hardy's *Jude the Obscure* (1894) attempts to live a free-love philosophy and also to become a teacher, but fails in both instances and gives in to social convention, in the end condemning her former behavior.

Grant Allen's *Woman Who Did* (1895) punishes the heroine, Herminia Barton, in her attempts to avoid the confines of marriage and rear an out-of-wedlock child. In the end, the unsympathetic daughter Dolores, now grown up, rejects her free-spirited mother, who then commits suicide in order to enable her daughter to marry a young man from a prominent family! In Allen's economy, Herminia's unorthodox lifestyle limits the social choices her daughter feels she can make. Despite Dolores's mother's and father's high birth class—they both come from well-connected families—Dolores cruelly tells her mother that she is done "associating with such a woman as you have been. No right-minded girl who respected herself could do it" (137). The social sanction of marriage is more important to the child than the actual people her parents are. Petty respectability and narrow-mindedness trump both parental love and impeccable social position.

Other British writers treated the subject with humor and light dismissal, including the playwright Sydney Grundy, whose *The New Woman* (1894) introduces men's and women's sexual freedom and equality in marriage in an elite setting. A drawing-room comedy, *The New Woman* satirizes a feckless, well-to-do woman and contrasts her with a docile former lady's maid who has married into the upper class. An admiring male contingent approvingly calls the former maid "every man's sort" of woman and "a woman—nothing more or less" (15, 19). Female self-fulfillment outside of pleasing a male is portrayed as dilettantish and self-indulgent.

In the United States New Woman fiction of the period seems less melodramatic and more matter-of-fact than the British offerings. William Dean Howells gave us a sympathetic lady doctor in *Dr. Breen's Practice* (1881), whereas the Boston-born Robert Herrick, disliking both capitalism and New Women, peopled his books with unpleasant and self-serving upper-class feminists and hardworking, moral, lower-class traditionalists, particularly in *One Woman's Life* (1913). Isabel Archer and Henrietta Stackpole in Henry James's 1881 *The*

Portrait of a Lady share a class dynamic with the two women in Grundy's play. Isabel, who has breeding and money, makes an unwise, confining marriage, even though she would like to broaden her experiences. Henrietta Stackpole—who, as her name implies, is less well bred than Isabel—is nonetheless a true New Woman since she works for a living as a journalist. Less glamorous, she has better luck making herself happy, with and without men.

In *The Bostonians* (1886), James creates an emotionally stunted middle-aged New Woman, Olive Chancellor, and a naive young New Woman, Verena Tarrant, who in the end marries above her class and gives up the cause. The portraits of New Women in *The Bostonians* are rather damning of the movement. The feminists in the novel, such as Miss Birdseye and Dr. Prance, live for social causes and inhabit a classless, unaesthetic world with little recognition by polite society. The wealthier Olive is presented more sympathetically, but James puts forward that hers is a lonely netherworld as she fights against her innate gentility and tries to forego the luxuries of her class. Further, the novel's ending suggests that lovely young girls such as the fiery suffrage speaker Verena either often do marry or even perhaps would do best to give up activist notions in order to marry and live henceforth as helpmates.

The backpedaling that characterizes the end of *The Bostonians* also occurs in Dorothy Canfield Fisher's 1915 novel, *The Bent Twig*, where lively, educated Sylvia Marshall marries a gentleman farmer and abandons any career aspirations. Irrepressible Californian Gertrude Atherton wrote several novels exploring the complexities of the new choices women had in this era, including the reality that most women's financial well-being and social status were inexorably tied to their ability to ensnare a husband. Atherton's 1912 creation Julia France tamely settles down by novel's end after being a leading speaker and organizer for suffrage. Similarly, in *The Miller of Old Church* (1911), Ellen Glasgow's Molly Merryweather ends up engaged to a successful local businessman, after declaring for years that she will never marry. The world is too much with these women, and after a taste of the pleasures and perils of life without a male protector, they flee back to convention and marriage, within or above their birth class. As regressive as these plot endings may sound, however, the mere presentation of alternative roles for women introduced readers of popular novels to New Woman ideas in nonstrident contexts.

An American character of more backbone is young Diana Merivale in David Graham Phillips's 1908 play, *The Worth of a Woman*. Admittedly, Diana has more family support than the dispirited female protagonists of *Summer* or

Maggie: A Girl of the Streets or even than the more comfortable women cited in the aforementioned novels. Diana has her father's unflinching support and a home in their comfortable midwestern ranch to fall back on, but even so she makes the brave move to reject her fiancé Julian's condescending offer to marry her once he discovers that the two of them have conceived a child. Here, as in several other New Woman novels, when class appears, it rears an ugly head. Julian is referred to as one of "the *Boston* Burroughs," from "a family of icebergs stranded in Back Bay," for whom "conventionality is a god" (10 [emphasis in the original], 21). In order to appreciate his bride's fierce belief in equality between the sexes, Julian has to look deeper than his training in "Boston upper-class snobbishness" and his formerly shallow understanding of women's characters and needs (21).

Willa Cather's 1915 novel, *The Song of the Lark,* is sometimes cited as a New Woman novel, and indeed Thea Kronborg lives out a life of career and personal ambition, eschewing family and, until middle age, marriage. But the effortlessness of her journey into the professions—territory that many women found fraught with anxiety and disappointment—though it makes the novel seem modern, makes it unrealistic for its era. In addition, the fact that Thea's career is opera singing makes her story less a victory for aspiring professional women than an androgynous bildungsroman of the growth of an artist. The class issues, too, that so concern later Cather novels are largely absent from *The Song of the Lark.*

· · ·

In fiction about African American women, stories published around the turn of the century well before the Harlem Renaissance often take for granted that a woman will work outside the home. New Woman–like activities are less of an anomaly. As early as 1859, Frances Ellen Watkins Harper's story "The Two Offers" presents a life of work for others being preferable to an unhappy marriage—interestingly, a theme in line with Louisa May Alcott's idealistic work ethic. Similarly, Pauline Hopkins depicts socially concerned women who work in *Contending Forces: A Romance Illustrative of Negro Life North and South,* although her female characters are somewhat more neurotic and less competent than some of those in stories by Fannie Barrier Williams or Jessie Fauset. Fauset's story "The Sleeper Wakes" (1920) is an interesting addition to feminist literature, because like Thea in *The Song of the Lark,* the middle-class African American heroine of this tale has little fear or conflict about having a professional role. After leaving an unhappy marriage to a white man, to whom she has "passed" for white, Amy Boldin finds self-respect and financial independence by becoming an expert dressmaker. In this story the economic and social freedoms that are contested in many Anglo New Women novels are presented as commonplace.

It seems that this nonchalance about an unmarried or even divorced middle-class black woman earning her own living is, in fact, due not to the slightly later publishing date of these stories but to the fact that in the African American community it was more accepted that women would work and therefore have personal autonomy. Thus, in its striking contrast to tales about white women from this time, "The Sleeper Wakes" is in many ways *not* a New Woman story, even though its orphaned female protagonist creates her own life through hard work and determination in the business world. There is little angst either about the social appropriateness of her autonomy or her succeeding by means of hard work and resourcefulness. The family and marital wrangling about women's independence and working outside the home foregrounded in Anglo writers' New Women fiction is restfully absent from much early African American fiction by women. Fauset has been criticized for being too class conscious and tied to Anglo standards, and therefore her work offers a nice contrast to Foote's, since both authors are concerned with their characters' maintaining or achieving a rigorous gentility.[7]

Asian women writers, too, usually took women working for a living for granted, but had some of the affectations of Fauset in their relation to class. Onoto Watanna (Winnifred Eaton) (1875–1954) even chose her pseudonym to create an alter ego as a Japanese noblewoman. *The Old Jinrikisha* (1900) is full of Japanese class and feudal stereotypes, samurai and honor, and pride and repression. Likewise, her more famous sister, Sui Sin Far (Edith Maude Eaton) (1865–1914), though she wrote stirring defenses of independence for women, kept traditional class, Asian and American, in the picture. Her 1899 story "A Chinese Ishmael" in *Overland Monthly*, for example, depicts a Chinese slave girl in old San Francisco who is in love with the son of a Chinese mandarin. Using a phrase Mary Hallock Foote could have employed, Sui Sin Far's young woman admiringly notes that her beloved has "the grace of the well-born" (n.p.). Sui Sin Far strove tirelessly to bridge the racist divide between Asian and white, usually dealing with more urgent issues for her heroines than the self-fulfillment and middle-class altruism of New Women.

The Third Sex

In *The Ground-Swell,* Foote presents the living arrangements of Katherine and her friends as decidedly avant-garde. Some of the young women, including Katherine, live with female roommates and have set up quasi marriages in the process. These "Boston marriages," like those of Sarah Orne Jewett and Annie Fields and of Willa Cather and Edith Lewis, are rendered in surprising detail in Foote's novel, though of course they lack sexual innuendo—Katherine is clearly heterosexual. Mrs. Cope herself notes somewhat blandly and without much comment that Katherine's "husband" is a woman named Sarah Huntwell, who in turn calls Katherine her "wife" (216, 189). Mrs. Cope explains that Sarah "kept their mutual accounts and paid the bills in manly fashion," and the mother's only comment is the dry aside, "This struck us as 'new'" (189). Judith Roman idealistically asserts that such same-sex relationships were often in fact free of the male-female power dynamic, having "complete reciprocity" (quoted in Blanchard 153). Mrs. Cope interprets the young women's close emotional ties with each other as signs of a "new" age but does not address the sexual or class implications of women who choose to live independently from a male-dominated family structure.

The term *third sex* actually crops up in *The Ground-Swell* when Katherine casually refers to the concept with a touch of humor, perhaps to pique her mother. She mentions it when relating to her mother and beau Tony her dream of founding a school for girls. The teachers, male and female, would be from all the social classes, she explains. The women teachers in particular would be of all sorts: mothers "and hostesses and great ladies and small ladies, and just plain women . . . even the 'third sex,'" she slyly throws in (130). Mrs. Cope and the unsophisticated Tony don't know what to make of this.

The term has had a long history. The idea of a "third sex" goes back at least to the third century, morphing into more modern usage in the eighteenth century to describe male homosexuals as well as certain women (Herdt 10).[8] In an 1868 letter to George Sand, Gustave Flaubert greets the woman writer with "oh you who are of the Third sex," and, implying that she has transcended sexual roles and thus can see into the hearts and souls of both sexes, goes on to ask her advice on gender matters (120). Also in 1868, Karl Heinrich Ulrichs uses the term in his seminal work *The Riddle of "Man-Manly" Love,* asserting that there are three sexes, and that for loving men, he belongs to the third (527).

The late nineteenth and early twentieth centuries saw a burgeoning of interest in and classification of alternative sexual practices, with *third sex* being used as a descriptor of homosexuality along with the now offensive *urning* or *invert* (Vicinus 484). In the later twentieth century, the term had been used sparingly until the rise of queer theory gave it new life.[9] It has had nonhomosexual reincarnations in such sociological books as Patricia A. McBroom's *Third Sex: The New Professional Woman* (1986), which details American women who succeed in hitherto male-only business venues.

In the era of *The Ground-Swell*, the term *third sex* did not always imply lesbian, but may have had those overtones, as Katherine's somewhat coy use of the term in conversation with her mother suggests. We can thus presume that "third sex" women were a subset of New Women, albeit not a particularly well-defined one. At any rate, with its pre- and posthomosexual history, the phrase has usually meant an outsider who does not conform to conventional sexual roles.

Foote's New Woman

In *The Ground-Swell*, Foote keeps the setting upper middle class, as when Mrs. Cope describes Katherine's New Women friends. Though she is critical of their dogged independence, Mrs. Cope paints them as charming, well-bred ladies. At a party they give, Mrs. Cope notes that the young women have "the self-confidence that perfect form, manner, social background gives," but she still comes away griping, "The ungrateful hussies, they will not marry" (214). With Gertrude Atherton, she may suspect that such women "are conscious of too many resources both within themselves and life; [and] after a man's novelty has worn off," they are "more likely than not—certainly apt!—to find him their inferior in brain, and almost inevitably in character" (*Julia France* 250). This echoes what Katherine suspects would be the case if she married the nonintellectual Tony.

Thus, Katherine opts out of the traditional procreative female path. Late-nineteenth-century Anna Julia Cooper describes this new lifestyle for women as "stepping from the pedestal of statue-like inactivity in the domestic shrine, and daring to think and move and speak,—to undertake to help shape, mold, and direct the thought of her age" (quoted in Hopkins, *The Magazine Novels* xiv). Katherine looks at the social conditions around her, assesses how they might be improved, and decides to get involved personally. Her mother has her own interpretation of this: "You [young things] think and speculate too much. You can't leave anything alone" (195). Mrs. Cope has the same exasperation as the middle-aged Colonel in Grundy's *New Woman,* who complains that "everything's a question nowadays! Nothing is sacred. . . . Existence is a problem to be investigated; in my youth, it was a life to be lived" (11). A privileged man might indeed complain about young women's wanting to live for more than blood lines and male comfort; he might naturally feel that any rethinking of traditional roles jeopardizes their contentment with the old dispensation.

But Katherine's lively mind is busy rethinking what others will not. She sees her sister marry into a wealthy family, and then have to cope with the drinking and womanizing of her playboy husband, which all but destroys her marriage. Katherine often argues with her mother on the merits of this detached point of view, joking at one point, "Children are my hobby, you know," which rankles her mother, eager for more grandchildren (112). This adventurous young woman wants to avoid the constant responsibility of children and insists to her mother, "If we go anywhere near it, if we let it touch us, it's a sure hold. You're never able to say you are free again" (112–13). This echoes the sentiments of young Mary Hallock Foote to her best friend Helena de Kay Gilder after the birth of Foote's first baby: "A woman is a slave the moment she has a child" (early Fall 1877). Katherine has problems with "marriage in the abstract," as some of Grundy's determined British feminists do in *The New Woman* (11). Nonetheless, Mrs. Cope insists to the bitter end that marriage and motherhood for Katherine would have "rounded out her womanhood," even though the girl has more expansive views of what womanhood might be (280). Atherton's 1912 protagonist Julia France explains this new point of view, as she tries to make clear to her conservative fiancé why marriage and children are no longer enough for women: "Their brains have become so complex that love alone cannot satisfy. They would have love plus so much more! If the choice must be made, they dare not cast for love, in their fear of disaster[;] . . . all their problems . . . never can be solved by love, marriage, children, the good old way. . . . [T]hey know that a greater need still is to fill their lives and use their brains" (418). This is exactly how Katherine feels, especially given that despite his earnest attempts at self-improvement, California shore man Tony lacks both her intellectual depth and her concern for social justice.

Nancy F. Cott describes the era's ideas in similar ways, for both men and women: "Such longing of the pampered or the intellectual to be in touch with vital things was found among men as well as women and expressed in reactionary and rebellious politics, but for educated women in particular it was an

expression of their alienation from the restricted genteel world conventionally allowed them" (33). Katherine Cope posits to her mother that by working
with poor and underprivileged children, she may help as many as a hundred
women feed and nurture their children better over her lifetime, but if she had
had her own children, she would be able to help only a handful. This concept
has been termed *social motherhood,* an aspect of the so-called social housekeeping in the Progressive Era in which women banded together, often across class
lines (Swerdlow and Lessinger 94). Nonetheless, such idealistic thinking cuts
no ice with Mrs. Cope. She counters to Katherine that her daughter's own
mere handful of children would have been more "remarkable . . . [and] choice"
individuals than any number of poor children. She tries to clinch the argument with a classic Footism, "Environment and teaching can't take the place
of blood," but Katherine will not back down, and by alluding to the character
of her sister's feckless but well-to-do husband undercuts such elitist and old-
fashioned sentiments (196). Thus, Foote lets new ideas have the upper hand, at
least provisionally.

Katherine's socially conscious view of parenting departs from the family-
centered nurturing of middle- and upper-class American and European life.
As advanced as it may seem at first, in fact it advocates a return to an almost
tribal, community-based practicum much like what Charlotte Perkins Gilman
details in *Herland* (1915): a mother stops being "completely wrapped up in her
own pink bundle of fascinating babyhood" and begins to feel connected to "the
common need of *all* the bundles" (quoted in D'Arcy and Landa 190; emphasis
in the original). Mrs. Cope, in fact, comprehends this aspiration toward com-
munality and notes that her daughter and her circle call themselves socialists,
but she does not take their claims entirely seriously. At a going-away dinner
where Katherine's New York friends sport "family jewels and gowns of rank
price," Mrs. Cope admits that the young women were "prepared, in theory at
least, to go in khaki and fling those jewels into the common heap," but she does
not think it is right that they are happily forsaking their class position (215).
She is distressed to see that "these maiden mothers who were giving away their
youth" also do not feel a need for genteel female signifiers such as marriage,
beaux, and even afternoon receiving gowns and long, impractical hair (167).[10]
Foote's purpose in making Katherine's circle of colleagues uniformly genteel
may have been to make Katherine's world less threatening than it might have
otherwise been portrayed.

It is true, however, that reformers and settlement workers in this era were often from well-to-do, educated backgrounds. Ironically, some paid to live in settlement houses with the poor. They rubbed shoulders with other native-born settlement or factory workers or with immigrant girls, who by dint of intelligence, self-education, or fortuitous mentoring rose to levels of responsibility in the various causes. Mrs. Cope calls Katherine's friends in New York both "sturdy workers [and] . . . mere charmers lapped in luxury," thus covering all bases (189). Many members of the Heterodoxy Club in New York had been born outside the United States or were from rural backwaters of the United States with few educational or cultural resources, but Foote does not complicate or enrich her upper-middle-class story with such variety. She avoids including anyone in Katherine's circle like "factory girl" Leona O'Reilly, for example, who worked for years in shirtwaist mills and became connected with the Social Reform Club and the Henry Street Settlement, or Rosa Schneiderman, who came from impoverished Russian Poland and ended up being a highly respected labor organizer. Katherine's friends are "wonderful, super-civilized young goddesses," as are Atherton's Julia France and her London Society suffragettes and Jack London's restless, lovely, and doomed Paula Desten in *The Little Lady of the Big House* (1915) (214). Foote avoids class mixing among *The Ground-Swell*'s activist women, unlike Henry James in *The Bostonians,* who delights in depicting Olive Chancellor's innate aristocracy, simple Miss Birdseye's lack of aesthetics and Olive's instinctive abhorrence of it, and the tawdry Tarrants' failures at upward mobility.

In *The Ground-Swell,* Foote shies away from realistic depictions of life in Katherine's slums, although one would think that Mrs. Cope would be curious to see her daughter on the job. Mrs. Cope and the reader remain ignorant of that world. Foote keeps the reader's gaze firmly on the sort of people who count for her, the Anglo elite. To complicate her *Century* magazine tale with the concerns of the impoverished and uneducated perhaps would be to drag it down to vulgarity. Although she deliberately averts her narrative's focus from the grittier side of life, naturally Foote was not ignorant of it herself. In a telling 1900 letter to Helena Gilder she allowed that she knew "as much about the men who tread those fields as a man could—more—but I don't know the fields and don't wish to appear to" (quoted in Graulich 46). In Foote's view, women, and especially married women, maintained respectability by at least appearing sheltered from crudeness and harsh realities.

· · ·

It sometimes seems that Foote wasn't sure what to do with an unmarried Katherine if she had been allowed to live. Toward the end of *The Ground-Swell,* Mrs. Cope says that she can envision the futures of her other two children, as bleak as they might be, but "Katherine's future I could not see" (221). Later, when Katherine has died of illness in France, Mrs. Cope assesses her children's present situations and futures, asserting that "Patty's story has scarcely begun; Cecy's pauses till Peter [her husband] comes back; *Tony is committed to his chosen work,* and Katherine's work is done" (280; emphasis added). The young women do not seem to exist to their own mother until their husbands come back from the war, but Mrs. Cope has no trouble believing that her dull, beloved Tony, whom the vibrant Katherine would not marry, is somehow able to have a full life defined solely by work. Mrs. Cope freely admits that with Tony Katherine would have married below her class. Yet she insists that there would have been greater glory in trying to broaden a provincial "shore-man" and raise his children on the isolated California coast than in being part of the rich cultural and interpersonal world of New York, with its needy immigrants and convivial New Women. But Katherine, though she is drawn to Tony, feels, like Molly in Glasgow's *Miller of Old Church,* that "it's not the man, but marriage that I don't like" and in youthful idealism turns her back on convention and status in favor of social conviction and personal growth (112).

Gertrude Atherton expresses dismay and even disdain for the kind of female dependence that Mrs. Cope tries to encourage Katherine to adopt. In *Julia France,* a wise old man cautions Julia's mother about encouraging a match with a dissolute but titled heir. He explains to the sheltered, provincial mother that the world is changing: "Women today are working out destinies for themselves. Now, personally, I should rather see my daughter a famous author, painter, singer, even . . . than suddenly elevated to a class to which she was not born, particularly if led there by the hand of a man like France" (9–10). Atherton grimly depicts the death of spirit that occurs for women who become isolated by marriage and are denied the opportunity to use their talents. They end up on the "scrap heap" and, if they have to work, may endure long hours, only to follow it with "long hours of drudgery in the home . . . where there seemed no object in living whatever" (186, 268). Atherton tackles thorny issues of drunkenness and husbands' absolute physical and financial power over wives with a force that points up the timidity of Foote's foray into issues of women's autonomy and dependence. With her usual archness, Atherton even derides fictional characters like Katherine Cope, noting that taking to settlement work is "the last resource of the novelist who wants to make his elevated heroine 'do something'" (104).

The autonomous Katherine has come to see marriage and family creation as entanglements to the self-fulfillment of a woman, though like Atherton's Julia France she is not sure what one does with the fact of attraction and love between the sexes. Neither young woman can imagine an equal, self-actualized partnership with a man. Julia lies awake one night and finds an inner wisdom that Katherine might champion: "She knew that several millions of her sex were forcing the world to recognize them as breadwinners, independently of any assistance from a man. It was magnificent, the opportunities of to-day, when compared with the meager resources of the past. . . . The twentieth century was theirs" (255). Margaret Mead writes in her autobiography of a similar sense of euphoria. She says that she and her peers felt "free to postpone marriage while we did other things, free from the need to bargain and hedge that had burdened and restricted women of earlier generations" (quoted in Conway 295–96). Period novelist Ella Hepworth Dixon proudly asserted that using one's body and housekeeping skills to leverage for a legitimate life was an artifact of the past: "If young and pleasing women are permitted by public opinion to go to college, to give parties, to read and discuss whatsoever seems good to them, and to go to theatres without masculine escort, they have most of the privileges—and others thrown in—for which the girl of twenty or thirty years ago was ready to barter herself for the first suitor who offered himself and the shelter of his name" (quoted in Showalter, *Sexual Anarchy* 39).

Still, Mrs. Cope feels that independence has its limits. Somehow it isn't *nice* for a well-bred woman to be spending her twenties single and devoted to the poor. For Mrs. Cope, the underprivileged are not as deserving as those of her daughter's own class and lineage. Likewise, James's painfully upper-crust suffragette Olive Chancellor recoils from the vulgarity of being a public figure in an era when middle- and upper-class women maintained their position by *not* appearing in the public eye. She has to steel herself to endure the uncomfortable streetcar and the commonplace women at Miss Birdseye's drab meetings. Julia France also wrestles with this issue when she first decides to devote herself to the cause. Her aunt reacts violently upon hearing that Julia plans to take up suffrage, declaring how inappropriate it is for women of their class to be "fightin' men and sleepin' in prison," ending with the ultimate dismissal: "It's a middle-class movement, anyhow" (297). Julia initially fears that her fellow suffragettes will have "coarse, vulgar [and] hard" faces and personalities, as *Punch* and the other era periodicals routinely depicted them, and is pleasantly surprised to find the stereotypes not borne out (301).

The matronly narrator in *The Ground-Swell* exhibits her distaste that young women like Katherine work for a living and with poor people at that, but Foote has missed a novelistic opportunity by not depicting Katherine's actual work more explicitly. The gross differences in temperament, taste, and lifestyle between the healthy, well-fed upper and middle classes of the period and the impoverished might have been used to bolster Foote's ambivalent attitude by portraying some of the negative consequences for women who worked. Illness, for example, was a considerable concern for those who labored with the poor, as was crime. Sarah Orne Jewett often had to treat the infections her partner, Annie Fields, developed, working, as Fields did, in the dirty and infected slums of Boston (Blanchard 159). Jane Addams, as much as she respected and validated the immigrants in her Hull House neighborhood of turn-of-the-century Chicago, had the honesty to note the ethnic clashes and unpleasantness that the urban poor lived with daily. She and journalists east and west detailed the appalling sanitation conditions in immigrant neighborhoods, conditions that the immigrants generally accepted, since they had little choice and conditions in the old country had not always been better. Without sinking to abject realism, then, Foote could have made the people Katherine works with stark or even alarming. The novel could have usefully included a description of Mrs. Cope accompanying Katherine on her rounds, for example, but it does not.

In *The Ground-Swell*, Foote's few depictions of the Other—urban poor, immigrant or otherwise—appear in ambiguous ways. They illustrate a romantic nineteenth-century attitude toward those who are different yet also reveal a realism that Foote's earlier novels lack. One example is a Portuguese squatter woman and her family that Mrs. Cope and her husband see on the beach in California. Mrs. Cope and her husband make up nicknames for her: "Mrs. Italy" and the "Purple Woman"—the latter due to her sole dress. Mrs. Cope observes that the woman has "a magnificent bare, brown arm and that she [walks like] a queen . . . like one of the Immortals" (95). Then Foote undercuts Mrs. Cope's naive condescension. Tony matter-of-factly tells them about the Purple Woman's squalid life, bursting the Copes' "leech-gatherer" mentality. He explains that their picturesque Amazon is in fact actually gathering limpets. She has seven children and no education, lives in a makeshift tent house, and never gets to bathe. Foote lets Katherine have the last word on the subject, further allowing a deromanticization of Foote's own lifelong classicizing tendency. Katherine jokes to Tony that it is her mother's wish for people like the limpet gatherer to meld with mainstream (Anglo) Americans and thereby improve the robustness of the nation. Tony himself would not have been considered a "mainstream" American in that era, since he is half Norwegian and half Hispanic. Thus, Katherine's joke makes the California-born Tony an outsider. Tony gets lumped with the hapless immigrant, and Katherine's later rejection of him disappoints Mrs. Cope and her eugenic vision. Nonetheless, in one sense Katherine's refusal to marry Tony validates another side of Mrs. Cope's vision, her conservative wish to so ardently avoid the groundswells of social as well as global change.

. . .

In the novel, Katherine Cope graduates from Bryn Mawr College before she starts social work in Manhattan. Bryn Mawr, along with Barnard, is one of the Seven Sisters, the first women's colleges in the United States, and, as Carroll Smith-Rosenberg notes, "we identify the New Woman most directly with the new women's colleges" (247). Margaret Mead was part of a group of Barnard undergraduate women living together off campus while attending college in 1921–1924, less than five years after *The Ground-Swell* was published. Mead and her schoolmates, like Katherine and her circle, wished to live and work together for social justice or for their chosen profession and felt strongly that marriage and children could easily derail such hopes and ambitions. The women who attended the new private eastern colleges were usually from upper-middle-class families; in fact, Bryn Mawr's founding document states that it was created for "young women of the upper classes" (Earnest 220). But if attitudes such as those of Willa Cather and Dorothy Canfield Fisher are any indication, women who attended the less elite midwestern or western schools emerged with as much sense of personal autonomy, even if they had less noblesse oblige. East or west, new possibilities and purpose propelled American New Women toward formerly forbidden personal and professional goals.

Sometimes New Women—in real life and also in fiction—lost momentum after college and were not sure what to do with all their precious training, but a fortunate few, who had vision or mentors or both, worked their way into the professions. Comfortably born Jane Addams did a grand tour of Europe with relatives after her schooling, but felt guilty for not being more productive and useful. It was during a subsequent trip to London that included a visit to a settlement house in the East End slums that she conceived of doing the same thing in Chicago. In Fisher's novel *The Bent Twig*, after college the protagonist Sylvia "stopped short, finding herself in company with a majority of her feminine classmates in a blind alley. '*Now* what?' they asked each other with sinking hearts" (234). Sylvia's sister goes straight into nursing school, but for Sylvia and her peers marriage is apparently the only means of escape from living with their families and working at dead-end jobs. For them, a woman's class position is still almost entirely dictated by whom she marries. Sylvia lacks the secure sense, however humble, of being the "daughter of a gentleman" that carries Louisa May Alcott's Jo March or Atherton's Julia France through trials and into a career. Some women writers, at least, felt that the traditionally male-identified nature of status was not essential to class position. Atherton, in particular, depicted women in several of her novels who, like herself, rise to or maintain a high social status, even if they lack (or have discarded!) a prominent husband. Such "odd women" do not fit into the traditional social roles and have to be proactive if they want to retain the kind of dignity that usually only marriage conferred.

Recall that recent historians and literary critics treat with some vigor the class and race exclusivity of fictional as well as real historic New Women and their organizations. As we have seen, some make the case that middle- and upper-class women forged authentic alliances with their less financially independent sisters, bonding over "social motherhood" and other pan-female issues (Swerdlow and Lessinger 95). Some, however, assert that working-class women and women of color often felt condescended to and were excluded from much of the freedom and social progress that elite Anglo women enjoyed. They note that white social workers often took a Lady Bountiful role with those less fortunate and had "an inadequate analysis of the importance of the socioeconomics of class in the continuation of poverty in the lives of minorities," as Lois Rudnick claims was the case even with Jane Addams (quoted in D'Arcy and Landa 191). It is only fair to point out that Blanche Wiesen Cook's research on Addams contradicts this. Cook cites an essay by Addams that clearly shows the Hull House founder's awareness of colonial and imperialist origins for much of the world's economic oppression (see D'Arcy and Landa).

Nonetheless, Rudnick posits that Jane Addams's "white, middle-class notions of 'uplift' sometimes led her to patronize, as well as to romanticize, her immigrant neighbors" (quoted in D'Arcy and Landa 191). We also see this in

The Ground-Swell with Mrs. Cope's fantasies about and labels for the Portuguese shore woman. This criticism is not infrequently leveled at feminist reformers by both contemporary writers and revisionist historians as well. Anzia Yezierska (1885–1970), for example, a German Jewish teacher, writer, journalist, social worker, and activist, satirizes the upper classes who condescendingly try to help the poor in her 1923 *Salome of the Tenements.* Fisher's book *The Bent Twig* expresses a view similar to Rudnick's. Educated, morally rigid, and casting about for a suitable career, the youthful Sylvia defends her avoidance of social work by exclaiming, "I could never bear the idea of interfering in people's lives to tell them what to do about their children and their husbands just because they were poor. It always seemed to me it was bad enough to be poor without having other people with a little more money messing around in your life" (406). This flippant dismissal of welfare and social work can be interpreted as a laissez-faire willingness to perpetuate the inhumane conditions in American cities, which demanded that *someone* improve them *somehow*, even if it was not going to be Fisher's heroine. Nonetheless, Foote's Mrs. Cope shares Sylvia's view of the proper scope of a respectable individual's involvement, and sees Katherine's work with underprivileged women as unnecessary meddling. Margaret Deland takes a similar stand in a 1910 *Atlantic Monthly* piece titled "The Change in the Feminine Ideal," in which she describes what happens when New Women daughters reject the homebound *"selflessness"* of their mothers and broaden their social and political consciousness: "This young person has gone to college, . . . is going to earn her own living, . . . [and] declines to be dependent upon a father and mother amply able to support her[; . . . She] will do settlement work; she won't go to church; she has views on marriage and the birth-rate, and she utters them calmly, while her mother blushes with embarrassment; she occupies herself, passionately, with everything except the things that used to occupy the minds of girls. . . . Restlessness! Restlessness!" (291).

Katherine's mother likewise feels that women should take on the selfless, wifely roles beckoning to them, and not go spreading their wings into broader, more public venues. When World War I breaks out, Mrs. Cope feels that it is correct for men to volunteer—after all, she is married to a military man and is conventionally patriotic. But she believes that other than unavoidable male heroics, the rest of the population should stay in their own spheres. The novel ends with an adamant assertion that Katherine's place should have been by Tony and not in a distant land helping strangers: "It was not enough for Katherine just to die, nursing dying soldiers; she should have nursed living children and helped Tony to broaden his life on the shore that meant work as well as peace and rest" (283).

But Katherine does not want peace and rest. Having what Deland would call "a more or less petulant criticism of life as it is lived," Katherine wants independence and the feeling that she is doing worthwhile work (290). And her soul mates on these adventures are not men, who might restrict her movements even if they maintained her in middle-class fashion, but third-sex women. Her closest friend is not a husband but wealthy older female cousin Helen, who, the narrative suggests, is at least unconventional and perhaps lesbian. Thus, Katherine frankly states to her mother, "Helen and I have always said we found each other in France. . . . [I]n France we were two hearts that beat as one" (212–13). This sort of bonding, "this modern friendship," in Mrs. Cope's disapproving words, will not produce bourgeois children to carry on the material strivings of Katherine's class (84).

If young Mary Hallock Foote and her dear friend from art school Helena de Kay Gilder had chosen each other as life companions instead of the well-connected young men who became their husbands, they would not have had the children they did, who went to the right schools and associated with the right people, thus perpetuating their families' class status. That the idea may have at least crossed Foote's mind can be discerned in a comment in an early letter to Helena. Helena had started seeing Richard Gilder, which Foote admitted put her out at first. But she told Helena that she had come to accept it, declaring, "We are too nearly married to let a *real* chill ever come between us" ([October 1873]).[11]

But Foote does not linger on Katherine's female companions, since her narrator, Mrs. Cope, wants to keep the focus on the traditional marriage plot. Mrs. Cope and perhaps Foote reveal their attitudes toward class in the characterization of Tony Kayding, Katherine's erstwhile love interest, who is considerably less "tony" than the New York New Women. He is a local California "shore-man," which apparently means to the Copes that he is provincial—he has not traveled or been formally educated. We are told that his apartment has an "atrocious" vase, and his books are lowbrow, since Mrs. Cope notes that "there was not one I would have carried down the hill!" (92). But the Copes come to believe that Tony is naturally genteel, saying that he has the "spirit and humility of a gentleman," a "wildness that could never be roughness" (129, 90). Nonetheless, General Cope becomes exasperated with his wife's matchmaking plans when she defends Tony by saying that he cannot help it since he is a "shore-man." Her husband shoots back, "And that's all he'll ever be." General Cope later adds, "He is n't our kind of folks" (144).

When Mrs. Cope is trying to "place" Tony when she first meets him, she uses the "politer word" for Tony's Hispanic mother—"early Californians"—but her husband straightforwardly says, "They were Mexicans, yes" (34). In a nice bit of oxymoron, Mrs. Cope terms Tony "pure mongrel, but he's remarkably pure." For her, no doubt some of his purity comes from the influence of an Anglo doctor foster father, who "kept him out of the streets" as a lad (122). And once Tony inherits money and land from the doctor, his tutelage under the Copes' status-conscious daughter Cecily adds a patina of sophistication and class to the "shore-man." As condescending as Mrs. Cope and apparently Foote are, they do allow that Tony deserves upward mobility, but only due to his humble will to self-improvement and almost obsequious deference to those he discerns are his social betters.

Since we know that both fictional and real New Women sometimes did link up with compatible mates, male and female, one suspects that in time a real-life Katherine might have found at least one enlightened man for a partner, but Foote does not present any in the novel. Tony the shore man is the only option. There are in fact signs that if she had lived, Katherine Cope would have probably followed some sort of a compromised path to middle-class marriage. By the time she goes off to France, she is weakening in her resolve to eschew traditional female roles and gives Tony some hope for a future together. In classic Foote fashion and in a move that would not have seemed out of place in Foote's allusive and mannered early Leadville novels, Katherine writes to Tony to give him a test of character when she learns he has inherited money and land. Like an Arthurian maiden, Katherine wants a sign of her lover's loyalty and disregard for worldly things. She asks Tony to divest himself of his inheritance to prove his love for her.

This odd request is similar to the situation in Fisher's *Bent Twig,* when the rich hero chooses on his own to give away his lucrative mine holdings in Colorado in order to live the moral life and his loyal, quasi–New Woman love interest, Sylvia, chooses to marry him anyway. This high-minded action is treated as a noble sacrifice for potential bride Sylvia, but if Bourdieu's notion of cultural capital is invoked, one sees that Sylvia will still have a well-educated, well-traveled, intelligent husband despite his new relative poverty, whereas Katherine would have to contend with the limited, unimaginative Tony thousands of miles from congenial friends and work. The cost of such a mismatched marriage to Katherine's joie de vivre may have seemed too high even for the conventional Foote. Nonetheless, a novel ending with Katherine continuing her single, happy, and socially dedicated life was not possible either, perhaps because it left an upper-middle-class girl unmarried. In an equivocating gesture, then, Foote kills Katherine off in France by means of an illness, and Katherine dies before she might have overturned the marriage plot with a more radical plan.

Ultimately, Foote's efforts to write about the New Woman come off as a sincere attempt on the theme, even if her treatment of it is class bound and a bit outdated for 1919. She allows a young woman to live an experimental life while at the same time not significantly challenging traditional notions of the feminine. Katherine's early death is so contrived that potential New Women reading the novel might have dismissed the ending as predictable and not realistic. Thus, instead of being chastened by the dire consequences of Katherine's risk taking, they might have taken inspiration from the way she fulfills her dreams before she recklessly volunteers to be in harm's way.

Foote's approach did not radically disrupt but rather gently expanded young women's possibilities. And although she did not explore them in depth, Foote nonetheless touched on many real New Woman concerns, such as girls attending college and delaying or avoiding marriage, the new field of social work, the revised clothing standards for women who work, and the dilemma of a woman's personal fulfillment versus her family duty. Why conservative, antisuffrage Foote chose to tackle a subject such as the New Woman at all is not entirely clear.[12] In a late letter she distanced herself from feminists by stating, "I am constantly amazed at the number of clever women nowadays who succeed in being charming as well. In my girlhood . . . they were usually rather queer, and very seldom good-looking! In these days, the Freaks are not as clever as they used to be and the charming women are more so" (MHF to "Mrs. Sanborn," December 20, 1938).[13]

After Foote's art training in New York City, marriage, and subsequent moves to western frontier towns in her youth, she kept abreast of the social issues of the day through frequent letters from friends, occasional visits to the East, and avid reading. Foote thus knew of social movements as far as that was possible living in small towns in Colorado, Idaho, and northern California. Although she remained traditional about women's roles, she may have had enough fond memories of being an independent wage earner herself in her urban twenties to be fascinated with the newest generation of liberated women. She gives us just a taste of a New Woman, and does it without seriously undercutting social conventions or class position. Her contribution to the New Woman novel, then, is the dashing if doomed character of Katherine Cope, living her own life as she wishes, whether with the underprivileged in New York or the soldiers in the trenches, and ultimately both fulfilling and escaping her mother's rigid standards of propriety and class expectations.

Chapter Six

The Early Correspondence of Mary Hallock Foote
and Helena de Kay Gilder

"We Find It Necessary to Keep Up the Little Forms of Civilization"

The letters between Mary Hallock Foote and Helena de Kay Gilder span almost fifty years and are mandatory study for an analysis of Foote's attitudes toward class. This is particularly true in light of the fact that she and Gilder came from different backgrounds. The cultivated but middle-class Foote often deferred to the superior social position that Gilder was born to and enhanced with a childhood spent mostly in Europe, brilliant marriage, substantial family inheritance in her thirties, and glittering contacts in the art and political worlds of late-nineteenth-century New York, Washington, D.C., and Newport, Rhode Island. Foote also favored Gilder in other ways, citing her artistic "genius," as she called it. She repeatedly expressed that Gilder had more talent than she, a gesture that in subtle ways confirms the difference in class position between the two women.

Helena and her poet-editor husband, Richard Watson Gilder, and Foote and her mining and irrigation engineer husband, Arthur De Wint Foote, lived in separate worlds that Mary Hallock Foote strove to connect with her letters. Mary Hallock Foote's family circumstances and social connections were more modest than Helena Gilder's, with an upbringing on the proud, yet marginally productive, Quaker farm in upstate New York and Foote's subsequent financially precarious stays in various western towns with her husband, children, and sometimes assorted unpaid family retainers. As Rodman Paul noted, Foote "paid a price" for her love of Helena Gilder and her dependence on the Gilders for literary contacts and contracts: "Already part of the genteel tradition when she first went west, her continued reliance on the Gilders, who were the embodiment of eastern culture, kept her subject to what would be called today the viewpoint of the Eastern Establishment, at a time when she was becoming known as a leading writer and illustrator of scenes that were regarded as being 'authentically western'" (introduction to *A Victorian Gentlewoman* 9). Wallace Stegner concurs, noting that "even as [she] paid attention to what [she] must do today and tomorrow, [she] heard the receding sound of what [she] had relinquished" (20).[1] If Foote had not had such strong eastern ties, she might have become more purely integrated into western life, clinging less to the eastern hierarchies and decorum that had informed her youth.

How different was Mary Austin just a few years later. Also raised with Victorian notions of refinement and respectability, she tried to cast off much of it in her remote desert cabin in southern California. She worked to accept and learn from the local cultures—Native American, Hispanic, and Anglo—drawing strength and depth from her new experiences. In contrast, Foote valorized "the genteel performance" and, in Richard Etulain's phrase, "utilize[d] western scenes to make comparisons with a static eastern society and culture" (Gatewood 182; Etulain, *Re-imagining* 13). Often quite aware of her narrow attitudes, however, Foote was honest about her own rigidity and inflexibility, which she conveyed in the sometimes conflicted letters. She perceived that she was loath to let go of the customs and values from her childhood, and remarked on it throughout her letters to Gilder.

Given the vicissitudes of time and erratic habits of preserving letters, especially by people not particularly famous, it is surprising that approximately four hundred of Mary Hallock Foote's letters to her best friend, Helena de Kay Gilder, survive, as well as around one hundred of Gilder's to Foote. They are in the process of being edited for publication.[2] This chapter will cover the early letters between Foote and Gilder, those written between 1868 and 1889. The early letters reveal the most about Foote's class attitudes, in that her first views of the West were the most class bound and also because Foote and her family moved several times during these early years, so she had more opportunity to encounter new people and places. At the outset of this copious correspondence, Foote was twenty-one, an eager young graduate of the Cooper Institute School of Design, where she met Helena de Kay. Their passionate if platonic friendship survived their marriages and Foote's removal to the West in the 1870s. By December 1889 Foote was forty-two, and both women had children and lived more than two thousand miles from each other—Foote in Boise and Gilder in New York City. They continued to correspond until Gilder's death in 1916.

Foote wrote also to Richard Gilder, Helena Gilder's husband and Foote's editor at *Century* magazine, and though mostly business related, her letters to him also included comments pertinent to an analysis of her class attitudes.[3] Although I will primarily cite the letters between the women friends, I also incorporate ideas from letters to Richard and other editors, and from *Edith*

Bonham, an odd 1917 novel that Foote wrote a year after Helena Gilder died, in which she explores and reinvents the various roles she and Helena Gilder played in each other's lives. In the story, the character similar to Foote, Anne, dies after childbirth in remote Idaho, and a character much like Helena Gilder, Edith Bonham, comes from the East to be governess to the two motherless children. After suitable mourning and misunderstandings, Edith marries her best friend's widowed husband. In reality, Helena and Arthur had little to say to one another; it would have been an unlikely pairing.

. . .

A discussion of the class concerns in the letters between Mary Hallock Foote and Helena de Kay Gilder is important since the letters show in a detailed, nuanced way how eastern norms were brought west and also how these norms were adapted, even for as conservative a woman as Foote. How she viewed the often rustic settlers in the West points up Foote's mainstream, undemocratic nineteenth-century notions of culture and refinement in ostensibly democratic America.[4] When her letters and novels allude to the power structures and social forces, they generally affirm a conservative, often elitist, and Anglo point of view. Soon, as Foote came to see the differences between her family and the less mobile inhabitants of her western towns, she realized that as "professional exiles" she and her family fitted nowhere and anywhere. As part of the new professional middle class, Foote and her family enacted the changing nature of the nation's elite in their ability to take advantage of improved transportation and communications.

Twentieth-century Foote critics focus on Foote's literary efforts but are not expansive about her private letters or the class concerns in them. Rodman Paul quotes from Foote's letters to many people, including Helena Gilder, in his astute introduction to Foote's autobiography, published in 1972, but other scholars were slow to mine this vein at first. With the rise of scholarly interest in women's history and the extraliterary, the remarkable correspondence between Foote and Helena Gilder—most of which has been at Stanford University since the 1950s—began to receive more attention. Later endeavors, including literary biographies of Foote in 1980 and 2002 and the first dissertation solely on Foote in 1997, began to use the letters as one of the sources with which to shed light on both her literary texts as well as the sociological and historical context of Foote's life and writings (see L. Johnson; Miller; Cothern, "Becoming Western"). This eventual inclusion of her letters into scholarship may in part have been due to Mary Ellen Williams Walsh's groundbreaking exposé in 1979 of Stegner's liberal appropriation of Foote's letters for his Pulitzer Prize–winning 1971 novel, *Angle of Repose*.[5] Once it became known that Foote's letters at Stanford and in other repositories had a wealth of detail for historians and, in particular, feminist historians, attention was forthcoming. Melody Graulich could declare that Foote's letters to Helena Gilder are her best writing, Richard Etulain quoted from the letters in an overview of western American fiction and art, and Lynn Cothern's Ph.D. dissertation, which takes a biographical approach to Foote's work, included the letters in an analysis of Foote's "psychic economy" and the gender issues enacted in her life ("Becoming Western" 3). There has been no sustained focus specifically on class issues in Foote's writing or her letters, however.

Carroll Smith-Rosenberg drew widespread attention to the Foote and Gilder correspondence by citing it prominently in her seminal 1975 essay "The Female World of Love and Ritual," stating, "This collection of letters radically transformed my approach to women's history" (27).[6] Smith-Rosenberg's academic goal was to achieve a more balanced understanding of history, with writings by women finally able to join the large store of male texts, but she did not address how Foote's or other women's letters bring to light the class concerns of their era. Nor did Nancy Evans Rushforth in her 1993 master's thesis, which has as its main focus Foote's letters to Gilder. Rushforth instead explores the power and gender implications of Stegner's wholesale "borrowings" of Foote's letters and also Foote's storytelling skill evidenced in the letters.

. . .

In her letters to Gilder, Foote endeavored to convey the fabric of her life as well as the "crude communities of transplanted lives" around her in the West, all the while indicating to her well-connected friend that she had not sunk as low as her eclectic neighbors (*The Led-Horse* 22). When Foote first went west to California, for example, she unashamedly condescended to the residents of New Almaden, and was only slightly more familiar ten years later in Boise. Class was many things to Foote, but it was particularly about sharing exclusive tastes with the right sort of people, and less about the more obvious signifiers such as wealth or conspicuous consumption. In her letters to Gilder, Foote frequently brought up class and taste, sometimes to draw her friend's attention to a shared aesthetic or, once she was in the West, often to describe the lack of it around her.

Foote preferred a life lived on the high plane of ideas and culture, and disliked having to be concerned with the "machinery of life" (MHF to HKG, July 1881). Like a proper Victorian lady, she preferred the private sphere to the sordid bustle of the industrializing outside world.[7] In *Edith Bonham* the narrator (the Helena-like character) thinks fondly of her aunt Essie's house in New York City, remembering its "silence of a well-bred mechanism that left one's thoughts free for immaterial things" (238). In her letters Foote complained to Gilder how much she disliked housework and wished the family could afford more servants, even noting that she minded having to make her own bed—"a part of the morning I hate" (December 13, 1885). When Foote told Gilder her plans for a rare vacation to Victoria, British Columbia, she noted, "I shall be so glad of a quiet old place like Vic. where I shall know nothing of the inner wheels" (April 21, 1889). According to Foote, people of quality sought such serene environments, and indeed could create them. She described a southern gentleman she met in New Almaden who had "a soft slow voice and accent [and] an immense amount of family pride which only shows in that repose and gentle satisfaction of manner which feels too sure of its own position to care to assert itself" (December 22, 1876). Those with the right kind of class inspire confidence in others, like Helena Gilder's husband, who, Foote declared, was one "of those rare ones who have never disappointed you or given you one pang—either in their lives or in their work, or in any ways of expressing themselves" (July 5, 1885).

Being "well-bred," having "background," and coming from a "good family" counted more for Foote than mere money (September 14, 1876; November 16, 1887; March 3, 1889). On the other hand, people of the upper class that Foote admired, such as her husband's relatives the Hagues, as well as the Gilders themselves, did have nice houses, possessions, and clothes, although they displayed them casually and did not brag about them (March 10, 1877). Theirs was a reticence Foote emulated, as when she was clearly thrilled that Helena Gilder had inherited a substantial income. Foote called it "joyful news" but in the next breath said, "I do not mean to make too much of money, but..." (June 12, 1880). Nonetheless, the inheritance enabled the Gilders to live even more comfortably than before, buy a larger house, and entertain on such a scale that they became friends with President and Mrs. Grover Cleveland. When Foote first came West, the Hagues impressed Foote with their well-appointed San Francisco home full of collectors' objects from around the world. In *Edith Bonham* Foote indulges her love of the expensive and the rare in a description of an ideal house. In rural Idaho the irrigation engineer much like Foote's husband builds for his new wife a large house, with good "simple lines," a garden complete with imported Japanese irises, and, most incongruously, a library with stained glass by noted New York artist John La Farge (an old mentor and friend of Helena's). Thus, as much as background and strength of character were important to Foote in the creation of an upper class, the material also figured.

. . .

We do not know exactly how Helena Gilder viewed her old friend in the West, and if she, too, felt the social as well as the geographic distance between them. She was affectionate in her letters, and clearly missed Foote, especially in their early days apart. The Gilders were in England when the Footes were first in Leadville, the two friends in their early thirties. In one letter Helena Gilder alluded to their unique bond. She explained to Mary that she did not have the Leadville address and so would send the letter to Mary Foote's aunt to send on to Colorado. This meant, apparently, that the letter might be read, and Gilder seemed to feel that she could not be as candid as usual. She said to Foote, "We are too old and *serious* to let them see our weaknesses for each other, so read between the lines" (September 29, 1879). Yet the Gilders certainly never visited the Footes, despite the trip to Europe and seasonal migrations to summer watering holes in the East. At one point when writing from Leadville, Foote broke off near the end of a letter and exclaimed to Gilder, "Oh! If this were only a place that you could ever come to!" (May 1880).

Foote family members speculate that Gilder may have felt that their two worlds were too different or indeed that she may have not found the West beguiling enough to visit (A. Gardiner interview). Once when Gilder was wondering aloud when she and Foote would be able to see each other again, she broke off: "How horrible if you should settle in Leadville and become a Westerner! I cannot believe it. It must never be and it shall not be" (September 29, 1879).

Gilder was very busy, with social and Art Students League commitments, as well as with her growing family and Richard's sometimes precarious health. The extant Gilder letters are full of family news, affectionate encouragement of Foote's drawing and writing, and descriptions of trips to England, France, and the eastern seaboard. Gilder usually eschewed the literary analysis that often peppered Foote's letters. From England Gilder commented, negatively, on meeting Henry James—"He is the same unsatisfactory person he always was"—but only fleetingly mentioned his work (January 1880).

Gilder was, of course, aware of class and gentility, and touched on them in her letters to Foote. She briefly described a female Pre-Raphaelite acquaintance in England as "very accomplished too and very well read," and she related the woman's experiences modeling for Dante Gabriel Rossetti and listening to Algernon Charles Swinburne read his poems (September 29, 1879). Of course, a real lady would never have posed for artists. Gilder's letters are peppered with references to famous people—she was friends with the young, glamorous first lady Mrs. Grover Cleveland and took art lessons from John La Farge himself. She had an oil portrait done by Winslow Homer,[8] who, according to Helena Gilder's granddaughter and namesake, Helena "Hylie" Pappenheimer, was love-struck and disappointed he could not marry her. The Gilders socialized with the sculptor Augustus Saint-Gaudens, and Helena's brother apparently was much enamored of poet Emma Lazarus, much to the scandal of all, including Foote, for whom Lazarus's Jewish faith was an insurmountable obstacle to a proper marriage to a de Kay.

. . .

The letters between Foote and Gilder are on the more literate end of the spectrum when compared to most other extant letters from nineteenth-century women. They are similar in volume and in tone to those of reformer Lucy Stone and her sister-in-law theologian Antoinette Brown Blackwell, in that they mention both personal and also more political, literary, and artistic news (see Stone and Blackwell). And sometimes Foote's reached the heights to which transcendental critic and editor Margaret Fuller rose, in her lyric descriptions of nature and in her analyses of literary ideas. Foote is less intellectual and broadly philosophical than Fuller. Speaking about the redwoods when she first went west, Foote effused, "It must take these old fellows a year to wake up in the morning—their day must last a hundred years and when they sleep the wars and trouble & tumult of Nations, . . . new races springing up, must be the dreams of a night. They seem to take great slow breathes of the sea wind that comes to them from miles away" (MHF to HKG and RWG, September 29, 1877).

Literature was never far from Foote's thoughts, as it helped sustain her in her western isolation. In one of Foote's many references to Emerson in the letters to Helena, she noted:

It is queer that we sh'd both be leaning restfully on that strong heart of a poet—I am thinking of Emerson though you will think of Richard [Gilder's husband]—You spoke of him in this letter of yours I have just read. On these days of our slowly awakening Spring, I find his music stirs the blood in my veins as the sap stirs under the bark and no poets' music ever woke a healthier vibration of the pulses. It is not emotional poetry—and yet I do not get such emotions anywhere else—almost—Nobody can write about a little child as he has—How his great soul must have been wrenched before threnody was born of its anguish—"Nail the wild star in its track on the half climbed Zodiac"—Sometimes I think this is one of the finest lines he, or any body else ever wrote, then a dozen other as good and better ones wake in my memory. What a tone he has! There is no instrument to compare it to. (Spring 1882)

Because of the high esteem in which Foote held her friend and their deep emotional attachment, she often wrote like this to Gilder, expressing considerable intensity. In Paula Blanchard's discussion of other deep friendships between women of the era, she comments on the bond between Sarah Orne Jewett and Annie Fields, noting that Jewett held it "with a significance that can only be called sacramental" (218). Foote's similar devotion to Gilder endows her letters with an authenticity and an honesty that are our gain. We have a letter from Foote's daughter Betty to her mother, about Mary and Helena's friendship. Betty noted that it had a "romance and a kind of glory like that the Greeks took in their epic friendships—Achilles and Patroclus" (September 20, 1924). The monumental importance of their bond was felt by Foote and Gilder themselves, lending an air of dignity and historical self-consciousness to their exchanges.

Unlike many women's letters from the western frontier, as well as the generally stilted correspondence of working-class women, the letters of Foote and Gilder are free of simplistic or sentimental religious piety and also of the gruesome details of nineteenth-century sickness and death. Nonetheless, due to Foote's frequent references to what someone wore or ate and other mundane facts, her letters sometimes sound like those of ordinary pioneer women. Foote relates the illnesses of her children, some of them severe, though she always avoided the melodramatic. Foote's contemporaries described her as eager to spend an evening in the parlor talking about books and culture with those she considered her peers, other professional exiles. Her letters to Gilder, however, even as they did mention authors and literature, also related the quotidian routine of her life, with an emphasis on delineating the social standing of her neighbors or her husband's colleagues. Being a good storyteller and wanting someone to share the ironies of her life in the West, Foote poured out to her friend analyses of provincial California, Colorado, and Idaho. Such efforts were similar in content and tone to those in her novels and stories. Give or take a bit of romanticizing, her descriptions of western locales in fiction echo her letters to Helena, and vice versa. Since Helena Gilder's letters to Foote usually were about her social life and travels more than intellectual pursuits, we may discern that Helena, in fact, may not have had as literary a bent as Foote. Wanting to entertain her social eastern friend, Foote reciprocated by relating her parallel if more modest social activities in the West. This slice of the early social structure of western mining towns reveals much about the values there, and in addition we can learn about women's roles and attitudes toward class, race, and immigration.

. . .

Before she came west, Foote had lived an isolated life with her family, excepting three years at art school in New York City. Her early letters to Gilder reflect that even in the Hudson Valley, there were many people with whom she did not want to interact. At one point she noted to Gilder that her family was having a party and would be "inviting all the neighbors [w]ho are inevitable" (January 20, 1880). She alluded to the fact that some local shopgirls had no taste, lamented that the region was overrun with strangers in the summer, and rejoiced upon hearing that a "cultivated" family might move in nearby (August 1871, November 1871, April 1869). At one point on a walk to town, Foote took shelter during a rainstorm in "a little tenant house" filled with small children and a scolding mother, and felt the family's stolidness acutely. She pettishly asked Gilder, "Did it ever occur to you that the so-called laboring class have really much less to do & think about than any other class above them?" (Summer 1873). As much as she condescended to them, however, Foote was able to sympathetically portray just such a working-class Hudson River family in a children's story five years later, "How Mandy Went Rowing with the 'Cap'n.'" The parents of young Mandy and Bub in the story live a happy if narrow life along the river, where the father fishes for shad and the mother does housework for another family. Foote's lack of empathy or deep interest in those less privileged than herself did not preclude her from writing about them, albeit with some detachment.

From New Almaden, California, in 1877, Foote's first western home, she noted to Gilder that she was pleased she and her husband lived a mile from the dusty town and thus were "spared all the business element of the place," with its makeshift crudity and constant drudgery (March[?] 1877). Foote was actually quite isolated, since her husband often worked overtime at establishing his engineering career in the mine. She spent her time drawing on her "blocks" for

New York commissions and ordering the meals that her maid—brought west for the purpose—cooked. She clearly liked her remove from the tumbled-down shacks of the miners and what she described as the hygienically questionable food sellers. She later had a nurse for their first baby, born in New Almaden. In a letter to Richard Gilder, she related proudly, "I was kept like a fine lady at New Almaden, with two women and a reasonably strong man to wait upon me" (early Fall 1877).

Foote found odd the segregated nature of New Almaden—there were separate "camps" for the Cornish, Mexican, and Chinese miners, with a manager's house, as well as the Footes' dwelling, set away from the others. And she had to laugh at the rigid social hierarchy in place when she learned how unusual it was that her husband's boss, the manager, and his wife had called on them—"a most unusual condescension in the Manager." Apparently, the men formerly in Arthur's position did not merit social calls. Foote said to Gilder, "Isn't it queer? Here we are, absolutly [sic] in the power of this mild, quiet-mannered gentleman, whom we would meet outside of this place, on terms of the easiest equality" (September 14, 1876). Like many people in that era, Foote and her husband felt constrained by the rigid social expectations of a company town. Not usually a champion of the underprivileged, even Foote was horrified to report that one old miner lost his job and had his house destroyed by mine goons one day for the crime of merely buying a stovepipe out of town and not at the company store.

At this point in her career, Foote had not started writing professionally and worked primarily as an illustrator. She was always on the lookout for suitable subjects to sketch and enthusiastically described to Helena and Richard Gilder the various ethnic elements of the dusty mining town, noting the picturesqueness of the tidy Chinese men in their pigtails, the sturdy, rough Cornish people, and the Mexican water carrier, "who wears a sheepskin apron. He is a jewel—a joy to me and a thing of marvelous ugliness." She observed, "These people never intrude, but I like to see them around—I like their strong, wholesome faces and voices when I meet them—They 'compose' better with the 'landscape' in its massive breadth, than the most refined specimens of culture would. I'm in despair because I cannot draw donkeys and mules" (March[?] 1877).

Thus, the way Foote related to the alien cultures around her was not by means of direct communication but through the eyes of her mannered art, which objectified her neighbors and kept them out of her intimate circle. She soon noted from Santa Cruz, "The people are nothing to us and never can be,

but the place owns us. I have never felt at rest since we came West until we got
here by the Sea. That is always the same. It *cannot* be new or crude or out of
tune" ([letter 12A], Fall 1877). She quoted from George Eliot to Gilder at one
point later that "all crudity is immoral," in an effort to find validation for her
sensibilities and exclusive habits (March 8, 1885).

· · ·

The issue of servants complicated Foote's interactions with the locals in the
West. Foote was grateful that white immigrants, as well as the Chinese, were
willing to serve as domestics. She was relieved that the Germans, Irish, and
Chinese, in particular, could be hired in "a region of no servant class . . . a place
where the ladies say 'ma'am' and the servants don't," as one of Foote's characters
describes it (*Edith Bonham* 21). Foote stereotyped immigrants with the usual
characteristics—Chinese, efficient; Germans, strong but coarse; Irish, feckless—but she was never anti-immigration per se. As long as immigrants kept
to a subservient role, which they apparently did with her, Foote appreciated
them. Would she have laughed at the British House of Lords peers sneering-
ly singing in Gilbert and Sullivan's 1882 *Iolanthe:* "Bow, bow, ye lower middle
classes, / Bow, ye tradesmen, bow, ye masses"? Perhaps. Foote's diction in the
letters indicates an attempt to distance herself psychologically by referring to
her nursemaid as "the female" or the cook as "the Chinaman" (November 19,
1882; October 1885). She noted to Gilder that her Chinese cooks were wonderful, because they were neat, "expressionless," and "noiseless and machine-like."
Only after the Chinese cooks had been with the family some time did they
acquire names in her letters, but Foote noted with approval that they still kept
their professional deference. "Charley is really quite one of the family," she explained about one cook, "but I never hear about his illnesses, if he ever has
any—I never know when he is tired or out of humor—He doesn't indulge in such
luxuries" (April 18, 1887).

 As a bride, Foote tried to adopt a confident tone about having servants,
blithely noting that her sister-in-law Mrs. Hague, who could well afford it, "isn't
such a fearful worker as most of the women here are. She has lots of help and
believes in it—So do I. I am not going to economize on servants" (January 1878).
And despite the Footes' often precarious financial situation, especially during
the Idaho years, by means of Foote's writing she managed to keep at least a
cook and governess in the household. It must have been difficult to find help
in rural Idaho, however. Foote found the egalitarian nature of society in the

West a bit off-putting, like Old Mrs. Harris in Cather's story: "Mrs. Harris was no longer living in a feudal society, where there were plenty of landless people glad to render service to the more fortunate, but in a snappy little Western democracy, where every man was as good as his neighbour and out to prove it" (*Obscure Destinies* n.p.).

Foote's dry comments about the public schools of Boise left no doubt that she did not want to sink to the lowest common denominator, democracy or no democracy. The much touted egalitarian nature of the West held little appeal, as she struggled to maintain an exclusive, patrician lifestyle among, as she termed it, "the natives [we] happen to be thrown with" (April 10, 1887). Upholding the enactment of class in the face of difficult material circumstances was important to Foote, as it is to Mrs. Harris, who works herself to the bone so that her daughter can be a woman of leisure. From her constrained circumstances in Idaho, Foote said to Gilder, "Isolated as we are, we find it necessary to keep up the little forms of civilization, as discipline is kept up on ship-board" (January 25, 1887).

On an early visit to San Francisco, Foote expressed some discomfort about the leveling of class she saw there, where "the very servants gamble in stocks" and sometimes end up as rich as their masters (December 7, 1876). She worried about the social changes she perceived and instinctively feared what Richard Ohmann calls the "new conditions . . . that obliterated old hierarchies and broke old social bonds" (152). Yet she felt the spell of San Francisco, noting that "the atmosphere seemed to relax one's fibers more easily" and admitting that "there is a mysterious fascination in the place—I could not help acknowledging it to myself in spite of prejudices" (December 7, 1876). If Arthur had been able to get a job in cosmopolitan San Francisco, Foote might have been happier in the West.

Had San Francisco been her permanent western home, however, Foote's lifelong class inflexibility might have only been reinforced. All through her letters, she had the detachment to perceive this inflexibility, but she saw it as an integral part of her heritage. She mentioned to Gilder once that as they are Quakers, "We *all* have that *narrowness*" (October 10, 1884). Rather than expand her criteria for social acceptance, Foote would be as she describes her character Edith Bonham, who was "of an older world than ours; she kept it in the background, but you felt that she had it, the memories of historic places and a richer human past than we could gather around us" (330). Foote wanted to stay connected to what she perceived to be the immutable touchstones of culture and history, and to do so required that she stay aloof from those who lacked such background. She praised Gilder for her consistency of character: "I so like the *sameness* of your view, through all the whirl around you," continuing, "It is so well-bred to keep one's head as you do, and take the measure of things and choose the best" (January 25, 1887). All very well, one might observe, since Helena Gilder had been trained from childhood to have elite tastes and, as an heiress, could afford them. But for Foote, such consistency demonstrated Gilder's strength of character, and she chose not to focus on economic explanations for Gilder's taste and traits.

. . .

To be fair, one might speculate about the extent to which Foote's exclusivity was partially due to longtime shyness or in fact due to her elitism. In the introduction to Foote's autobiography, Rodman Paul speculates that Foote was merely reticent, as does Lee Ann Johnson in her biography, but Foote's enjoyment of socializing with those who shared her interests and perceived social station belied that. Thomas Donaldson, who met her twice in the West, once in Leadville and once in the Boise canyon, noted how friendly and talkative she was, full of humor and effervescence. Foote was not comfortable socializing with those different from herself, however. She also had a low tolerance for too much interaction, even with peers, and repeatedly wondered at and scolded about the Gilders' relentless round of parties and receptions in fashionable eastern watering holes. Several times, in vain, she invited the Gilders to come to relax with her for a month or two in remote Idaho, in hopes of warding off both Helena's and Richard Gilder's occasional fatigue and illnesses.

Foote noted repeatedly in her correspondence to Gilder that people tired her, and that she disliked crowds and social commitments. This was true in Milton on her family's farm even before she came to mind it in little western towns. From Milton at age twenty-five, Foote declared, "I am strong and well but people wear upon me more than I can tell you" (September 15, 1873). In the first western locations Foote lived in, the stratified mining towns, she was actually relieved that there were few peers with whom she must socialize, although she enjoyed occasional conversations with visiting engineers and other cultured professionals. She twice wrote to Gilder that she preferred the decorative, rough immigrants, whom she could use as models for her sketching, to the "commonplace primness" of the middle-class manager's house (Fall 1876;

March 1877). She retained the antisocial tendencies from her youth, and her later distaste for Boise was to some degree personal and not mere snobbery. From Boise, she admitted to Helena that "Arthur says I need to see more people and it is very true—and it is equally true that I'm getting dreadfully thin-skinned and *dread people!* You will see. Perhaps it *is* the spell of the Canon" ([letter 356] January 8, 1888). Foote's lifelong insistence on exclusivity thus derived in part from her psychological makeup and not only from snobbery.

Still, Foote had little use for most local people and avoided much contact with them. She used various methods of keeping herself and her family separated from the vagaries of the local population. Her battle with "calls," those time-wasting, de rigueur social visits, was one she waged all her life in the West. She did not like to receive or return calls from the local women, and repeatedly complained to Gilder that such social rituals were laughable and a waste of time. Early on, after receiving her first call from a couple in New Almaden, she sniffed, "They are nice enough to see once in a great while—but I dont [*sic*] think I shall care for any of the people here" (July 18, 1876). A few years later in Leadville, Colorado, Foote did not return social calls made to her and blithely noted to Gilder that "I dont [*sic*] make calls. I simply will not, and so the ladies who don't like it stay away. Those who I like best, however, come just the same" (June 12, 1880). Ohmann notes that by this time, the formal call was becoming rarer, and by 1895 it survived only for congratulations and deaths. Yet in the provincial West, Foote continued to endure them. For Gilder's amusement, she described the numerous New Year's calls inflicted on her one year by local Boise ladies and condescendingly related: "They left behind them the most amusing collection of 'Happy New Year!' cards. I enclose one of the modest specimens" ([letter 281] May 1, 1885). Ohmann asserts that "modernizing, middle class people gradually came to see the highly scripted performance of respectability as confining and unnecessary," as did Foote herself in some ways (153). Perhaps those in Boise based their behavior on outmoded norms. It must be remembered, of course, that Foote was busy working most of the time in the West, and did not have time for idle socializing. At first she spent her time making illustrations for various New York and Boston publishers' commissions, but soon after began her dogged routine of writing what she called "potboilers"—her stories and novels—in order to keep her family solvent in the face of her husband's job instability (*Edith Bonham* 43).

. . .

In any event, Foote made no bones about being miserable for most of the Idaho years, for many reasons. First of all, she missed the complicated hierarchies and social density of the East—what Pierre Bourdieu calls "class fractions"—joking that in Boise, "there is one [social] set and everybody is in it" (January 5, 1885). Also about Boise she noted to Gilder that "it is curious how little 'shading' there is, either in the society, or the public life of the place" (April 21, 1889). Foote would have shared the sentiments of a member of an elite African American family in Baltimore: "I sometimes think of my girlhood days when mothers would insist that their children only associate with refined people. . . . There are some who think that a good suit of clothes . . . is all one needs to enter refined company, but back of it should be a respect for all those conventions which make for respectable living" (Mrs. Hester Griffin quoted in Gatewood 183). Genteel conversation and knowledge of and deference to tradition were part of the fabric of life Foote missed in Boise. The historyless and self-satisfied settlers failed to stimulate her educated mind and aesthetic palate.

As Paula Petrik notes in a study of social history of women in Helena, Montana, although class was "a slippery concept at best on the frontier where an individual could rise swiftly to 'capitalist,' tumble to laborer, and rise yet again—all in a single year," opulence and a showy display of wealth usually characterized those who rose thus (xvii, 15; see also Roberts). The Boise ladies' pretensions to gentility, their elaborate dresses and provincial hats, their love of social chatter, and their ill-bred children eventually drove Foote to encourage her husband to build houses for the family away from town, at first ten miles east in the river canyon near his irrigation works and later on the Mesa overlooking the city. She paid for at least one of the houses' construction with money from her novel sales.

. . .

In the many letters from Foote and Gilder's correspondence Foote never stopped complaining about the lack of culture and taste in Idaho. She lamented the loud people and loud clothes, men with dyed hair and families living in squalor (June 15, 1884). Over the eleven years there, the Footes moved every few years due to the ups and downs of Arthur Foote's irrigation schemes. Sometimes they lived with Mary Hallock Foote's sister Bessie and her family in town in order to lower expenses. From comments in her children's stories, it is clear that Foote felt at a disadvantage in this peripatetic limbo, having to bring up her children without the stability of grandparents at the Hallock and Foote family compounds in New York and Connecticut, respectively. In addition, Foote felt humiliated because her husband had apparently managed to "get left" in a rural western backwater with no career prospects. His life "pauses," as she explains about some unlucky men in the West, and "the conspicuous tests, moral and physical," that exist there, threaten his family's security and indeed honor (*The Idaho Stories* 301). Soon Arthur's drinking on the job causes Foote great worry, and she finally admits to Gilder that he might lose his position entirely if he has a relapse. In a rare and sudden moment of abject emotion, she exclaimed, "Oh Hy . . . all I ask is *barest safety*—and respectability—on the *outside*" (August 8, 1889). Although quite desperate, she seemed to care only about appearances, and was willing to suffer privately as long as the outward show was maintained.

In less extreme moments, Foote was also concerned with respectability and joked about the spectacle of herself being "on the seat of Propriety" (April 7, 1889). Yet she detailed to Gilder how careful one had to be about maintaining one's social position. "The dressmakers here are the queerest lot," she started out in one Boise letter.

> I had one good one whom I had to give up because it transpired that her customers were sadly mixed. She worked for the ladies of the town and Arthur did not like me to "try on" at the house where the professionals also went to try on their robes of purple and green. I *thought* there were some queer looking clothes lying around, when I went there but supposed it to be the taste of the West. The present one is very respectable, but doesn't know anything and is very lofty and condescending as befits the wife of an overland stage driver. (April 4, 1886)

The description of the new seamstress is an example of Foote's condescension to the provincial pretensions that she found so exasperating about Boise, yet one wonders if others in the town found her as full of affectations in her own way. Nonetheless, Foote clearly wanted to stay above reproach, and at one point, when "an old Leadville acquaintance—not a very reputable one," called on the Footes in Boise, Foote mused to Gilder, "I wonder whether I am a person you ought to know—I am getting such a mixed set of acquaintances!" (Summer[?] 1887).

Still, Foote did not test the waters of eccentricity too deeply, and at one point apparently dropped friends in Boise when they faced disgrace. A Mr. Camp had been dismissed from his job as territorial assayer because of embezzling charges, and his wife and children—who were regular playmates of the Foote children—had to leave town to live on a remote ranch. Foote did not mention any attempt on her part to keep up the acquaintance, merely noting to Gilder how sad it was, and how they "seemed so affectionate and simple-hearted" but "have come to a most horrible end socially" (May 28, 1885). Thus, whether due to Foote's and particularly her husband's moral rectitude or to local pressure, public impropriety severed the friendship. In *Edith Bonham* the narrator asserts that in Boise, "We've no classes, but we have public opinion chopped out to fit the masses" (199). One might think that living apart from the town, Foote would not care if her neighbors looked askance, but in *Edith Bonham*, as well as in another Idaho story, Foote depicts the care female characters must take of their reputation in a small place much like Boise ("On a Side Track," in *The Cup of Trembling*).[9] In both cases, a lady has been too much talked about for being seen in the innocent and platonic company of a man not her husband. The mere appearance of impropriety in the two tales is enough to set in motion the actions of the honorable to rectify the situation.

The ethos of Victorian respectability and the looming shadow of its opposite, scandal, took on a personal urgency for Foote during the long Idaho years in which she tried to keep her family fed and together. Sometimes she ridiculed the concept of respectability, as when she avers in *Edith Bonham* that respectability is merely being "dressed in a certain way and married to someone rich" (203). At one point she joked to Gilder that a certain job her husband was considering with the Geological Survey was "very respectable, you know" (April 12, 1889). Even allowing for a bit of coyness here, Foote was quite serious about keeping up appearances in Idaho, especially as it became more and more of a challenge. Louisa May Alcott comments, from experience no doubt, that it can be difficult for "decayed gentlefolk" to "earn their bread without the entire sacrifice of taste and talent which makes poverty so hard for such to bear" ("How I Went" n.p.). Foote made sure that her own taste and talent did not go to waste by using every ounce of it to write and draw for the *Century* and *St. Nicholas* checks that sustained her family and its gentility.

So it continued that the people of Boise, who have been known in recent years to celebrate a Mary Hallock Foote Day, did not elicit much empathy or sympathy from Foote when she lived there. In *Edith Bonham* the character based on Foote bitterly exclaims, "Take a town like Boisé and persons who are not above the average even there, who have never heard of your rules. . . . I trust no one" (33). In an essay warning "pretty girls" from the East not to marry western men, Foote explains the problems for cultured women in the West: "Even the ordeal of taste is not to be despised—taste, which environs and consoles and unites and stimulates women in the East, and which disunites and tortures and sets them at defiance, with one another, in the West" (*The Idaho Stories* 299). Foote herself was part of that disunity. For her Idaho story "The Harshaw Bride," she apologized to her publisher for the "rowdy" narrator, an ordinary Idaho matron, hoping that the piece "will not disgust you in the person of the slangy little woman who tells it,—which I do assure you she isn't Mrs. Foote! . . . But she's awfully natural, Mrs. Tom Daly, I do assure you. I know/knew [*sic*] lots of her out here, and her husband too. They are almost our commonest type" (MHF to Robert Underwood Johnson, May 13, 1895).[10] To this reader the "Harshaw Bride" narrator seems a bit voluble but not particularly "common," so Foote must have been particularly sensitive to shades of verbal refinement not apparent to all.

To Helena, Foote called the local Boise women "very kindhearted but fearfully poky and provincial" and said they "dress like Yahoos" (May 19, 1884; September 15, 1889). She continued: "Something is always wrong, poor things. Their ideals are all wrong to begin with" (September 15, 1889). This last comment is typical of Foote, vaguely holding up many aspects of material life to so-called ideals, and thus conflating moral, literary, social, and aesthetic standards with the sartorial. The West and western people did not stand a chance of making the grade, since almost by definition they lacked knowledge of her specific, highly textured upbringing and its "ideals."

Similarly, Foote explained to Gilder just before Christmas 1887 that she could not find anything suitable in the Boise stores to send the Gilders; between the shoddy local goods and worn-out Native American relics available, she laments, "We have too many barbaric things in proportion to things which speak of sweetness and light" (December 16, 1887). By "sweetness and light," Matthew Arnold's catchphrase, Foote meant beautiful, well-made items that might grace expensive homes like the Gilders.' Alan Trachtenberg points out, however, that civilization loses a good deal if it is made up of only sweetness and light.[11] As middle-class nineteenth-century Americans sought to better themselves and absorb packaged culture, such as in the Chautauqua movement, they came to define culture as the manifestations of idealized human endeavor, in part following Arnold's dictum that it "is *a study of perfection*" (Buckler 459; emphasis in the original). The era's sanitized versions of history and human endeavor depressed William James, who lamented the absence of the dark side of human nature in them, the *Hebraic* side, per Arnold. But Foote did not want to write about the dark side and preferred her culture exalted. When confronted with Native Americans camped around Boise, she declared to Gilder some eight years after first going west that she "hate[d] these wild peoples," but upon reading Bancroft's *Myths and Antiquities of the Native Races*, she admitted "it must be confessed some of their legends and myths are fine" (October 10, 1884). Foote could appreciate the purportedly barbaric if it was digested through a translating and mediating lens. She needed those lenses, however, since their strengths were not evident to her in the prosaic or squalid real thing.

. . .

Foote was not sure if culture could survive at all in the West. In the novella *The Fate of a Voice* (1889), a young opera singer allows all her careful training to wither away when she marries an irrigation engineer and goes to live in an Idaho canyon. This is Foote's allegory that high culture was next to impossible to enact in the wilderness, in places with no facilities, no tradition, no audience. In *Edith Bonham* Foote's affectionate descriptions of old New York society pepper the text, as cosmopolitan Edith, the Helena character, tries to find her feet in remote Idaho. Despite her joy as governess to her dead friend's children, Edith observes that the people of Boise seem shallow and petty; she sometimes longs for her "old set, the talkers" in New York, who, for all their urban self-centeredness, "had imagination, if they chose to use it, [and] they had subtlety" (215). On a visit east, an aunt tells Edith that she should return to "circles where the talk is deep, and simple, and strange to an outsider—where there is a reticence and a grace of the times that do not come again; where elegance is understood, and manners have become a manner as old and myste-rious as the past that made it" (242). Foote clearly revered the fact that Helena was lucky enough to live in this charmed, upper-class environment. This pas-sage echoes Olive Chancellor in Henry James's *Bostonians*, as she sits one eve-ning in an elegant salon as the sun sets over the Charles River in Back Bay. She reflects, "Civilization, under such influence, in such a setting, appeared to have done its work; harmony ruled the scene; human life ceased to be a struggle" (156). The structural economic inequalities that coexist with and indeed make possible such soirees are momentarily forgotten, even by someone as vigilant as the egalitarian Olive. Thus, culture for Miss Chancellor as well as for Foote does not usually serve as a "democratizing influence," in Trachtenberg's phrase, but is an exclusive and uplifting path to finer ideas and ideals, ideals of which the uneducated and lower classes, Foote at least feels, have little notion or understanding (141). Trachtenberg notes, "The emergent idea of the cultured life made it increasingly difficult . . . for its devotees even to *see* the rest of the world, let alone see it critically. Stock notions of 'the other half' were implanted in the evolving middle-class consensus" (144).

And indeed, although Foote might have occasionally empathized with the plight of some local people, she did not take much interest or even *see* most of her neighbors in the West. When first in California, she wrote to Gilder, "The country makes a deep impression, but the people scarcely any at all—I feel as if Arthur were the only human being here. . . . The place is full of strange faces" (September 3, 1876). In another early letter, from the West Coast, she said, "I have never seen a place in my large experience so heaped with advantages by Nature and so meagre in human interest. How *can* the people be so stupid, with such beauty around them!" (October 29, 1877). A month later, she continued in the same vein: "I hope I am not prejudiced against western society, but except for a very small set in s. f. [San Francisco] I have seen none that could be called anything but an incongruous mixture of incongruent elements." Foote then mentioned that there were many "good plain folks" in Santa Cruz, "who ought to make you feel happy—whom you ought to want to be with—and don't!" (November 1877). She cringed at someone she met in New Almaden, a man who called himself a major, yet he was "one of those people who worry you because he is so nearly a gentleman, and yet so fatally *not* one" (April 12, 1877). A few years later when an acquaintance from Leadville wrote to her, Foote complained to Helena that Miss Ward insisted on pouring out her soul in "gushing letters. I feel very old and cynical when I read them. But surely we didn't write our hearts out to friends of a day, did we? Perhaps it is 'Western'" ([letter 230] January 20, 1880).

Foote could understand people from different backgrounds or other cultures only on condition that they had the requisite manners and background of the Anglo upper class. In New Almaden, an Austrian baron came to visit the mining works, and Foote initially found it very "disagreeable" that hospitality dictated she lend him her bedroom in which to change his clothes. The baron later sat and talked European politics with the couple, however, and Foote sheepishly admitted to Gilder that "I felt ashamed of myself when he proved to be so gentle and delicately bred" (September 14, 1876). But, of course, most of the populace of isolated western towns were not European royalty, and Foote ignored them as much as she could.

. . .

After more than a decade in the West, Foote found a paradigm for herself, her husband, and the other engineers, surveyors, and educated people she met in the West who were not pioneers or homesteaders. She termed them "professional exiles" (December 7, 1876). Historian Richard Ohmann calls them the professional middle class. Clark C. Spence, in the intriguingly titled *Mining Engineers and the American West: The Lace-Boot Brigade, 1849–1933*, describes the peripatetic, patrician, and sometimes opulent life of the West's first engineers, detailing their superior education and cultural sophistication. In this era, engineers the world over were making their often imperialist mark, from India to South America, from Africa to Russia.

At first, Foote did not know how to understand this exiled society and explored her attitudes in letters to Gilder, perhaps in an attempt to gain clarity. She first met these kinds of people in San Francisco at the gracious home of her husband's brother-in-law expert mining consultant James D. Hague and his wife. She described them as "men who have been educated abroad and have lived everywhere. They dont [sic] care particularly about San Francisco or any other place"—"they were not 'Western' or local in any sense." Foote added, "I feel very unsettled in my views of Western society since seeing them," thus admitting that the cognitive dissonance she was experiencing left her not knowing what to think if she let go of her preconceived expectations about the West. She continued: "I wonder if this letter will sound strange to you and unlike me—I felt unlike myself all the time we were away [in San Francisco]—it is venturing into strange waters" (December 7, 1876).

When she further discovered that these clever men had tolerant mates who did not dread the constant relocations, she was truly confused. The cultured eastern wives talked to her about how they coped living so far from their birthplaces, but they were not bitter and felt proud that they made the best of things, although Foote thought she saw a certain "pathetic sense of being alien" in their talk. She noted insightfully to Gilder that these "very charming women—well-bred, gentle, and very adaptable . . . seem to have fewer prejudices than we have" (December 7, 1876). Prejudices were a luxury in a West often too demanding to allow them.

Foote was not one to keep an open mind and stay comfortable with ambiguous situations, however, and so, after some years in the West, she was able to categorize these professionals and scientists and their adaptable wives into a class of their own. It comforted her but also haunted her that she had found an identity that she could connect to her eastern roots. She and the other professional exiles were high-class gypsies living "on the crust of much that lay beneath," as she termed it about Leadville in her autobiography (*A Victorian Gentlewoman* 197).

Some eleven years after her initial discussion of this phenomenon with Gilder, Foote explained herself more fully:

> It came to me one evening at [the Wilds'] house—Mrs Wild sitting in the hammock . . . in a charming Paris gown (made over, so she said) singing Spanish songs to the accompaniment of her guitar, tilting herself slightly in the hammock, looking so awfully *civilized*—it occurred to me that there is a class of Americans not yet classified—strangers in their native land, exiles under their own flag—The relations of these people with other exiles, with the natives they happen to be thrown with, their semi-estrangement from the East—their pride and their despair in the life they lead. . . . The most bewildering thought is that perhaps we belong to this unclassified class ourselves. What if we should find that we cannot live East because we have lived too long in the West. (April 10, 1887)

It is interesting that after more than a decade spent mostly in the West Foote had to classify the situation at all, that she was driven to do it, and that she still felt so deracinated. She intuited despair in her fellow exiles, but as we have seen with the couples at the Hagues' house, some did not seem to mind the life at all. As William Bevis notes, for successful Americans the more elite one is, the less one is identified with any particular region of the country. It follows that to be local and regional is to be "marginal" and not compatible with the necessary "liquidity" of exchanges of marketable skills, mobile manpower, and hard data that capitalism requires (21). Foote and her husband were on the cutting edge of this trend, but the strain of it took a toll on the shy, cultivated Foote.

Professionals in the West, as well as those of more modest backgrounds who aspired to upward mobility, were the direct or indirect bearers of national and business cultural norms. They reached all over the West with their elite standards, so that by the end of the century, "Eastern corporations had virtually accomplished their control of Western enterprises," according to Trachtenberg (24). Stephen M. Voynick observes the same dynamic in mining enterprises, noting that in the early days a single man and his hand-panned claim or other professional mining skills could make a living. By the late 1870s, however, the best an independent miner could hope for was finding a good lode in his spare time from his day-laboring job and selling it for a good profit to large, consolidated, and eastern-backed corporations or syndicates. Foote certainly was part of this exchange, both in Leadville and Idaho. In the introduction to *The Led-*

Horse Claim the narrator speaks frankly of "the ark of the mining industry . . . awaiting the olive-leaf of Eastern capital" with its "uncertain doves of promise" (9). In a later Idaho irrigation story, "The Watchman," a homesteading family who has lived in contented isolation for years is forced to acquiesce to the large-scale irrigation and infrastructure plans that an eastern company has for their arid valley. These seemingly merely economic issues have cultural and class implications, since those who succeeded in the West had to ally themselves in some way with power structures that were not usually based there. Sociologist Thomas D. Hall calls this "dependency theory" and shows how economic colonization in the American Southwest to some degree determined and skewed original, more egalitarian existing social relations in the region by creating an unhealthy dependency on remote centers of power and capital (Limerick, Milner, and Rankin 199).

. . .

Foote's artistic, financial, and indeed psychological dependence on the East defined most aspects of her personal and professional existence. She repeatedly and emphatically stressed to Gilder that this or that associate of the family was *not* local or western, thus giving a pejorative twist to such descriptors. She imported an English governess whose family she knew for her three children rather than expose them to the local Boise schools or even an unknown American tutor. She later sent her son to boarding school in the East, the first year "entirely on the strength of the blessed Century checks," so that he would have the advantages of contact with the old elite (August 8, 1889). Foote spent much of a long letter to Gilder explaining why the boarding school she and her husband picked, St. Paul's, in Concord, New Hampshire, was the best. She had met several of its graduates, one of whom on a visit to the West exhibited "breeding" that stood the "test" (March 28, 1888). As C. Wright Mills asserts, "The school—rather than the upper-class family—is perhaps the most important agency for transmitting the traditions of the upper social classes" (quoted in White 22). Foote believed that St. Paul's would instill character and an "unaffected, manly tone" in their son, and stated with pride that it had such high standards that "the boys respect it," which resulted in "not, I think, a bad sort of snobbishness" (March 28, 1888).

Foote was not alone in her belief that the right kind of school would instill the proper traits in boys. George Van Santvoord, the influential headmaster of the Hotchkiss School in Connecticut, stated, "To be a gentleman, to be a person of character—that is the most important thing we can teach you here" (quoted in Birmingham 249). Foote said in her autobiography that when, after young Arthur Foote's first term at St. Paul's, the distinguished headmaster wrote that "'Arthur is a good and gentlemanly child.' . . . We delighted in that phrase!" (*A Victorian Gentlewoman* 317). Foote wanted a secure social and professional assurance for her boy, a position legal historian G. Edward White defines, quoting Mills: "Individuals who had passed through the boarding-school-university-club route came to assume a 'manner of simplicity and the easy dignity that can arise only out of an inner certainty that one's being is a definitely established fact of one's world, from which one cannot be excluded, ignored, snubbed, or paid off'" (30).

Foote was fully aware the opportunities her children would miss if they did not have the requisite upper-middle-class off-site educations, as her portrayal of the adolescent children of an engineer in the Idaho-based *The Chosen Valley* (1892) attests. The girl Dolly feels inadequate to live anywhere but her remote canyon. She admits that without education or specialized training, the best she can do is marry well, explaining that "I should not care to marry beneath a certain class, the class I'm supposed to belong to, yet I have not been bred like the women of that class. I should never feel at home with them" (527). The son of the unsuccessful engineer, young Alan, is angrier. He blusters to an acquaintance who has just returned from engineering school in Europe, "Have n't you been everywhere that I want to go? and seen everything, and had the chance I ought to have had?" (118). Foote wanted to avoid such fates for her children, and in fact did.

. . .

Foote had the self-deprecation to joke to Gilder about the family's purported exclusivity in their Idaho canyon, noting that when the spring runoff made the river impassable and the carriage roads dangerous, "our camp is quite fastidious—We are nothing if not picturesque, and exclusive" (June 26, 1885). But she was quite serious about keeping her children away from the "dreadful vulgarity" of the Boise children (July 19, 1888). Like the townspeople in Cather's "Old Mrs. Harris" who do not want their children playing with the motley offspring of the sexually loose laundress, Foote fears contamination by what Mrs. Harris terms "ill-bred and unclassified" western neighbors (*Obscure Destinies* n.p.).

As for the children's parents, Foote maintained a distance from most of the adults as well. She found most local people painfully provincial and appallingly unaware of the things that made life worth living for her—art, books, intelligent conversation, and aesthetic discernment. Her fellow professional exiles were the only ones to hold any interest for her, and they were naturally few and far between in the rural areas in which she lived. In Leadville the Footes attended an "'assembly'—a select? (yes very select for a place like this)," at which she noted, once again self-deprecatingly, "I suppose every body here secretly wonders when they first come if there *are* any people here nice enough for them to associate with and are greatly surprised to find themselves by no means exceptional." She found a few kindred souls among her husband's professional friends in Leadville, but was careful to place people in a social hierarchy for Gilder: a Mr. Litchfield is "one of the characteristic types of the place—a young man of fine education, good family & prospects as an Engineer," whereas another man is described as "Robert the weak Englishman of low degree who attends to the horses" (May 28, 1979). Like quirky Dr. Obet in Cooper's *Prairie,* she must categorize everyone into a tidy hierarchy.

Young Mr. Litchfield exhibited a property that Foote mentioned again and again in letters and her novels: he was an innate gentleman. She explained to Gilder that even though he was living in a rude cabin in Leadville with a mining partner and looking after his own domestic needs, Litchfield was "concealing the gentleman as much as a gentleman can be concealed by such 'lendings'" (May 28, 1879). Foote mentioned later the pride she had in her husband and his assistant in Idaho when her third child was almost due. The men behaved solicitously to her in the remote canyon, keeping a horse ready day and night for two weeks to go for the doctor when the child came. She concluded, "It was a test of the delicacy and inborn and bred gentlemanliness of our men" (March 6, 1887).

As in her early novels about Leadville, Foote liked to believe in innate gentility, and when events proved her assessments of people wrong, she was at a loss. The Footes initially got to know the governor of Idaho, who "has a character, a lovely wife, & everything dignified," and when the governor was discovered to lack political integrity, Foote was humiliated "in light of the mistake we made in the Governor's character" (January 5, 1885; March 1885). Likewise, when Foote finally confessed to Gilder that her husband's drinking problem had caused problems for years and had occasionally jeopardized his job, she had no explanation for her years of alluding to the fineness of his breeding and character. She had kept up the fiction that he was of a superior stock and that even the major disappointments of uncertain irrigation projects in Idaho had not been able to weaken his character. Perhaps this is why despite Arthur's weaknesses and failures, Foote stayed with her flawed man.

. . .

The power inequity that existed between Gilder and Foote from the beginning became more pronounced after Foote went West. It was an inequity originating from their different social circles, levels of wealth, artistic talent, and, also, it might be added, by Foote's insistence on upholding those differences. As Gilder herself affectionately noted in an early letter to Foote: "With you, I live in an atmosphere so rosy with your affection . . . that the ideal Helena whom you think you see almost exists in virtue of your desire that it should, and I am better and stronger for it, my dearest" ([Staten Island, Summer 1873]). Foote continued this exalted view of her friend all her life and often referred to Gilder and her family members as "noble" (Easter Sunday 1885; November 10, 1885). Whenever she received new photographs of the Gilder children or news of the Gilders' activities, Foote frequently assured her friend that it was visually obvious that their breeding and character were of the highest sort. One would think that having put Gilder and her family on a pedestal, Foote might at some point have become disillusioned with her "ideal," but this does not appear to have happened. Gilder's charming ways persisted as a standard by which all people, children, marriages, femininity, and artistic talent were measured. By contrast, Foote's glowing bridal faith in her husband during the early New Almaden years gave way to stoic despair in the difficult Boise era. Foote had no such unpleasant or unaccountable disappointment in the local people in the West, it may be observed, since she had low expectations for them to begin with. That they often fell short of her ideals was an ongoing source of occasional exasperation and frequent humor for Foote, but not disillusion.

After Foote has been in the West many years, she ruefully described herself as having become "Western and narrow," and wondered how the cosmopolitan Gilder would find her when they finally met again (November 16, 1887). Foote subtly but frequently alluded to their unequal social positions in her letters, as well as to their differing propensities for socializing. Whatever their respective classes, the two women did, indeed, have differing temperaments, Helena de Kay Gilder honestly enjoying the social limelight and Mary Hallock Foote preferring a more private, family-oriented circle similar to the one she had grown up with. Gilder moved in the most elite circles both in the United States and in Europe, and Foote, for all her gentility and culture, had much humbler connections. Early in their relationship, a young Foote referred to Gilder's "illustrious family" and noted that her own Quaker blood was more homespun (July 1871; January 1874).

Foote respected the artistic as well as the elite, and the fact that Gilder and her brother Charley, as well as Gilder's husband, created art and poetry meant more to Foote than mere wealth might have. As has been demonstrated, for Foote the best art elevates people, history, and geography. She talked a good deal in the letters about her own and Gilder's "Art." It was this strong cultural connection with all the Gilders that deepened Foote's lifelong communication with them. She was never merely a social hanger-on, but an intelligent admirer of their creative selves, who saw, or believed she saw, into their inner characters by means of their artistic creations. Foote analyzed and praised Charley's and Richard's writings as they were published in Richard's *Century* magazine, and she continually encouraged Helena Gilder to keep up her art, especially after marriage. Ever the Arnoldian, Foote averred that art raises a person above his peers, proposing that Charley Gilder's "high & sad nature, so impossible to *mix* with the average, seems to point to a separate & unusual destiny for him" (January 1874). She considered Richard's poems excellent because they "seem often so grand and impersonal as if no one had written them but as if they had always been written." Richard's "pure high soul" transcends the mundane, and transported her to an exalted plane (January 10, 1886). She stated with awe that Helena and Richard Gilder "make Art a thing as holy as religion" (June 1881). She also mentioned to Helena the authors who were "god-like" to her— Ralph Waldo Emerson and Robert Browning—and she admired Ivan Turgenev because of his "masterly impersonality" (Spring 1870; September 21, 1877).

Conventional transatlantic cultural ideas such as these have class repercussions. Foote adhered to what Trachtenberg calls the "healing properties identified with high culture," a concept that he asserts served to alienate rich and poor in America at this time. He continues, "When narrowly defined as art, polite conversation and manners, genteel styles of speech and dress, culture seemed antithetical to the rough and tumble of everyday life" (145). Foote's constant struggle in the West was to maintain a zealously guarded island of refinement and polish in towns that were full of those she called "Philistines" and "Yahoos" (September 18, 1887; September 15, 1889). She thus defended the social structure that kept her own cultural capital current and useful in maintaining her lifestyle. By avoiding crudity, one made a virtue out of such avoidance and damned those whose poverty or lack of education make crudity the norm. The fact is ignored that it was much more difficult for working-class people to achieve the standards of gentility and propriety that the middle and upper class took for granted.

· · ·

In the end, Foote's aesthetic judgments validated the elitism and exclusivity in her life and work, since she used them to dismiss any efforts less professional or not tied to eastern American literary and cultural standards. Thomas Donaldson, who settled in Boise in 1869, recounted the cultural self-sufficiency of the early days of the region, when a dance, a church sing-along, or an amateur theatrical night was an event to be cherished. But Foote was firmly tied to her eastern roots, and, like Gertrude Atherton's provincial ingenues in *The Californians* who yearn for New York and European shops and society, Foote often exhibited a sense of inferiority about her adopted region. This was particularly manifested in the way that she compared Gilder's life to her own in the letters. Although she ruefully admitted it was more difficult to determine people's social status in the West than in the East, Foote doggedly continued doing so, pointing out when this or that acquaintance had connections to the East and even to Gilder herself (November 28, 1884; September 18, 1887; March 9, 1889).

Foote had the self-consciousness to see the humorous side of this purported name-dropping, but kept doing it nonetheless (June 8, 1887). She could never forget that the Gilders were her "distinguished friends" and that they moved among "certain people of importance," whereas she herself stayed put in the Boise canyon with her family and a few handpicked associates and servants (September 18, 1887; January 9, 1887). She feared that news of her family's canyon activities and of her husband's tepid success and outright failures was dull indeed compared to Gilder's letters of dinners at the White House, dressmaking in Paris, and galas in New York. "I meander on about our *no* doings when your affairs are so much better worth talked about—It isn't a fair exchange," Foote wryly stated (September 18, 1887). Homegrown observations, new traditions and exigencies, none of it seemed valid to Foote. She could not lead where later Laura Ingalls Wilder, Elinor Pruitt Stewart, and Anne Ellis would go: accounts of ordinary yet interesting western lives. In one letter where Foote was detailing the social whirl in Boise, she broke off and exclaimed to Gilder, "But you cannot care for this" (November 16, 1887). Compared to Gilder's life, her Idaho existence "reels with stillness," and she perceptively noted that "the sense of contrast is picturesque—it—runs through our lives" (September 18, 1887). In a gesture implying that it was somehow her own responsibility to close the gap, Foote wrote, "Your world is so different. The difficulty is always on my side" (December 16, 1887).

Foote's insistence on hierarchy and eastern connections may indicate she was grasping at a world that she felt was slipping hopelessly away from her western life. From Idaho she wrote to Gilder: "I told you our plan of house building and taking up land out here. It is a good thing to do, but it is not the happiest thing in all ways. It commits us to more years in the West; and at first I felt that it was another stroke of fate—and that we were being whirled apart. And I felt a sort of bitterness against your world, which has become so complex since the old days. I ought to have remembered that there is a fatality in your life as in mine" ([letter 356] January 8, 1888). Foote was forty-one here and four years into the eleven-year frustration that Idaho became for Arthur and the family. A few months later during the same year Foote was planning a trip east but had some trepidation about seeing Gilder again. She worried that her letters were too frank and gave her friend "wounds." She then confessed, "I must love you on my knees for a while before I deserve to ask you to take me in your arms again" (March 3, 1888). This startling and humbling image shows where Foote believed the power lay in their friendship, and that she was somehow unworthy.

. . .

Foote reveled in hearing about the Gilders' activities, some of which she even read about in the society page of the local Boise newspapers. She commented that she wished the mail had not been promptly delivered one day, so a letter of Gilder's written on White House stationery might have been left out "'keerless-like' at the offices downtown" to impress the provincials in Boise (December 16, 1887). Foote kept her head and did not fawn over Gilder about her social connections but clearly was pleased by her friend's claims to fame. But it was Gilder and not Foote who truly "lived on the crust of much that lay beneath" (*A Victorian Gentlewoman* 197). To the upper class, position meant not just wealth and power but also "membership in an exclusive social network" (Ostrander 5). The Gilders' set, even as sketchily as it can be discerned from the Mary Hallock Foote–Helena de Kay Gilder letters, indicates the truth of this. The Gilders saw certain people in New York in the winter, and met the same crowd in coastal Marion, Massachusetts, in the summer, where they and the Clevelands had summer homes, as well as in the grand "cottages" of Newport, Rhode Island. Richard Gilder, as one of the "gentleman publishers" of the era and editor of the prestigious *Century* magazine, had a suitably genteel job with which to move among the artists and notables of the day. If Foote had married a man who had been a business success, she, too, might have made a life among this elite. Like the impoverished March girls in *Little Women,* Foote was the daughter of a gentleman and thus "a gentlewoman by birth" (248). As it was, Foote had at least some entrée into the upper-class network, through both the Gilders as well as through her husband's family, particularly his successful brother-in-law James D. Hague.

Perhaps Foote's persistent determination to keep her family exclusive and connected to eastern centers of power helped in the long run. It demonstrated to people such as the Hagues and others who could do her husband some good that if Arthur's talented wife refused to "go native" in the West, then perhaps they could trust him to manage their mining or irrigation projects. Due to Arthur Foote's own patrician upbringing, he himself attracted men of a certain refined class to his projects in the West, even though he lacked the social finesse to keep those far away with influence and money interested in his projects. At one point Foote complained to Gilder that "Richard helps you, but my 'men folks' dont [*sic*] help me a bit" (July 5, 1889). It was up to Foote to use the earnings from her drawings and writings to maintain her family's standard of living, as it was up to her to keep alive the family's connections to powerful friends and relations who might invest in her husband's projects.

In this era, the role of women in what Gertrude Atherton calls the "aristocratic middle class" was, not surprisingly, more constrained than that of their less elite sisters. What elite women could and could not do—a frequent concern in Foote's novels and in her letters to Helena—was still being studied in the late twentieth century, and "rigid gender differentiation and gender stratification" still dictate behavior in the American upper class (Ostrander 6). One hundred years earlier, these societal constraints were even more in force, especially for women. We see this in Helena Gilder's pursuits, and although Foote lived in the West where she might have let some of these rules go, her life, too, reflected eastern standards of propriety. When Gilder wrote that she was giving up serious artistic ambitions upon her marriage to Richard, Foote was conventional enough to see the inevitability of such a decision. Yet she still felt that Gilder's marriage was in some sense a tragedy for her friend's "genius." For years after the marriage, as well as after the Gilders started a family, Foote continued to write letters to Helena Gilder encouraging her to keep up her art. Foote chose to share a feminist friend's initial reaction to Gilder's marriage by presenting the friend's argument: "*Any* woman can marry but few are so manifestly cut out for greatness in Art" as Gilder (February 1874). Thus, Foote's class beliefs warred with her appreciation of her friend's creative genius.

A proper lady should have a husband, however. Foote considered women who never married or who married late odd, even if she admired them—women like Foote's own aunt Philadelphia, her husband's cousin Katherine, and Foote's "eccentric" landlady in Santa Cruz, Brook Farm alumna Georgiana Kirby (April 12, 1877). At the same time, Foote earnestly believed in Gilder's artistic ability— "your light shines brighter," she said to her—and felt it a shame for her to hide her light under a bushel (April 18, 1887). Foote's and Gilder's tacit acceptance of Gilder's new role as social maven and networking helpmeet to her husband's career shows just how limited the life choices were for a woman who wanted to stay in high society. That Edith Wharton, Foote's contemporary, could both write and play society hostess is a tribute to Wharton's determination. But it must be noted that Wharton did not publish until she was forty years old, remained childless, and in the end settled in France, whence another creative nineteenth-century American woman, the unmarried Mary Cassatt, had earlier fled to preserve her artistic vision.

...

Even as Mary Hallock Foote spent much time and effort in remote parts of the American West maintaining the class position of her own eastern youth and perpetuating it in her children, she also came to love aspects of her adopted region. Her cultivated eastern character based on Helena Gilder, Edith Bonham, allows that the West has a "tremendous force, concealed somehow" (263). In her letters and her novels, Foote often waxed rhapsodic about the western landscape, but it was unusual for her to praise much about the culture in the West. After moving outside of Boise, "the little stupid town," as she termed it to Gilder, she could enjoy the mountains and muse that "there is certainly a simplicity of view out here which one cannot help to a certain extent, sharing. Life is younger, fresher, less subtle, *far* less intellectual but also less timid and self-conscious." Foote had just mentioned that when she read the writings of William Dean Howells and Henry James, she had "a sort of resisting feeling—isn't it queer?" The work of regionalists Charles Egbert Craddock (Mary Noailles Murfree) and Joel Chandler Harris, however, gave her "a more genuine emotion," in spite of the fact that "they haven't of course the perfection of method or the breadth of Howells or James but they do not, on the other hand, make you wish you were a Pagan, nourished in a creed outworn—so that you might catch glimpses of 'something less forlorn'" (October 10, 1884). Foote acknowledged that the old modes of interpreting human behavior and social norms did not exactly apply to the experiments in settlement and reinvention that were the West. A few years later she continued in the same vein: "There are no new sorrows and needs here, but they have greater relief and are more conspicuous and dramatic. That isn't the side of the life out here altogether for poets to treat of. The movement [is] in its largeness, not individual tragedies or even race tragedies—for in the main, the movement of life in the West is hopeful and strong. . . . There are stagnant spots, halts, and deserters in every march, but the march moves on" ([letter 356] January 8, 1888). These moments display a rare acceptance on Foote's part of the emotional power of the new, and the aridity of the traditional and magisterial. She temporarily abandoned her prejudices about her locale and defended it over the well-worn paths illuminated by the literary gods of her age. She preferred the social density of the milieu that produced the mannered complexity of Henry James and the Gilders, but she could sometimes also appreciate the honesty and simplicity of a less complicated worldview.

In many ways it is a loss for the Far West that Foote clung to her social pretensions and stratified outlook as much as she did. If she had seen her new territories less through the eyes of New York and more through the eyes of California, Colorado, and Idaho, she might have let go the need to live and write according to Helena Gilder's values and have grown into a more expansive set of standards. All her adult life, however, Foote kept up the role of the "Victorian gentlewoman in the Far West," the title aptly chosen for her autobiography in 1972. In the end, the Foote-Gilder letters reveal the love and longing of an exiled gentlewoman for the East—its culture and depth, old class hierarchies and traditional norms, Anglo elite and older history. Foote's emotional and professional dependence on the Gilders was a crucial part of her makeup, and certainly contributed significantly to her inability to acclimate body, psyche, and soul to the West.

As we have seen it, Foote's letters to Helena usually validated eastern class privilege and lamented the differences in geography and culture between herself and her distant friend. From her novels we hear similar themes. Perhaps this is partially due to what Foote thought Gilder and her audience wanted to hear, however. If Foote had had a western correspondent to whom she was as attached as she was to Gilder, she might have focused in her letters more on what the West had to offer. Likewise, if the audience for her novels had been primarily westerners, she might have looked past class and been more inspired to look deeper into the West's core. As it was, she tried to convey her West through eastern eyes, for eastern eyes, a practice that reveals as much about the East as the West. Her role as professional exile kept her heart in New York, even as her backdrops were the dry wastes of sagebrush and Ponderosa pine. The result is fiction and letters that reflect the wistfulness if not also the downright pain of relocation and a stubborn resolve to keep and re-create as much of the lost world as possible.

. . .

At the end of this analysis of Mary Hallock Foote's views on social class, a querulous question about western literature attributed to Owen Wister comes to mind: "Must it be perpetual tea-cups?" he is said to have asked (Lukacs 17). For Foote, the answer was yes and no. Yes, she was part of the inevitable grafting of the West to eastern and European literary and economic forces to make the new "untamed" regions safe and palatable for family magazine readers, armchair travelers, and cautious investors. Indeed, the process has still not been completed, though we are much further along since Foote laid down her Quaker-capped head for the last time in 1938. Despite suburban sprawl and other postindustrial ills, the West remains different from the industrial and over-populated East. It asserts its own identity even into the twenty-first century, as more populist and provincial yet still less elitist and class ridden than the East. Foote would have doubtless decried these "improvements" to the West, as her former cultural vacuum was subsumed into the cyberspace of globalization.

But back to Wister's question: the other answer is no. On occasion Foote did abandon the teacups in their dusty formal parlors and go in search of a more down-to-earth West. Most of her descriptions of western locales stand on their own, for example, without a need for comparison to well-watered regions. And, increasingly, she presented some hearty western characters, "haunted by no fleshpots of the past," as Foote termed those who lacked her pining for the East and its ways ("A Cloud on the Mountain," in *In Exile* 156). They would not have known how to handle a teacup if they found one and might very well have thrown it into a canyon in disgust.

Still, Foote rarely questioned the value of refinement, cultivation, and social exclusivity. In her unsought status as one of the new professional exiles, she lamented the crass attempts at upward mobility around her and hoped that good character from old family ties would carry the day. At seventy-six she could look back and still say that even as her western "camps . . . became to us in every sense of the word Homes; yet [they] were never without their curious haunting longings for the old ones in the East. Once you have it in your blood, you never get it out" (MHF to Ferris Greenblatt, May 6, 1923).[12] Accordingly, in her fiction, the old romancer kept the East and its status touchstones uppermost in her protagonists' minds. But in the background she could not help but honestly convey social and regional changes. Foote's fears and frustrations about this indeterminacy show through as on a palimpsest as she attempted to reclaim and elevate the significance of her own family history and culture. As Burton J. Bledstein puts it, "In a sense all class identities became a matter of economic and emotional confidence—a kind of confidence game—based on resources and credit" (Bledstein and Johnston 8). Foote had resources and credit only in the form of cultural capital. Nonetheless, it was enough and gave her confidence, whereas the twist of fate of her background and talents gave her the ability to support herself and her family. You might say she rose to it; she had fame thrust upon her. The reading public wanted to hear an accessible, genteel version of exotic westernness, so Foote gave them mannered scenarios set in the stratified mining settlements of California, the snowcapped reaches of Colorado, the sere wastes of Idaho, and, later, in the "golden rolling hills of California."[13]

It is interesting to track how power and influence have come and gone and come again to Foote's beloved Hudson River backwater. The province changed from an eighteenth-century royalist stronghold to a region of yeoman farmers in Foote's childhood, to a largely abandoned rurality in the mid-twentieth century, to a gentrified present, with art museums and second homes raising the property values of those old Quaker landowners. The competing forces of elitism and upward mobility that affected Foote still shape the United States more than a hundred years later. When I went searching for traces of Foote along the Hudson, I found dilapidated and restored eighteenth- and nineteenth-century buildings, including Foote's own Hallock homestead, but also postmodern art facilities and a huge local African American weekend fair by the wide, serene river. Such cycles of use illustrate how situated anyone is in an era and locale. What now may seem immutable standards and traditions will pass away, or at least evolve, whether we embrace or jettison them, and whether or not we find our own angle of repose within them.

Preface

1. See Ohmann's assertion that since the late nineteenth century, advertisers' strategies for various elite and even nonelite consumer goods have made American society seem, though it actually is not, "classless through consumption" (80).

Introduction

1. For an excellent and thorough overview of Foote's artistic career, see Rainey.

2. See these Nevada County (Calif.) Library online sources for a general overview of Foote's life: Fjeldsted; "Mary Hallock Foote."

3. See also a less than complimentary analysis of the gentlemen publishers of these magazines who "perceived themselves as the arbiters of Anglo-American taste and the protectors of white privilege" (Cane and Alves).

4. For more on this much discussed topic, see Fetterley. See also Coultrap-McQuin, who asserts that women "did not compromise their womanhood by being writers" (quoted in Amireh 112). Alcott discusses this issue in "How I Went Out to Service," in which a daughter of a gentleman goes to work as a housemaid. In Alcott's *Work,* the approved genteel professions, modeled more or less cheerfully, include teaching, piecework sewing, nursing, horticulture, charity projects, and the roles of governess and companion. Kelly, however, believes that women were "ambivalent," their professional and personal lives "conflicted."

5. Unless noted otherwise, all correspondence from Mary Hallock Foote is from the Mary Hallock Foote Papers, courtesy of the Department of Special Collections and University Archives, Stanford University Libraries, hereafter cited parenthetically by date in the text.

6. Ehrhardt makes this point, too, citing Ohmann, that "'even the most formulaic stories' in mass market publications articulate ideological and political concerns" (9).

7. Joan Wallach Scott notes that analyzing marginalized texts becomes more effective when one adopts the "methodologies . . . in interdisciplinary borrowings from sociology, demography, and ethnography" (21).

8. Concerning so-called island communities as well as a seminal history of the Progressive Era, see Wiebe.

9. For an enjoyable treatment of the rise of sentiment and its effect on women and nineteenth-century capitalism, see Nelson.

10. See the works of Sui Sin Far (Edith Maude Eaton), such as "A Chinese Ishmael" (1899) and "Mrs. Spring Fragrance" (1912), and those of Watanna Onoto (Winnifred

Eaton), such as *The Old Jinrikisha* (1900) and *Tama* (1910). See also Jessie (Redmon) Fauset, "The Sleeper Awakes."

11. For a discussion of snobbery and elitism within the black community, see Graham.

Chapter One.
Foote's Cultural Moment

1. See the politically correct ire of Noreen Groover in "'There Was a Part for Her in the Indian Life': Mary Austin, Regionalism, and the Problems of Appropriation," in Inness and Royer. For a reasoned revisionist analysis of Cather's elitism and Anglocentrism, see Piacentino.

2. Valerie Walkerdine is a prolific and wide-ranging historian and social scientist at the University of Cardiff, Wales.

3. See Robert Coles's surprising research on children of affluence.

4. "A Touch of Sun" was published in *Century* in January 1900 and published in a book of Foote's collected short stories in 1903.

5. Perhaps some of Foote's stories might be made into Merchant-Ivory productions, as James's and Wharton's novels have been, highlighting the social and aesthetic contrasts between the sumptuous East and the spare West. The western scenes would need a different director, perhaps the ghost of John Ford or Howard Hawks.

6. See Susan Lee Johnson's excellent *Roaring Camp* and Brian Roberts's *American Alchemy* for fuller treatment of social interactions between the races and ethnicities in early western extraction communities.

7. In all fairness, many Anglos and Anglo writers in this era considered Spanish "blood" suspect, including Kate Douglas Wiggen in *Rebecca of Sunnybrook Farm*.

Chapter Two.
Literary Allusions in Foote's Leadville Novels

1. Used with kind permission of John Gorka, Blues Palace Music (ASCAP), *Land of the Bottom Line* (Windham Hill, 1990).

Chapter Three.
Gender Roles in the Leadville Novels

1. MS Am 1925 (611), by permission of the Houghton Library, Harvard University.

2. Ibid.

3. See also Roberts on how middle-class morality and conventional expectations worked their way into freewheeling gold rush camps.

4. Container 6, Benjamin Holt Ticknor Papers, Manuscript Division, Library of Congress, Washington, D.C.

Chapter Four.
Class for the Kids

1. See particularly the stories "A Hole in the Wall" and "The Princess and the Brownie" in Alcott, *A Round Dozen.*

2. Lee Ann Johnson's discussion of Foote's first story, "The Picture in the Fireplace Bedroom," is the most thorough. Johnson astutely assesses the personal parallels between Foote and the story's young protagonist, but she does not discuss the class issues implicit in the tale.

3. For an enthusiastic overview of the magazine, as well as useful links, see "A Tribute to *St. Nicholas,* a Magazine for Young Folks."

4. *Century/St. Nicholas* (December 1877–October 1878).

5. See A. T. Dudley's football tale, "The Generous Side," or Alice Wellington Rollins's "Oh, Uncle Phillip," in which the literate young ladies at Uncle Philip's niece's day school write letters during the summer vacation.

6. This was a particularly American kind of modernization, one might add, since in Europe many regions kept their goods production small and local, thus thriving into the twenty-first century with human-scale communities coexisting with increased manufacturing and trade. Europe retained in large part the continuity and sense of family history that Foote so cherished.

7. MS Am 1925 (611), by permission of the Houghton Library, Harvard University.

8. Ibid.

Chapter Five.
The Ground-Swell, the New Woman, and Social Class

1. See Tonkovich on the promotion of domesticity in women writers who made their living by writing.

2. Richard Ohmann even claims that the controversy about New Women had all but disappeared from the popular press by 1900, having been discussed and ridiculed ad infinitum. Most women's historians do not concur, however, asserting that the term had currency up past World War I. Nonetheless, see Ohmann's excellent work *Selling Culture.*

3. James D. Hague Collection, Huntington Library, San Marino, California.

4. See Matthews as well as the discussion threads on H-Women on H-Net, May–June 1997 and September 2003, http://www.h-net.msu.edu.

5. See Phelps's *Silent Partner* (1871) or *The Story of Avis* (1877).

6. For more context, see Nowlin. Nowlin discusses Wharton and modernism, and America breaking away from European "culture" in this charged era. He asserts that even Emma Goldman and the avant-garde in Greenwich Village were somewhat elitist when it came to culture and the masses, claiming that those interested in culture in

the United States were often unwittingly "apologists for the genteel tradition" (95n20). While some thinkers of the time felt that Americans should base their culture on Anglo traditions (as Foote did), some believed that the melting pot of European immigrants had more to offer. Cather certainly made an effort to bring these immigrant traditions into the western American literature mix.

7. Much of the African American fiction published at this time was similar to Fauset's in tone and content. It often explored African American issues in settings that took for granted respectable and upwardly mobile values. The stories and novels serialized in the *Colored American Magazine* around the turn of the twentieth century were aimed at the African American middle and upper classes (see Hopkins, *The Magazine Novels*). Even Christmas stories in black magazines serialized from this period often have underlying themes of achieving respectability and "uplifting the race" (see Collier-Thomas).

8. For more on this history, see Herdt; Vicinus.

9. See, for example, Herdt, which presents a potpourri of the concept, analyzing (among other things) eunuchs during the Byzantine empire, sapphists in nineteenth-century London, *hijras* in India, and Native American berdaches.

10. Foote does not address the popular debate about the new less restrictive women's clothing in this novel. The West harbored some women who enjoyed its somewhat less stringent dress codes, and some even exploring cross-dressing possibilities. See Riedel and Guardino's "Wild West Women" Web site for a popular summary of the latter.

11. James D. Hague Collection, Huntington Library, San Marino, California. It was from comments like these in the letters between Foote and Gilder that Carroll Smith-Rosenberg inferred a passionate attachment—part of "The Female World of Love and Ritual"—between the two women (53).

12. Foote noted in a letter to someone who wanted her to donate her work for the suffrage cause that she did not want "to contribute towards the campaign for municipal suffrage, not being entirely in sympathy with it as a means towards the progress of woman" (MHF to Alice B. Stockham, August 15, 1887, MSS 223, courtesy Albertsons Library, Boise State University, http://library.boisestate.edu/special/footeletter.htm).

13. James D. Hague Collection, Huntington Library, San Marino, California.

Chapter Six.
The Early Correspondence of Mary Hallock Foote
and Helena de Kay Gilder

1. This is Stegner's description of his fictional characters based on Foote and Helena and Richard Gilder, but I believe it accurately reflects the Mary Hallock Foote's situation.

2. The publication of the Foote-Gilder letters is a story in itself, with the project having been started by various members of the Foote family more than thirty years ago, later receiving the collaboration of Mary Ellen Walsh Williams of Idaho State Univer-

sity at Pocatello. Most of Foote's original letters to Gilder are at Stanford, with some at the Huntington Library in Pasadena. Gilder's are at the Lilly Library of the University of Indiana. Foote's great-granddaughter Ann Gardiner of Berkeley has just finished the transcriptions and, like her mother and brother before her, labored many years on them. Professor Melody Graulich of Utah State University finally has charge of all the boxes of microfilm, transcripts of varying accuracy, and contextual notes for the project amassed over many years by many individuals. She and her graduate students hope to finish the project in 2009 or 2010.

3. The letters I cite between Richard Watson Gilder and Foote are part of her professional correspondence to him at *Century,* and are now in the Houghton Library at Harvard University.

4. I am indebted to the ideas in Alan Trachtenberg's *Incorporation of America: Culture and Society in the Gilded Age.*

5. This research was first presented at the 1979 Western American Literature conference.

6. Originally published in *Signs: Journal of Women in Culture and Society* 1.1 (1975).

7. Gillian Brown's and others' notion that capitalism and the public workplace are deindividualizing and not conducive to an integrated self would resonate with Foote.

8. Now in the Thyssen-Bornemisza Museum in Madrid, Spain, across from the Prado Museum.

9. That the incident is so specific and so similar in the two stories makes one wonder if indeed something like it happened in Boise to one of Foote's husband's associates. Stegner's depiction in *Angle of Repose* of Susan Burling Ward's attraction to a colleague of her husband seem to have had some basis in fact, since Foote discreetly conveys to Helena that she and the children greatly enjoyed the literate company of one of them and that she had some anxieties about her relations with him. Nonetheless, it is my view (and that of the Foote family descendants) that Foote did not actually engage in any compromising behavior.

10. Mary Hallock Foote Collection, Huntington Library, San Marino, California.

11. Trachtenberg's ideas are in a discussion that initially analyzes William James's distaste for the self-improvement culture that the New York State Chautauqua seminars promoted; they were too facile and lowbrow for James.

12. MS Am 1925 (611) by permission of the Houghton Library, Harvard University.

13. From "The Redtailed Hawk," written by George Schroder, Grass Valley, California. Recorded by Kate Wolf and the Wildwood Flower, in *Back Roads* (Owl, 1976; rereleased by Rhino Records, 1994).

Sources by Mary Hallock Foote

"The Children's Claim." *St. Nicholas* (January 1880): 238–45.

The Chosen Valley. Boston: Houghton Mifflin, 1892.

Coeur d'Alene. Boston: Houghton Mifflin, 1894. Reprint, New York: ams Press, 1976.

The Cup of Trembling, and Other Stories. 1895. Reprint, Freeport, N.Y.: Books for Libraries Press, 1970.

The Desert and the Sown. Boston: Houghton Mifflin, 1902.

Edith Bonham. Boston: Houghton Mifflin, 1917.

"A Four-Leaved Clover in the Desert." *St. Nicholas* (May 1894): 644–50.

The Ground-Swell. Boston: Houghton Mifflin, 1919.

"How Mandy Went Rowing With the 'Cap'n.'" *St. Nicholas* (May 1878): 448–53.

The Idaho Stories and Far West Illustrations of Mary Hallock Foote. Edited by Barbara Cragg, Dennis M. Walsh, and Mary Ellen Walsh. Pocatello: Idaho State University Press, 1988.

In Exile, and Other Stories. 1894. Reprint, New York: Garrett Press, 1969.

John Bodewin's Testimony. Boston: Ticknor, 1886.

"The Last Assembly Ball" and "The Fate of a Voice." Boston: Houghton Mifflin, 1889.

The Led-Horse Claim: A Romance of a Mining Camp. 1882. Ridgewood, N.J.: Gregg, 1968.

The Little Fig-Tree Stories. Boston: Houghton Mifflin, 1899.

"Menhaden Sketches: Summer at Christmas-Time." *St. Nicholas* (December 1884): 116–24.

"A 'Muchacho' of the Mexican Camp." *St. Nicholas* (December 1878): 79–81.

A Picked Company. Boston: Houghton Mifflin, 1912.

The Prodigal. Boston: Houghton Mifflin, 1900.

The Royal Americans. Boston: Houghton Mifflin, 1910.

A Touch of Sun, and Other Stories. Boston: Houghton Mifflin, 1903. Reprint, Freeport, N.Y.: Books for Libraries, 1972.

The Valley Road. Boston: Houghton Mifflin, 1915.

A Victorian Gentlewoman in the Far West: The Reminiscences of Mary Hallock Foote. Edited by Rodman Paul. San Marino, Calif.: Huntington Library, 1972.

Other Sources

Adey, Lio. "Class-Conditioning in Nineteenth-Century Hymnals for Children." *Mosaic: A Journal for the Interdisciplinary Study of Literature* 18.3 (1985): 87–99.

Alcott, Louisa May. "How I Went Out to Service." 1874. http://www.blackmask.com/books42c/howservice.htm.

———. "Jack and Jill." *St. Nicholas* (December 1879): 89–95.

———. *Little Women*. 1868. Oxford: Oxford University Press, 1994.

———. "An Old-Fashioned Thanksgiving." In *A "St. Nicholas" Anthology: The Early Years*, edited by Burton C. Frye, 5–16. New York: Meredith Press, 1969.

———. *A Round Dozen*. Edited by Anne Thaxter Eaton. New York: Viking, 1963.

———. *Under the Lilacs*. 1878. Boston: Little, Brown Young Readers, 1996.

———. *Work: A Story of Experience*. 1873. http://www.gutenberg.org.

Allen, Grant. *The Woman Who Did*. 1895. Introduction by Sarah Wintle. Oxford: Oxford University Press, 1995.

Amal, Amireh. *The Factory Girl and the Seamstress: Imagining Gender and Class in Nineteenth-Century American Fiction*. New York: Garland, Taylor, and Francis, 2000.

Ammons, Elizabeth. *Conflicting Stories: American Women Writers at the Turn into the Twentieth Century*. New York: Oxford University Press, 1991.

Antelyes, Peter. *Tales of Adventurous Enterprise: Washington Irving and the Poetics of Western Expansion*. New York: Columbia University Press, 1990.

Ardis, Ann L., and Leslie W. Lewis, eds. *The Politics of Modernism: Against the New Conformists*. New York: Verso, 1989.

———. *Women's Experience of Modernity, 1875–1945*. Baltimore: Johns Hopkins University Press, 2003.

Armstrong, Regina. "Representative American Women Novelists." *Critic* (August 1900): 131–41.

Atherton, Gertrude. *Adventures of a Novelist*. New York: Blue Ribbon, 1932.

———. *The Aristocrats*. London: John Lane, 1901.

———. *The Californians*. 1898. Reprint, Ridgewood, N.J.: Gregg Press, 1968.

———. *Julia France and Her Times*. New York: Macmillan, 1912.

Barnard, Robert. *A Talent to Deceive: An Appreciation of Agatha Christie*. New York: Dodd, Mead, 1980.

Benn, Mary Lou. "Mary Hallock Foote: Pioneer Woman Novelist." Master's thesis, University of Wyoming, 1955.

Benson, Jackson J. *Wallace Stegner: His Life and Work*. New York: Penguin, 1996.

Bevis, William. "Region, Power, Place." In *Reading the West: New Essays on the Literature of the American West*, edited by Michael Kowalewski, 21–43. Cambridge: Cambridge University Press, 1996.

Birmingham, Stephen. *America's Secret Aristocracy*. Boston: Little, Brown, 1987.

Blair, Edward. *Leadville: Colorado's Magic City*. Boulder: Pruett, 1980.

Blanchard, Paula. *Sarah Orne Jewett: Her World and Her Works*. Reading, Mass.: Addison-Wesley, 1994.

Bledstein, Burton J., and Robert D. Johnston, eds. *The Middling Sorts: Explorations in the History of the American Middle Class*. New York: Routledge, 2001.

Blend, Benay. "A Victorian Gentlewoman in the Rocky Mountain West: Ambiguity in the Work of Mary Hallock Foote." In *Reading Under the Sign of Nature: New Essays in Ecocriticism,* edited by John Tallmadge and Henry Harrington. Salt Lake City: University of Utah Press, 2000.

Blumberg, Paul, ed. *The Impact of Social Class: A Book of Readings.* New York: Harper and Row, 1972.

Blumin, Stuart Mack. *The Emergence of the Middle Class: Social Experience in the American City, 1760–1900.* Cambridge: Cambridge University Press, 1989.

Bolt, Christine. *The Women's Movements in the United States and Britain From the 1790s to the 1920s.* Amherst: University of Massachusetts Press, 1993.

Botton, Alain de. *Status Anxiety.* New York: Hamish Hamilton, 2004.

Bourdieu, Pierre. *Distinction: A Social Critique of the Judgment of Taste.* Cambridge: Harvard University Press, 1984.

——. *The State Nobility: Elite Schools in the Field of Power.* Translated by Lauretta C. Clough. Sanford: Stanford University Press, 1989.

Brodhead, Richard H. "Regionalism and the Upper Class." In *Rethinking Class: Literary Studies and Social Formation,* edited by Wai Chee Dimock and Michael T. Gilmore. New York: Columbia University Press, 1994.

Brown, Gillian. *Domestic Individualism: Imagining Self in Nineteenth-Century America.* Berkeley and Los Angeles: University of California Press, 1990.

Buckler, William E. *Prose of the Victorian Period.* Boston: Houghton Mifflin, 1958.

Bush, Casey. "Cultural Clearcut: The Lost Novels of Mary Hallock Foote." Review on Bear Deluxe Web site of *Mary Hallock Foote: Author-Illustrator of the American West,* by Darlis Miller. 2003.

Butts, Dennis, ed. *Stories and Society: Children's Literature in Its Social Context.* New York: St. Martin's, 1992.

Calvert, Peter. *The Concept of Class: An Historical Introduction.* New York: St. Martin's, 1982.

Cane, Aleta Feinsod, and Susan Alves, eds. *"The Only Efficient Instrument": American Women Writers and the Periodical, 1837–1916.* Iowa City: Iowa University Press, 2001.

Casper, Scott E., Jeffrey D. Groves, Stephen W. Nissenbaum, and Michael Winship, eds. *A History of the Book in America.* Vol. 3, *The Industrial Book, 1840–1880.* Chapel Hill: University of North Carolina Press, 2007.

Cather, Willa. *Death Comes for the Archbishop.* 1927. Reprint, New York: Alfred A. Knopf, 1950.

——. *A Lost Lady.* 1923. Reprint, New York: Vintage, 1972.

——. *My Antonia.* 1918. Reprint, Cambridge, Mass.: Riverside Press, 1949.

——. *Not Under Forty.* 1936. Reprint, Lincoln: University of Nebraska Press, 1988.

——. *Obscure Destinies.* 1932. http://www.underthesun.cc/Classics/Cather/ObscureDestinies/ObscureDestinies7.html.

——. "Old Mrs. Harris." In *American Women Regionalists, 1850–1910,* edited by Judith Fetterley and Marjorie Pryse, 597–637. New York: W. W. Norton, 1992.

——. *O Pioneers!* 1913. Reprint, Boston: Houghton Mifflin, 1987.

——. *Shadows on the Rock.* 1931. Reprint, New York: Vintage, 1971.

——. *The Song of the Lark.* 1915. Reprint, Lincoln: University of Nebraska Press, 1978.

Chopin, Kate. *A Shameful Affair, and Other Stories.* Edited by Janet Beer. London: Phoenix Orion, 1998.

Clifford, James. "On Collecting Art and Culture." In *Out There: Marginalization and Contemporary Cultures,* edited by Russell Ferguson Russell, Martha Gever, Trinh T. Minh-ha, and Cornel West, 141–69. New York: New Museum of Contemporary Art, 1990.

Coles, Robert. "Children of Affluence." *Atlantic* (September 1977): 52–66.

Collier-Thomas, Bettye, ed. *A Treasury of African-American Christmas Stories.* Illustrated by James Reynolds. New York: Henry Holt, 1997.

Conway, Jill Ker, ed. *Written by Herself: Autobiographies of American Women, an Anthology.* New York: Vintage, 1992.

Cook, Blanche Wiesen. *Women and Support Networks.* New York: Out and Out Books, 1979.

Cooke, Rose Terry. *How Celia Changed Her Mind, and Other Stories.* Edited by Elizabeth Ammons. New Brunswick: Rutgers University Press, 1986.

Cooper, James Fenimore. *The Prairie: A Tale.* 1827. New York: Holt, Rinehart, and Winston, 1966.

Corrigan, Robert W., ed. *Laurel British Drama: The Nineteenth Century.* New York: Dell, 1967.

Cothern, Lynn. "Becoming Western: Gender and Generation in Mary Hallock Foote's Dual Career." Ph.D. diss., George Washington University, 1997.

——. "Traveler and Tourist: Foote and Crane in Mexico." Paper presented at the Western Literature Association conference, Wichita, Kansas, 1993.

Cott, Nancy F. *The Grounding of Modern Feminism.* New Haven: Yale University Press, 1987.

Coultrap-McQuin, Susan. *Doing Literary Business: American Women Writers in the Nineteenth Century.* Chapel Hill: University of North Carolina Press, 1990.

Cragg, Barbara, Dennis M. Walsh, and Mary Ellen Walsh, eds. *The Idaho Stories and Far West Illustrations of Mary Hallock Foote.* Pocatello: Idaho State University Press, 1988.

Crane, Stephen. *Maggie: A Girl of the Streets (a Story of New York).* Edited by Herbert Van Thal. 1893. Reprint, London: Cassell, 1966.

Danneberg, Julie. *Women Writers of the West: Five Chroniclers of the American Frontier.* Notable Western Women Series. Golden, Colo.: Fulcrum, 2003.

D'Arcy, Chantal Cornut-Gentille, and José Ángel García Landa. *Gender, I-deology: Essays on Theory, Fiction, and Film.* Amsterdam and Atlanta: Rodopi, 1996.

David, Richard H. "Midsummer Pirates." *St. Nicholas* (August 1889).

Davidson, Levette Jay. "Letters From Authors." *Colorado Magazine* 19.4 (1942): 122–25.

Deland, Margaret. "The Change in the Feminine Ideal." *Atlantic Monthly,* March 1910, 289–302.

Diedrichs, Gary W. "Hear No Evil, See No Evil, Speak No Evil." *Cleveland Magazine* (December 1977). http://www.clevelandmagazine.com/editorial/thismonth_features.asp?docid=268.

Dimock, Wai Chee, and Michael T. Gilmore, eds. *Rethinking Class: Literary Studies and Social Formation.* New York: Columbia University Press, 1994.

Donaldson, Thomas. *Idaho of Yesterday.* Caldwell, Idaho: Caxton Printers, 1941.

Dorset, Phyllis Flanders. *The New Eldorado: The Story of Colorado's Gold and Silver Rushes.* New York: Macmillan, 1970.

Dublin, Thomas, ed. *Farm to Factory: Women's Letters, 1830–1860.* New York: Columbia University Press, 1981.

Dudley, A. T. "The Generous Side." *St. Nicholás* (November 1894): 22–29.

Dufva [Quantic], Diane. "Fact vs. Fiction: Leadville, Colorado, As a Setting for Fiction." Master's thesis, Kansas State University, 1966.

Earnest, Ernest. *The American Eve in Fact and Fiction, 1775–1914.* Urbana: University of Illinois Press, 1974.

Eder, Klaus. *The New Politics of Class: Social Movements and Cultural Dynamics in Advanced Societies.* London: Sage Publications, 1993.

Edgell, Stephen. *Class.* London and New York: Routledge, 1993.

Edwards, Paul. "20th Century Workplace Relations: Class Struggle Without Classes." In *Renewing Class Analysis,* edited by Fiona Devine, John Scott, Mike Savage, and Rosemary Crompton. Sociological Review Monographs. Oxford: Blackwell, 2000.

Egli, Ida Rae. "Early Western Literary Women." In *Updating the Literary West.* Fort Worth: Texas Christian University Press, 1997.

Ehrhardt, Julia C. *Writers of Conviction: The Personal Politics of Zona Gale, Dorothy Canfield Fisher, Rose Wilder Lane, and Josephine Herbst.* Columbia: University of Missouri Press, 2004.

Eliot, George. *Middlemarch: A Study in Provincial Life.* 1872. Edited by Gordon S. Haight. Boston: Houghton Mifflin, 1956.

Ellis, Anne. *The Life of an Ordinary Woman.* Lincoln: University of Nebraska Press, 1929.

Etulain, Richard W. "Mary Hallock Foote (1847–1938)." *American Literary Realism* 15.2 (1972): 145–50.

———. *Re-imagining the Modern American West: A Century of Fiction, History, and Art.* Tucson: University of Arizona Press, 1996.

Fauset, Jessie. "The Sleeper Wakes." *Crisis* 20 (August–October 1920): 168–73, 226–29, 267–74.

Fetterley, Judith. *Provisions: A Reader From 19th-Century American Women*. Bloomington: Indiana University Press, 1985.

Fetterley, Judith, and Marjorie Pryse, eds. *American Women Regionalists, 1850–1910*.
New York: W. W. Norton, 1992.

Fisher, Dorothy Canfield. *The Bent Twig*. New York: Henry Holt, 1915.

Fitzgerald, F. Scott. *Babylon Revised, and Other Stories*. New York: Scribner-Collier-
Macmillan, 1960.

Fjeldsted. Steve. "Mary Hallock Foote: Artist, Author, Spouse, and Mother." http://
new.mynevadacounty.com/library/index.cfm?ccs=602andcs=1105.

Flaubert, Gustave. *The Letters of Gustave Flaubert, 1857–1880*. Translated and edited
by Francis Steegmuller. Cambridge: Harvard University Press, Belknap Press, 1982.

Floyd, Janet. "Mining the West: Bret Harte and Mary Hallock Foote." In *Soft Canons:
American Women Writers and the Masculine Tradition*, edited by Karen L. Kilcup.
Iowa City: University of Iowa Press, 1999.

———. "A Sympathetic Misunderstanding? Mary Hallock Foote's Mining West." *Frontiers: A Journal of Women's Studies* 22.3 (2001): 148–67.

———. *Writing the Pioneer Woman*. Columbia: University of Missouri Press, 2002.

Fradkin, Philip L. *Wallace Stegner and the American West*. New York: Alfred A. Knopf,
2008.

Freedman, Estelle. "Separatism As Strategy: Female Institution Building and American Feminism, 1870–1930." *Feminist Studies* 5.3 (1979): 512–29.

Freedman, Ruth, and Patricia Klaus. "Blessed or Not? The New Spinster in England
and the United States in the Late Nineteenth and Early Twentieth Centuries."
Journal of Family History 9.4 (1984): 394–414.

Frye, Burton C., ed. *A "St. Nicholas" Anthology: The Early Years*. New York: Meredith
Press, 1969.

Fuller, Margaret. *The Letters of Margaret Fuller*. Edited by Robert N. Hudspeth. 6 vols.
Ithaca: Cornell University Press, 1983–1994.

Gaines, Kevin. "Black American Racial Uplift Ideology As 'Civilizing Mission': Pauline
E. Hopkins on Race and Imperialism." In *Cultures of United States Imperialism*,
edited by Amy Kaplan and Donald Pease. Durham: Duke University Press, 1993.

———. *Uplifting the Race: Black Leadership, Politics, and Culture in the Twentieth Century*. Chapel Hill: University of North Carolina Press, 1996.

Gardiner, Ann. Telephone interview. November 1999.

Gardiner, Evelyn. Personal interview. July 1992.

———. Telephone interview. August 1999.

Gatewood, Willard B. *Aristocrats of Color: The Black Elite, 1880–1920*. Bloomington:
Indiana University Press, 1990.

Giele, Janet Zollinger. *Two Paths to Women's Equality: Temperance, Suffrage, and the
Origins of Modern Feminism*. New York: Twayne, 1995.

Gilbert, Sandra M., and Susan Gubar, eds. *No Man's Land: The Place of the Women*

Writer in the Twentieth Century. Vol. 3, *Letters From the Front*. New Haven: Yale University Press, 1994.

———. *The Norton Anthology of Literature by Women: The Tradition in English*. New York: W. W. Norton, 1985.

Gilbert, William, and Arthur Sullivan. "Loudly Let the Trumpet Bray." *Iolanthe* (1882). Transcribed by Helga J. Perry. http://www.savoyoperas.org.uk/iolanthe/io2.html.

Gilder, Helena de Kay. "Author Illustrators." *Book Buyer* 9.7 (1894): 338–42.

———. Letters to Mary Hallock Foote. Gilder Collection. Lilly Library, University of Indiana, Bloomington.

Gilman, Charlotte Perkins. *Herland*. 1915. Introduction by Ann J. Lane. New York: Pantheon, 1979.

———. *The Home: Its Work and Influence*. Urbana: University of Illinois Press, 1972.

Glasgow, Ellen. *The Miller of Old Church*. Garden City, N.Y. Doubleday, Doran, 1911.

Goldsmith, Elizabeth C., ed. *Writing the Female Voice: Essays on Epistolary Literature*. Boston: Northeastern University Press, 1989.

Goodman, Susan. *Civil Wars: American Novelists and Manners, 1880–1940*. Baltimore: Johns Hopkins University Press, 2003.

Gorka, John. *Land of the Bottom Line*. Blues Palace Music, Windham Hill Records, 1990.

Graham, Lawrence Otis. *Our Kind of People: Inside America's Black Upper Class*. New York: Harper Perennial, 1999.

Grand, Sarah. *The Heavenly Twins*. 1894. Ann Arbor: University of Michigan Press, 1992.

Graulich, Melody. "Legacy Profile: Mary Hallock Foote (1847–1938)." *Legacy* 3.2 (1986): 43–62.

Gray, Patrice K. "The Lure of Romance and the Temptation of Feminine Sensibility: Literary Heroines in Selected Popular and 'Serious' American Novels, 1895–1915." *DAI* (Emory University) (1981): 2130.

Gruber, Laura Katherine. "'The Naturalistic Impulse': Limitations of Gender and Landscape in Mary Hallock Foote's Idaho Stories." *Western American Literature* 38.4 (Winter 2004): 353–73.

Grundy, Sydney. *The New Woman: An Original Comedy, in Four Acts*. London: Chiswick Press, 1894.

Guy-Sheftall, Beverly, ed. *Words of Fire: An Anthology of African-American Feminist Thought*. New York: New Press, 1995.

Hall, Peter Dobkin. *The Organization of American Culture, 1700–1900: Private Institutions, Elites, and the Origins of American Nationality*. New York: New York University Press, 1982.

Hall, Sands. *Fair Use*. Nevada City, Calif.: n.p., 2001.

———. Personal correspondence. July 2003.

———. http://www.sandshall.com.

Hamer, Judith A., and Martin J. Hamer, eds. *Centers of the Self: Stories by Black American Women, From the Nineteenth Century to the Present.* New York: Hill and Wang, Farrar, Straus, and Giroux, 1994.

Hardy, Thomas. *Jude the Obscure.* 1895. Reprint, New York: Modern Library, 1995.

Harris, Susan K. *19th Century American Women's Novels: Interpretive Strategies.* New York: Cambridge University Press, 1990.

Heller, Adele, and Lois Rudnick, eds. *1915, the Cultural Moment: The New Politics, the New Woman, the New Psychology, the New Art, and the New Theater in America.* New Brunswick: Rutgers University Press, 1991.

Herdt, Gilbert, ed. *Third Sex, Third Gender: Beyond Sexual Dimorphism in Culture and History.* New York: Zone Books, 1994.

Hine, Robert V. *The American West: An Interpretive History.* Boston: Little, Brown, 1973.

Hochman, Eleanor. *Fictional Females: Mirrors and Models; The Changing Image of Women in American Novels From 1789 to 1939.* Self-published, 2002.

Hodges, Harold M., Jr. *Social Stratification: Class in America.* Cambridge, Mass.: Schenkman, 1953.

Hopkins, Pauline. *Contending Forces: A Romance Illustrative of Negro Life North and South.* 1900. New York: Oxford University Press, 1988.

———. *The Magazine Novels of Pauline Hopkins.* Introduction by Hazel V. Carby. New York: Oxford University Press, 1988.

Howe, Edgar Watson. *The Story of a Country Town.* Atchison, Kans.: Howe and Co., 1883.

Howells, William Dean. *Chance Acquaintance.* Boston: Osgood, 1873.

———. *The Rise of Silas Lapham.* 1885. http://www.classicauthors.net/Howells/SilasLapham/SilasLapham1.html.

"An Indian Mother." *St. Nicholas* (November 1973): 29.

Ingersoll, Ernest. "Camp of the Carbonates." *Scribner's* 18.6 (Oct. 1879): 801–24.

Inness, Sherrie A. "Looking Westward: Geographical Distinctions in the Regional Short Fiction of Mary Foote and Mary Austin." *Studies in Short Fiction* 35.4 (Fall 1998): 319–30.

Inness, Sherrie A., and Diana Royer, eds. *Breaking Boundaries: New Perspectives on Women's Regional Writing.* Iowa City: University of Iowa Press, 1997.

Irving, Washington. *The Sketchbooks of Geoffrey Crayon, Gent.* Introduction by Andrew B. Myers. 1848. Reprint, Tarrytown, N.Y.: Sleepy Hollow Press, 1981.

James, Edward T., Janet Wilson James, and Paul S. Boyer, eds. *Notable American Women: A Biographical Dictionary, 1607–1950.* Vol. 1. Cambridge: Harvard University Press, Belknap Press, 1971.

James, Henry. *The Bostonians.* 1886. Introduction by Irving Howe. Reprint, New York: Modern Library, 1956.

——. *The Portrait of a Lady.* 1881. Reprint, New York: Modern Library, Random House, 1909.

——. *Washington Square.* 1880. Reprint, New York: Penguin, 1984.

Jehlen, Myra. *Class and Character in Faulkner's South.* New York: Columbia University Press, 1976.

Johnson, Lee Ann. *Mary Hallock Foote.* Boston: Twayne / G. K. Hall, 1980.

Johnson, Nan. *Gendered and Rhetorical Space in American Life, 1866–1910.* Carbondale: Southern Illinois University Press, 2002.

Johnson, Susan Lee. *Roaring Camp: The Social World of the California Gold Rush.* New York: W. W. Norton, 2000.

Jones, Sharon L. *Rereading the Harlem Renaissance: Race, Class, and Gender in the Fiction of Jessie Fauset, Zora Neale Hurston, and Dorothy West.* Contributions in Afro-American Studies, no. 207. Westport, Conn.: Greenwood, 2002.

Kahl, Joseph A. *The American Class Structure.* New York: Holt, Rinehart, and Winston, 1953.

Kaplan, Amy. *The Social Construction of American Realism.* Chicago: University of Chicago Press, 1988.

Karell, Linda K. "The Postmodern Author on Stage: Fair Use and Wallace Stegner." *American Drama* 14.2 (2005): 70–89.

——. *Writing Together/Writing Apart: Collaboration in Western American Literature.* Lincoln: University of Nebraska Press, 2002.

Kasson, John F. *Rudeness and Civility: Manners in Nineteenth-Century Urban America.* New York: Hill and Wang, Farrar, Straus, and Giroux, 1990.

Kelly, Mary. *Private Woman, Public Stage: Literary Domesticity in Nineteenth-Century America.* New York: Oxford University Press, 1984.

Kirkland, Caroline. *A New Home—Who'll Follow? Glimpses of Western Life.* 1839. Edited by William Osborne. Reprint, New Haven, Conn.: College and University Press, 1965.

Kolodny, Annette. "Dancing Through the Minefield." In *The New Feminist Criticism: Essays on Women, Literature, and Theory,* edited by Elaine Showalter. New York: Pantheon, 1985.

Lagemann, Ellen Condliffe. *A Generation of Reformers: Education in the Lives of Progressive Reformers.* Cambridge: Harvard University Press, 1979.

Latimer, Margary. *Guardian Angel, and Other Stories.* Afterwords by Nancy Loughridge, Meridel Le Sueur, and Louis Kampt. New York: Feminist Press, 1984.

Lee, Harper. *To Kill a Mockingbird.* New York: Warner, 1960.

Lee, Robert Edson. *From West to East: Studies in the Literature of the American West.* Urbana: University of Illinois Press, 1966.

Limerick, Patricia Nelson. *The Legacy of Conquest: The Unbroken Past of the American West.* New York: W. W. Norton, 1987.

Limerick, Patricia Nelson, Clyde A. Milner II, and Charles E. Rankin, eds. *Trails: Toward a New Western History*. Lawrence: University Press of Kansas, 1991.

"Literature." *Critic*, n.s., 19.590 (1893): 379.

London, Jack. *The Little Lady of the Big House*. New York: Grosset and Dunlap, 1915.

Lukacs, John. *A Thread of Years*. New Haven: Yale University Press, 1998.

MacIntosh, Peggy. "White Privilege: Unpacking the Invisible Knapsack." 1988. http://seamonkey.ed.asu.edu/~mcisaac/emc598ge/Unpacking.html.

MacLeod, Anne Scott. *American Childhood: Essays on Children's Literature of the Nineteenth and Twentieth Centuries*. Athens: University of Georgia Press. 1994.

Maguire, James H. *Mary Hallock Foote*. Boise State College Western Writers Series 2. Boise: Boise State College Press, 1972.

Mangum, Teresa. *Married, Middle-Brow, and Militant: Sarah Grand and the New Woman Novel*. Ann Arbor: University of Michigan Press, 1999.

Mapel-Bloomberg, Kristin. "American Women Writers, 1890 to 1939: Modernism and Mythology." http://www.geocities.com/Wellesley/7327/modernism.html.

Marchalonis, Shirley, ed. *Patrons and Protegés: Gender, Friendship, and Writing in Nineteenth-Century America*. New Brunswick: Rutgers University Press, 1988.

Marshall, Edward. "Locoed." *St. Nicholas* (November 1894): 55–64.

Marx, Leo. *The Machine in the Garden: Technology and the Pastoral Ideal in America*. London: Oxford University Press, 1964.

"Mary Hallock Foote, Writer and Illustrator, 1847–1938." http://new.mynevadacounty.com/library/index.cfm?ccs=1018.

Matthews, Jean V. *The Rise of the New Woman: The Woman's Movement in America, 1875–1930*. American Ways Series. Chicago: Ivan R. Dee, 2003.

McBroom, Patricia A. *The Third Sex: The New Professional Woman*. New York: Morrow, 1986.

McNall, Scott G., Rhonda F. Levine, and Rick Fantasia. *Bringing Class Back In*. Boulder: Westview, 1991.

Michaels, Walter Benn. *Our America: Nativism, Modernism, and Pluralism*. Durham: Duke University Press, 1995.

Miller, D. W. "A Ghetto Childhood Inspires the Research of a Yale Sociologist." *Chronicle of Higher Education* (March 19, 1999): a15–a16.

Miller, Darlis. *Mary Hallock Foote: Author-Illustrator of the American West*. Norman: University of Oklahoma Press, 2002.

Miller, Olive Thorne. "A Summer Home for Poor Children." *St. Nicholas* (June 1880): 647–53.

Monroe, Anne Shannon. *The World I Saw*. Garden City, N.Y.: Doubleday, Doran, 1928.

Motz, Marilyn Ferris, and Pat Browne, eds. *Making the American Home: Middle Class Women and Domestic Material Culture, 1840–1940*. Bowling Green: Bowling Green State University Popular Press, 1988.

Moynihan, Ruth B., Susan Armitage, and Christiane Fischer Dichamp, eds. *So Much to

Be Done: Women Settlers on the Mining and Ranching Frontier. Lincoln: University of Nebraska Press, 1990.

Murolo, Priscilla. *The Common Ground of Womanhood: Class, Gender, and Working Girls' Clubs, 1884–1928.* Urbana: University of Illinois Press, 1997.

Murphy, Mary. *Mining Cultures: Men, Women, and Leisure in Butte, 1914–41.* Urbana: University of Illinois Press, 1997.

Myres, Sandra L. *Westering Women and the Frontier Experience, 1800–1915.* Albuquerque: University of New Mexico Press, 1982.

Nelson, Elizabeth White. *Market Sentiments: Middle-Class Market Culture in Nineteenth-Century America.* Washington, D.C.: Smithsonian Books, 2004.

Nowlin, Michael. "Edith Wharton's Higher Provincialism: *French Ways* for Americans and the Ends of *The Age of Innocence.*" *Journal of American Studies* 38.1 (April 2004): 89–108.

Nugent, Walter. "Frontiers and Empires in the Late 19th Century." *Western Historical Quarterly* 20 (1989): 393–408.

Ohmann, Richard. *Selling Culture: Magazines, Markets, and Class at the Turn of the Century.* London: Verso, 1996.

Ostrander, Susan A. *Women of the Upper Class.* Philadelphia: Temple University Press, 1984.

Pappenheimer, Hylie. Personal interview. August 1993.

Pearson, Carol B. "Narrative Biography of Mary Hallock Foote, Based on Her Reminiscences and Letters." Ca. 1972. James D. Hague Collection. Huntington Library, San Marino, Calif.

Petrik, Paula. *No Step Backward: Women and Family on the Rocky Mountain Mining Frontier, Helena, Montana, 1865–1900.* Helena: Montana Historical Society Press, 1987.

Pfister, Joel. *The Production of Personal Life: Class, Gender, and the Psychological in Hawthorne's Fiction.* Stanford: Stanford University Press, 1991.

Phelps, Elizabeth Stuart. *Silent Partner.* Boston: Osgood, 1871.

———. *The Story of Avis.* 1877. New Brunswick: Rutgers University Press, 1985.

Phillips, David Graham. *"The Worth of a Woman," a Play in Four Acts, Followed by "A Point of Law, a Dramatic Incident."* New York: D. Appleton, 1908.

Piacentino, Ed. Review of *The Stuff of Our Forebears: Willa Cather's Southern Heritage,* by Joyce McDonald. *South Atlantic Review* (Southern Modern Language Association) 64.3 (Summer 1999). Available online at http://www.samla.org/sar/piacentino64-3.html.

"Pissarro Collector Buoyed by Recovery, Not Publicity." http://www.museum-security.org/reports/06298.html.

Poovey, Mary. *The Proper Lady and the Woman Writer: Ideology As Style in the Works of Mary Wollstonecraft, Mary Shelley, and Jane Austen.* Chicago: University of Chicago Press, 1984.

Porter, David H. "Cather on Cather II: Two Recent Acquisitions at Drew University." *Willa Cather Pioneer Memorial and Educational Foundation Newsletter and Review* 46.3 (Winter–Spring 2003): 49+.

Rabin, Jessica G. "Camelot, Back Creek, and Sweet Water: Arthurian Archetypes and Southern Sensibility in Willa Cather's *A Lost Lady*." *Willa Cather Pioneer Memorial and Educational Foundation Newsletter and Review* 42.2 (Fall 1998): 39–44.

Rainey, Sue. "Mary Hallock Foote: A Leading Illustrator of the 1870s and 1880s." *Winterthur Portfolio* 41.23 (Summer–Autumn 2007): 97–140.

Reesman, Jeanne Campbell. *Speaking the Other Self: American Women Writers.* Athens: University of Georgia Press, 1997.

Reynolds, Susan Slater. "Tangle of Repose." *Los Angeles Times Sunday Magazine,* March 23, 2003: 14+.

Richardson, Selma K., ed. *Research About Nineteenth-Century Children and Books.* Portrait Studies. Urbana: University of Illinois Press, 1980.

Ridgely, J. V. *Nineteenth-Century Southern Literature.* Lexington: University Press of Kentucky, 1980.

Riedel, Marilyn, and M. Constance Guardino III. http://users.wi.net/~maracon/lesson2.html.

Roberts, Brian. *American Alchemy: The California Gold Rush and Middle-Class Culture.* Chapel Hill: University of North Carolina Press, 2000.

Robinson, Lillian S. *Sex, Class, and Culture.* Bloomington: Indiana University Press, 1978.

Rollins, Alice Wellington. "Oh, Uncle Philip." In *Prairie Tales Retold From "St. Nicholas,"* 59–73. New York: Century, 1928.

Rosaldo, Renato. *Culture and Truth: The Remaking of Social Analysis.* Boston: Beacon, 1989.

Ross, Gwendolyn DeCamp. "Mary Hallock Foote: Literary Historian of the Mining Camps." Master's thesis, University of Texas–Arlington, 1970.

Rubin, Merle. Review of *Civil Wars: American Novelists and Manners, 1880–1940,* by Susan Goodman. http://www.washtimes.com/books/20030628-041130-9388r.htm.

Rushforth, Nancy Evans. "With Her Own Hand: The Correspondence of Mary Hallock Foote." Master's thesis, Brigham Young University, 1993.

Sandoz, Mari. *Old Jules.* Lincoln: University of Nebraska Press, 1962.

Schlesinger, Arthur M. *Learning How to Behave: A Historical Study of American Etiquette Books.* New York: Cooper Square Publishers, 1968.

Schlissel, Lillian. *Women's Diaries of the Westward Journey.* New York: Schocken, 1982.

Schwarz, Judith. *Radical Feminists of Heterodoxy: Greenwich Village, 1912–1940.* Norwich, Vt.: New Victoria, 1986.

Scott, Joan Wallach. *Gender and the Politics of History.* New York: Columbia University Press, 1988.

Scott, Walter. *Ivanhoe: A Romance.* 1819. Afterword by Compton Mackenzie. Reprint, New York: Signet, 1962.

Seidel, Michael. *Exile and the Narrative Imagination.* New Haven: Yale University Press, 1986.

Senf, Carol A. Introduction to *The Heavenly Twins,* by Sarah Grand. 1894. Reprint, Ann Arbor: University of Michigan Press, 1992.

Showalter, Elaine. "American Gynocriticism." *American Literary History* 1 (1993): 111–28.

———. *Sexual Anarchy: Gender and Culture at the Fin de Siècle.* New York: Penguin, 1990.

Singh, Rashna B. *Goodly Is Our Heritage: Children's Literature, Empire, and the Certitude of Character.* Lanham, Md.: Scarecrow Press, 2004.

Smith-Rosenberg, Carroll. *Disorderly Conduct: Visions of Gender in Victorian America.* New York: Alfred A. Knopf, 1985.

Sorensen, Virginia. *The Evening and the Morning.* New York: Harcourt Brace, 1949.

Spence, Clark C. *Mining Engineers and the American West: The Lace-Boot Brigade, 1849–1933.* New Haven: Yale University Press, 1970.

Spofford, Harriet Prescott. *The Amber Gods, and Other Stories.* Edited by Alfred Bendixon. New Brunswick: Rutgers University Press, 1989.

Stansell, Christine. *City of Women: Sex and Class in New York, 1789–1860.* New York: Alfred A. Knopf, 1986.

Stegner, Wallace. *Angle of Repose.* Garden City, N.Y.: Doubleday, 1971.

———. *Selected American Prose: The Realistic Movement, 1841–1900.* New York: Holt, Rinehart, and Winston, 1958.

Stegner, Wallace, and Richard W. Etulain. *Conversations with Wallace Stegner on Western History and Literature.* Rev. ed. Salt Lake City: University of Utah Press, 1983.

Stone, Lucy, and Antoinette Brown Blackwell. *Friends and Sisters: Letters Between Lucy Stone and Antoinette Brown Blackwell, 1846–93.* Edited by Carol Lasser and Marlene Deahl Merrill. Urbana: University of Illinois Press, 1987.

Stoneburner, Carol, and John Stoneburner, eds. *The Influence of Quaker Women on American History: Biographical Studies.* Lewiston, Maine: Edwin Mellen Press, 1986.

Sui Sin Far. "A Chinese Ishmael." 1899. Electronic Text Center, University of Virginia Library. http://etext.virginia.edu/toc/modeng/public/FarChin.html.

Sui Sin Far, Amy Ling, and Annette White Parks. *Mrs. Spring Fragrance, and Other Stories.* Asian American Experience. Urbana: University of Illinois Press, 1995.

Swerdlow, Amy, and Hanna Lessinger, eds. *Class, Race, and Sex: The Dynamics of Control.* Boston: G. K. Hall / Barnard College Women's Center, 1983.

Swift, Agnes, and Sally Swift. Personal interview. May 1992.

Sykes, Hope Williams. *Second Hoeing.* New York: Putnam's, 1935.

Thoreau, Henry David. *The Selected Works of Thoreau.* Edited by Walter Harding. Boston: Houghton Mifflin, 1975.

———. *Walden; or, Life in the Woods.* 1854. Reprint, Boston: Bibliophile Society, 1909.

———. "Walking." *Atlantic Monthly,* June 1862. http://www.eserver.org/thoreau/walking2.html.

Tompkins, Jane. *West of Everything: The Inner Life of Westerns.* New York: Oxford University Press, 1992.

Tonkovich, Nicole. *Domesticity With a Difference: The Nonfiction of Catherine Beecher, Sarah J. Hale, Fanny Fern, and Margaret Fuller.* Jackson: University Press of Mississippi, 1997.

Trachtenberg, Alan. *The Incorporation of America: Culture and Society in the Gilded Age.* New York: Hill and Wang, Farrar, Straus, and Giroux, 1982.

"A Tribute to *St. Nicholas,* a Magazine for Young Folks." http://flyingdreams.home.mindspring.com/nick.htm.

Ulrichs, Karl Heinrich. *The Riddle of "Man-Manly" Love: The Pioneering Work on Male Homosexuality.* Vol. 2. Translated by Michael A. Lombardi-Nash. Foreword by Vern L. Bullough. Buffalo: Prometheus Books, 1994.

"Using Newspapers for Genealogical Research." *West Virginia Archives and History News* 2.1 (March 2001). http://www.wvculture.org/history/0301news.htm.

Van Doren, Carl. "William Dean Howells." Chap. 6, sec. 2, in *The American Novel.* New York: Macmillan, 1921. http://www.bartleby.com/187/9.html.

Vicinus, Martha. "'They Wonder to Which Sex I Belong': The Historical Roots of Modern Lesbian Identity." *Feminist Studies* 3 (1992): 467–97.

Voynick, Stephen M. *Leadville: A Miner's Epic.* Missoula: Mountain Press, 1984.

Walkerdine, Valerie. "Syllabus for SY 1402 Lecture 5." University of Manchester. http://www.les1.man.ac.uk/cms/sy1402/documents/ lecture%205%20-%20for%20intranet.doc.

Walsh, Mary Ellen Williams. "*Angle of Repose* and the Writings of Mary Hallock Foote: A Source Study." In *Critical Essays on Wallace Stegner,* edited by Anthony Arthur. Boston: G. K. Hall, 1982.

Washington, Mary Helen. Introduction to *A Voice From the South,* by Anna Julia Cooper. New York: Oxford University Press, 1988.

Wasserman, Loretta. "Cather's Semitism." http://cather.unl.edu/scholarship/cs/vol2/semitism.htm.

Watanna, Onoto [Winnifred Eaton]. *The Old Jinrikisha.* 1900. Electronic Text Center, University of Virginia Library. http://etext.virginia.edu/users/browse/toc/EatJinr.html.

———. *Tama.* New York: Harper and Brothers, 1910.

Werner, Craig. "The Old South, 1815–1840." In *The History of Southern Literature,* edited by Louis D. Rubin Jr. et al. Baton Rouge: Louisiana State University Press, 1985.

West, Elliot. *Growing Up With the Country: Childhood on the Far Western Frontier.* Albuquerque: University of New Mexico Press, 1989.

Wexler, Laura. "Tender Violence: Domestic Fiction and Educational Reform." In *The Culture of Sentiment: Race, Gender, and Sentimentality in 19th Century America,* edited by Shirley Samuels. New York: Oxford University Press, 1992.

Wharton, Edith. *Collected Stories, 1891–1910.* Edited by Maureen Howard. New York: Library of America, 2001.

———. *Hudson River Bracketed.* New York: Grosset and Dunlap, 1929.

———. *Sanctuary.* New York: Scribner's, 1903.

———. *Summer: A Novel.* New York: Appleton, 1947.

White, G. Edward. *The Eastern Establishment and the Western Experience: The West of Frederic Remington, Theodore Roosevelt, and Owen Wister.* New Haven: Yale University Press, 1968.

Wiebe, Robert. *The Search for Order, 1877–1920.* New York: Hill and Wang, 1967.

Wiggen, Kate Douglas. *Rebecca of Sunnybrook Farm.* Boston: Houghton Mifflin, 1903.

Wilder, Laura Ingalls. *The Little House in the Big Woods.* 1932. Reprint, New York: Harper and Brothers, 1953.

Wingate, Mary G. "Ya-Sek." *St. Nicholas* (November 1873): 30–31.

Wister, Owen. "The Evolution of the Cow-Puncher." *Harper's* (1895). http://gaslight .mtroyal.ab.ca/gaslight/evolcowp.htm.

Wood, Mary E. "Spiders and Mice: Nature, Class, and the City in Mary Austin's *The Promised Land.*" *Isle* 9.1 (Winter 2002): 45–68.